RADICAL DEPRIVATION ON TRIAL

This book is an empirical study of contributions by courts in the Global South to comparative constitutionalism. It offers an analytical and comparative framework for understanding these constitutional innovations and illustrates them with a detailed qualitative study of the most ambitious case in constitutional adjudication in Latin America over the last decade: the Colombian Constitutional Court's structural injunction affecting the rights of more than four million internally displaced people (IDPs) in Colombia, and its implementation process. Although the ruling (known as T25 in Colombia) was handed down in 2004, its monitoring process continues to this day. This book traces the case's evolution over the last ten years, from its origin to its effects on law, policy, politics, and public opinion.

It also compares the implementation and effects of T25 with those of other structural rulings on the right to health, the right to food, prison overcrowding, and the right to housing in Colombia, India, and South Africa. The far-reaching insights from this case study will be of interest to scholars of comparative constitutionalism as well as leading constitutional courts in Latin America, Africa, and Asia.

César Rodríguez-Garavito is an associate professor and founding director of the Program on Global Justice and Human Rights at the University of the Andes (Colombia), and a founding member of the Center for Law, Justice, and Society (Dejusticia). He has published widely on law, social movements, and human rights. He is the author or editor of several books including *Law and Society in Latin America* (2015), *Balancing Wealth and Health* (2014), and *Law and Globalization from Below* (2005).

Diana Rodríguez-Franco is a PhD candidate in sociology at Northwestern University and a researcher at the Center for Law, Justice, and Society (Dejusticia). Her research focuses on the political economy of development, comparative environmental politics, sociology of law, and human rights. She is the author of several articles including *Internal Wars, Taxation, and State Building* (2015), *Globalizing Intellectual Property Rights: The Politics of Law and Public Health* (2012), and *Dependency Theory* (with James Mahoney, forthcoming).

Comparative Constitutional Law and Policy

Series Editors:

Comparative constitutional law is an intellectually vibrant field that encompasses an increasingly broad array of approaches and methodologies. This series collects analytically innovative and empirically grounded work from scholars of comparative constitutionalism across academic disciplines. Books in the series include theoretically informed studies of single constitutional jurisdictions, comparative studies of constitutional law and institutions, and edited collections of original essays that respond to challenging theoretical and empirical questions in the field.

Volumes in the Series:

Perils of Judicial Self-Government in Transitional Societies David Kosař

Engaging with Social Rights Brian Ray

Making We the People Chaihark Hahm and Sung Ho Kim

Radical Deprivation on Trial Cesar Rodriguez-Garavito and Diana Rodríguez-Franco

Unstable Constitutionalism Edited by Mark Tushnet and Madhav Khosla

Magna Carta and its Modern Legacy Edited by Robert Hazell and James Melton

International Courts and the Performance of International Agreements Clifford Carrubba and Matthew Gabel

Reputation and Judicial Tactics Shai Dothan

Constitutions and Religious Freedom Frank Cross

Constitutionalism in Asia in the Early Twenty-First Century Edited by Albert Chen

Social Difference and Constitutionalism in Pan-Asia Edited by Susan H. Williams

Constitutions in Authoritarian Regimes Edited by Tom Ginsburg and Alberto Simpser

Presidential Legislation in India Shubhankar Dam

Social and Political Foundations of Constitutions Edited by Denis J. Galligan and Mila Versteeg

Consequential Courts Edited by Diana Kapiszewski, Gordon Silverstein and Robert A. Kagan

Comparative Constitutional Design Edited by Tom Ginsburg

Radical Deprivation on Trial

THE IMPACT OF JUDICIAL ACTIVISM ON SOCIOECONOMIC RIGHTS IN THE GLOBAL SOUTH

CÉSAR RODRÍGUEZ-GARAVITO
University of the Andes and Dejusticia

DIANA RODRÍGUEZ-FRANCO
Northwestern University and Dejusticia

CAMBRIDGE
UNIVERSITY PRESS

CAMBRIDGE
UNIVERSITY PRESS

32 Avenue of the Americas, New York, NY 10013–2473, USA

Cambridge University Press is part of the University of Cambridge.

It furthers the University's mission by disseminating knowledge in the pursuit of education, learning, and research at the highest international levels of excellence.

www.cambridge.org
Information on this title: www.cambridge.org/9781107078888

First published 2015

A catalog record for this publication is available from the British Library.

ISBN 978-1-107-07888-8 Hardback

Contents

Acknowledgments

The work that culminates in this book has been as intense as it was challenging. Intense because the field research took us from court and government offices in the center of Bogotá to cities and neighborhoods in the Colombian periphery where the victims of forced displacement live with one of the greatest humanitarian emergencies in the world. Challenging because what we found along the way in Colombia and other countries of the Global South, where courts have challenged radical deprivation, did not easily fit within the models that comparative constitutional studies have created to conceptualize the connections between these different places.

This book attempts to trace these connections through a detailed analysis of the Colombian Constitutional Court's decisions regarding forced displacement, which many have recognized as one of its most notable and innovative contributions to contemporary constitutionalism. What impact has it had on public policy, public opinion, and, lastly, the displaced population's condition? What does this case study tell us about classic questions regarding the role of law and courts in social transformation, or about judicial activism's legitimacy and usefulness? What political, legal, economic, and social effects do the aforementioned judicial interventions have on structural social problems such as these? Lastly, how does it compare to similar cases in India, South Africa, and other countries of the Global South?

In the following pages we explain our analytic framework and the empirical evidence with which we have tried to respond to these questions. But first, we would like to express our deep and hearty gratitude to all the people that supported us in this effort, without whom this endeavor would have undoubtedly been harder and less fascinating. First, we would like to thank our colleagues and friends in the Center for Law, Justice, and Society (Dejusticia), who have accompanied us since the project's beginning with ideas and suggestions. We give special thanks for the unconditional support from Carolina Bernal, Mauricio García-Villegas, Diana Guzmán, Diego López, Natalia Orduz, Javier Revelo, Camilo Sánchez, and Rodrigo Uprimny. We also thank the researchers that have contributed to specific aspects of the study: Carlos Andrés Baquero, Julián Berrío, Luisa Ferreira, Catalina Góngora, Patrick M. Higgins, Sean Luna McAdams, Magnolia Prada, Hernán Ramirez, and Benjamin Saper.

We have been privileged to count on four experts' guidance in traversing the various complexities of forced displacement: Andrés Celis, Luis Jorge Garay, Luis Eduardo Pérez, and Clara Elena Reales. We thank them for generously sharing their knowledge with us. Lastly, the members of the Constitutional Court's Special Monitoring Chamber, in particular Lucía Delgado, Ingrid Santos, and Félix Torres, were extremely generous with their time and knowledge when we were updating the book.

For detailed and generous comments on earlier drafts of Chapter 1, we would like to thank Daniel Brinks, Jackie Dugard, Siri Gloppen, Patrick Heller, and Malcolm Langford. For permission to reprint in Chapters 1 and 8 parts of an earlier article (Rodríguez-Garavito 2011a), we are grateful to the Texas Law Review Association.

All those that agreed to be interviewed were equally generous, sharing their experiences and providing us with an essential data source for our study. We thank the judges, public officials, displaced population organizations' leaders, human rights activists, and all others who amongst the demands of daily life kindly opened the doors to their offices or homes to us.

The support of the Ford Foundation, especially Martín Abregú and Felipe Agüero, made possible the action-research projects that resulted in this book. Our deep gratitude also to Zachary Elkins, Tom Ginsburg, and Ran Hirschl for welcoming our work into Cambridge's *Comparative Constitutional Law and Policy* series, and to John Berger for his invaluable guidance throughout the editorial process.

Finally, the most important acknowledgments, the ones that come from the heart but cannot adequately be put into words. César dedicates this book to Ulpi, for filling every place and moment with sweetness and joy. Diana dedicates it to Michel, for valuing and supporting this and other efforts with love and tenderness. If this book helps, even the slightest bit, to ameliorate the situation of those forcefully uprooted from their homes, we know that they both will think it was worth the work.

Abbreviations

ACCI	Colombian Agency for International Cooperation *Agencia Colombiana de Cooperación Internacional*
Afrodes	Colombian Association of Displaced Afro-Colombians *Asociación de Afrocolombianos Desplazados*
Bancoldex	Colombian Foreign Trade Bank *Banco de Comercio Exterior de Colombia*
CCC	Colombian Constitutional Court
CERREM	Committee for the Evaluation of Risks and Recommendation of Measures *Comité de Evaluación de Riesgo y Recomendación de Medidas*
Cijus	Socio-Legal Research Centre of the University of the Andes *Centro de Investigaciones Sociojurídicas de la Universidad de los Andes*
CNAIPD	National Council for Integral Assistance to the Displaced Population *Consejo Nacional de Atención Integral a la Población Desplazada*
Codhes	Consultancy for Human Rights and Displacement *Consultoría para los Derechos Humanos y el Desplazamiento*
Conpes	National Council for Social and Economic Policy

	El Consejo Nacional de Política Económica y Social
Dejusticia	Center of Law, Justice and Society *Centro de Estudios de Derecho, Justicia y Sociedad*
DNP	National Planning Department *Departamento Nacional de Planeación*
EHA	Emergency Humanitarian Aid
ENDS	National Demographic and Health Survey *Encuesta Nacional de Demografía y Salud*
ENV	National Verification Survey *Encuesta Nacional de Verificación*
FARC	Revolutionary Armed Forces of Colombia *Fuerzas Armadas Revolucionarias de Colombia*
HRW	Human Rights Watch
ICBF	Colombian Institute for Family Welfare *Instituto Colombiano de Bienestar Familiar*
ICRC	International Committee of the Red Cross
IDMC	Internal Displacement Monitoring Center
IDP	Internally Displaced Person
Incoder	Colombian Institute of Rural Development *Instituto Colombiano de Desarrollo Rural*
MIJ	Ministry of the Interior and Justice *Ministerio del Interior y Justicia*
Monitoring Commission	Monitoring Commission on Public Policy on Forced Displacement *Comisión de Seguimiento a la Política Pública sobre Desplazamiento Forzado*
National Assistance Plan	National Assistance Plan to the Population Displaced by Violence *Plan Nacional de Atención Integral a la Población Desplazada por la Violencia* (Decree 250 of 2005)
National Roundtable	National Roundtable for the Strengthening of Displaced Persons' Organizations *Mesa Nacional de Fortalecimiento de Organizaciones de Población Desplazada*
NDP	National Development Plan

	Plan Nacional de Desarrollo
NGO	Non-Governmental Organization
ONIC	National Indigenous Organization of Colombia *Organización Nacional Indígena de Colombia*
OPD	Displaced Population Organizations *Organizaciones de la población desplazada*
PIU	Singular Integral Plan *Plan Integral Único*
The Program	National Program for the Integral Assistance to the Population Displaced by Violence *Programa Nacional de Atención Integral a la Población Desplazada por la Violencia* (Conpes document 2804 of 1995)
RUPD	Singular Registry of Displaced Population *Registro Único de Población Desplazada*
SAHRC	South African Human Rights Commission
SENA	National Apprenticeship Service *Servicio Nacional de Aprendizaje*
SER	Socioeconomic Rights
SGSS	General Health and Social Security System *Sistema General de Seguridad Social*
SNAIPD	National System for Assistance to the Displaced Population *Sistema Nacional de Atención Integral a la Población Desplazada*
SNAPIV	National System of Assistance and Reparation to Victims *Sistema Nacional de Atención y Reparación Integral a las Víctimas*
Social Action Agency	Presidential Agency for Social Action and International Cooperation *Agencia Presidencial para la Acción Social y la Cooperación Internacional*
UBN	Unmet Basic Needs
UNCDES	Unit of Prosecutors against Crimes for Disappearance and Forced Displacement *Unidad Nacional contra el Desplazamiento y la Desaparición Forzada*

UNHCR	United Nations Refugee Agency
UNHRC	United National Human Rights Council
WFP	United Nations World Food Program
WOLA	Washington Office on Latin America

PART I

STUDYING IMPACT: ACTIVIST COURTS ADDRESSING RADICAL DEPRIVATION

1

The Impact of Judicial Activism on Socioeconomic Rights in the Global South: An Analytical Framework

Shortly after 3:00 P.M. on Monday, July 28, 2014, Danelly Estupiñán, a leading figure in the Afro-Colombian social movement, stepped onto the platform of the Colombian Constitutional Court's courtroom in the heart of Bogotá. Flanked by ten other representatives of victims of forced displacement, she addressed the three Court justices presiding over the hearing, as well as the nearly 100 of us who were packed into the room – journalists, state officials, activists, scholars, and lawyers.

"The Court's ruling gave us a voice," she said, referring to the 2004 judgment on internally displaced persons (IDPs), the tenth anniversary of which was the occasion for the Court hearing. "It has been the type of validation and support that black communities had been waiting for" in the face of the massive forced displacement spurred by the worsening of Colombia's five-decade internal armed conflict in the early 2000s. We had met Ms. Estupiñán five years earlier in the city of Buenaventura and knew well what she was referring to: the gruesome killings, the daily intimidation, and the massive dispossession caused by right-wing paramilitary squads, leftist guerrillas, the Colombian armed forces, and drug-trafficking mafias as they fought over the control of land and resources in her city, the main Colombian port on the Pacific coast and one of the most dangerous places in the world (Human Rights Watch 2014).

Ms. Estupiñán herself is a member of the population of more than five million IDPs, the second largest in the world after Syria's (UNCHR 2013: 24). As she recounted the plight of her community, she recalled how the Court's ruling, as well as the numerous follow-up decisions and public hearings organized by the Court, had been a catalyst for important (albeit insufficient) improvements in state policies and the situation of IDPs over the last decade.

The path that led up to the hearing started in January 2004 when the Colombian Constitutional Court (CCC) aggregated the constitutional writs of protection (*tutelas*)[1] filed by 1,150 displaced families and handed down its most ambitious ruling in its two decades of existence: Judgment T-025 of 2004 (hereafter, T25). In this decision, the CCC declared that the humanitarian emergency embodied by massive forced displacement of millions of people constituted an "unconstitutional state of affairs." In other words, the Court ruled that IDPs' dramatic circumstances conformed to a generalized state of human rights violations associated with systemic failures in state action.

As the complaints that reached the Court from all corners of Colombia showed, the state lacked a serious and coordinated policy for offering emergency aid to IDPs. Nor was there reliable information on the number of IDPs or the situations they were facing. Moreover, the budget allocated to the issue was clearly insufficient. To address the root causes behind this state of affairs, the Court mandated a series of structural measures that, as we will see, spawned a lengthy implementation and follow-up process that continues today.

T25 was not the CCC's first structural decision declaring an unconstitutional state of affairs (Rodríguez-Garavito 2009b). Since 1997, the Court has handed down seven decisions of this kind, in greatly varying circumstances including massive prison overcrowding (Judgment T-153 of 1998), government's non compliance with its obligation to register public officials in the social security system (Judgment SU-090 of 2000), and lack of protection for human rights defenders (Judgment T-590 of 1998). In other decisions, the CCC has aggregated different *tutela* actions and has ordered long-term structural remedies without formally declaring an unconstitutional state of affairs. It did so most recently in Judgment T-760 of 2008, which mandated that the government institute public policies aimed at addressing the fundamental flaws of the health care system. These failures had led to more than 100,000 *tutela* actions per year, whereby patients would demand that courts fulfill their right to health by ordering public and private providers to grant them services or medicines that the providers had refused (Rodríguez-Garavito 2013; Lamprea 2015).

Partly because of its intervention in these cases, and partly because of its progressive rulings in more than 22,000 constitutional actions since its establishment in 1992,[2] scholars frequently include the work of the CCC in contemporary comparative constitutional studies (Coomans 2006; Gargarella 2006; International Commission of Jurists 2008; Langford 2009; Young 2012).

[1] Tutela actions are judicial mechanisms established by the 1991 Constitution to process complaints regarding the violation of constitutional rights. The Constitutional Court has discretionary power to pick tutela decisions for review among those handed down by lower courts.

[2] The exact figure (22,199 rulings between 1992 and 2013) includes decisions on writs of protection (*tutelas*) and decisions on constitutional challenges brought by citizens against acts of Congress (abstract review of constitutionality). See www.corteconstitucional.gov.co/relatoria/estadisticas.php (last viewed on October 31, 2014).

In a paradoxical turn in comparative legal history, one of the countries with the gravest human rights violations has become a net exporter of constitutional jurisprudence and of innovative institutional approaches to ensure the fulfillment of human rights at the domestic level.

1.1. RADICAL DEPRIVATION ON TRIAL

Although the CCC has not explicitly drawn on comparative constitutional law to develop its doctrine of unconstitutional states of affairs,[3] there are clear similarities between its jurisprudence and the doctrine of structural injunctive remedies in public interest litigation in jurisdictions such as India and the United States (Chitalkar and Gauri forthcoming; Sabel and Simon 2004). The study of the CCC's jurisprudence, therefore, affords a privileged vantage point on current scholarly and policy debates about judicial activism in general and about the impact of activist court rulings in particular. It also provides fertile ground for theoretical and empirical reflection on constitutional innovations in the Global South, which have received much less scholarly attention in comparative constitutional studies than have developments in North America and Europe.

We posit that this variety of activism, although particularly visible in the CCC's jurisprudence, forms part of an emerging trend in Latin America and other regions of the Global South (Rodríguez-Garavito 2011a). Embodied most clearly by court rulings in structural cases that address widespread violations of socioeconomic rights (SERs), this type of progressive neoconstitutionalism has unfolded with different names and features in different parts of the Global South (Bilchitz 2013; Bonilla 2013; Rodríguez-Garavito 2011b; Vilhena, Baxi, and Viljoen 2013). Together with the incorporation of SERs in national constitutions, these judicial interventions constitute key institutional innovations aimed at redressing fundamental socioeconomic injustices embodied by the deprivation of basic material conditions of a dignified life suffered, among others, by millions of slum dwellers, members of racial and ethnic minorities, malnourished children, victims of gender discrimination and sexual violence, refugees and IDPs, the chronically underemployed, legions of workers in the informal economy, disenfranchised migrants, and people without access to quality education, healthcare, and sanitation. Compounded by mounting inequality in the Global South and the North, as well as the uneven effects of climate change, these are the forms of radical deprivation that we allude to in the title to this book.

[3] Interview with former justice Manuel José Cepeda (author of the T25 opinion), May 27, 2014.

As Walzer has noted, "the problem is that inequality commonly translates into domination and radical deprivation. But the verb 'translates' here describes a socially mediated process, which is fostered or inhibited by the structure of its mediations" (1995: 19). We claim that courts are increasingly central characters in this mediation process, and can act as inhibitors of such a translation. We borrow from the title of a pioneer book on transitional justice by Argentine constitutional scholar Carlos Nino – *Radical Evil on Trial* (1998) – to argue that, just as many courts took on an important role in dealing with mass atrocities in transitions from authoritarian governments and armed conflicts starting in the 1980s, they are increasingly involved in dealing with mass violations of SERs.

We thus focus on particularly visible and ambitious court interventions. In stepping into the fray of core distributional debates, courts contribute not only to defining the contours of legal and economic systems, but also to the fate of literally millions of citizens whose basic material conditions of life are at stake. It is through this type of structural cases that radical deprivation is brought to trial.

Borrowing from the literature on structural remedies in U.S. public interest litigation, we define structural cases as those that (1) affect a large number of people who allege a violation of their rights, either directly or through organizations that litigate the cause; (2) implicate multiple government agencies found to be responsible for pervasive public policy failures that contribute to such rights violations; and (3) involve structural injunctive remedies, i.e., enforcement orders whereby courts instruct various government agencies to take coordinated actions to protect the entire affected population and not just the specific complainants in the case (Chayes 1976; Sabel and Simon 2004).[4]

We focus on structural cases for two additional reasons. First, in the face of increasing judicialization of SERs, structural rulings offer a procedural alternative to the case-by-case adjudication of thousands of individual cases that risk overwhelming the capacity of courts and yielding contradictory outcomes, especially in civil law legal systems where apex courts' rulings are not binding on lower courts. They thus provide a potentially useful option for the effective judicial enforcement of SERs by focusing on systemic causes of

[4] By focusing on these macro-cases we do not mean to suggest that they are the only or the most important cases for guaranteeing SERs. In fact, as several scholars have shown, the fate of SERs' fulfillment depends equally on a multitude of individual and common everyday cases (that may never get to court), from the payment of an adequate pension to a retiree to the provision of a public service without discrimination based on gender, race, national origin, or other reasons (see Abramovich 2005; International Commission of Jurists 2008).

rights violations and promoting corresponding structural institutional remedies. Second, especially when courts retain supervisory jurisdiction over the case and monitor implementation of their ruling through follow-up decisions and monitoring mechanisms (as the CCC did in T25), structural cases can foster meaningful dialogue and collaboration among state and civil society actors around complex distributional problems, which in turn hold better prospects for sustainable improvements in SERs protection.

Among the best-known examples of structural cases on SERs is the jurisprudence of the Supreme Court of India, which has addressed massive socioeconomic problems such as hunger and malnutrition (Baxi 2013; Muralidhar 2008; Shankar and Mehta 2008). Particularly relevant for our purposes is the fact that the Indian Supreme Court has sought to deepen the impact of its jurisprudence by appointing commissioners in charge of promoting the implementation of its rulings (Shankar 2013). Similarly, the South African Constitutional Court has become a central institutional forum for promoting rights such as housing and health, and for nudging the state to take actions against the economic and social legacy of apartheid (Berger 2008; Liebenberg 2010). The South African Constitutional Court has also elicited international attention in judicial and scholarly circles, as demonstrated by the reliance of its jurisprudence on U.S. and European constitutional theory (Dixon 2007; Fredman 2008; Sunstein 2004).

In Latin America, judicial activism on SERs has become increasingly prominent over the last two decades (Gargarella 2015; Rodríguez-Garavito 2015; Uprimny 2015). In countries as different as Brazil and Costa Rica, courts have decisively shaped the provision of fundamental social services such as health care (Brinks and Forbath 2013; Ferraz 2009; Lamprea 2014; Wilson 2005). In Argentina, some courts have undertaken structural cases and experimented with public mechanisms to monitor the implementation of activist judgments such as *Verbitsky*, on prison overcrowding, and *Riachuelo*, on environmental degradation (CELS 2008; Farstein et al. 2010; Bergallo 2005).

1.2. THE BOOK'S QUESTIONS AND STRUCTURE

The international literature on the justiciability of SERs has multiplied in proportion to the proliferation of activist rulings (Langford 2009). Two angles of analysis have dominated this scholarship. First, some contributions have concentrated on making a theoretical case for the justiciability of SERs in light of the demands of democratic theory and the reality of social contexts marked by deep economic and political inequalities (Arango 2003; Bilchitz 2007).

Second, a number of works have entered into the discussion from the perspective of human rights doctrine, which has given greater precision to judicial standards for upholding SERs and encouraged the utilization of these rights by judicial organs and supervisory bodies at both the national and international levels (Abramovich and Courtis 2002; International Commission of Jurists 2008).

These perspectives have considerably advanced the conceptual clarity and the justiciability of SERs. Nevertheless, the almost exclusive emphasis on the production phase of judgments has created an analytical and practical blind spot: the implementation stage of rulings. For this reason, there is a paucity of studies on the fate of activist decisions after they are issued (Langford, Rodríguez-Garavito, and Rossi forthcoming).[5] What happens to the orders contained in these judgments once they leave the courtroom? To what extent do public officials follow the judgments and adopt new courses of conduct in order to protect SERs? What impact do the rulings have on the state, civil society, social movements, and public opinion? Ultimately, do they contribute to realizing SERs and addressing radical deprivation?

These are the questions we consider in this book. Therefore, as Tushnet (2012) has noted, our study goes "past the question which U.S. scholars typically focus on – *whether* courts should enforce second-generation rights – to consider *how* to do so." We thus seek to contribute to the growing sub-field of comparative constitutional studies by applying the tools of social science research to analyze the impact of constitutional adjudication. This type of study sheds new light on questions "[o]ften excluded from the canonical discourse ... such as the real-life impact of constitutional jurisprudence and its efficacy in planting the seeds of social change; ... the actors and factors involved in demanding or bringing about constitutional transformation; ... its impact on the legitimacy of the courts" (Hirschl 2013). Departing from a law- or court-centered approach, the following chapters explore multiple actors beyond the court, such as public officials, activists, policymakers, and leaders of the IDP population targeted by the ruling.

To help unpack the black box of the implementation and impact of structural rulings, we will proceed in three steps. In Part I, we begin by laying out our analytical framework (this chapter) and our case study (Chapter 2). In dialogue with socio-legal and comparative constitutional literature on judicial activism, we offer a typology of effects of judicial rulings and illustrate it with evidence from T25.

[5] Some exceptions are Gauri and Brinks (2008), Uprimny and García Villegas (2004), and the studies in Langford et al.(forthcoming).

In Part II (Chapters 3–7), we present the detailed empirical evidence of our study about the impact of the decade-long implementation of T25. Based on our analytical framework, we document its direct, indirect, material, and symbolic effects. The sequence of the chapters is organized in such a way that we move from direct to indirect effects; in analyzing each effect, we comment on its material and symbolic dimensions.

In Part III, we draw lessons from our case study for the broader comparative debate on judicial activism on SERs. In Chapter 8, we turn to an explanatory question: what accounts for the different levels of impact of SER rulings? Why do some decisions – like T25 – have deep and multifarious effects, while others remain on paper? In order to strengthen the explanatory leverage and generalizability of the findings of our case study, we compare the implementation process and effects of T25 with those of other structural rulings of the CCC (i.e., T-153 of 1998 on prison overcrowding, and T-760 of 2008 on health care), as well as those of comparable rulings by the Indian Supreme Court and the South African Constitutional Court (i.e., the *PUCL* case on the right to food in India,[6] and the *Grootboom* case on the right to housing in South Africa[7]). Based on this comparative analysis, we make an empirical case for a specific variety of court intervention (which we call "dialogic judicial activism"), which we argue can satisfactorily address criticisms against courts' legitimacy and capacity to enforce SERs.

In Chapter 9, we close by recapping our conclusions and drawing their implications for future judicial interventions aiming to solve structural socioeconomic problems. We point toward both the potential of judicial activism and the political and institutional conundrums that activist courts in the Global South are likely to encounter as they nudge other branches of power to effectively realize SERs.

This is the analytical and geographic terrain on which our inquiry is inscribed. However, since the terms "judicial activism" and "Global South" can take different meanings, before proceeding it is important to specify how we use them in this book.

1.3. JUDICIAL ACTIVISM IN THE GLOBAL SOUTH

Judicial activism as a concept is doubly equivocal. Descriptively, it has been widely used, both in academic literature and public discourse, to refer to very different levels and forms of judicial intervention (Shankar 2013: 98).

[6] *PUCL v. Union of India* (writ petition No. 196 of 2001).
[7] *Government of the Republic of South Africa v. Grootboom*, 2001 (1) SA 46 (CC).

The normative implications the term usually carries further complicate this diversity of meaning, where describing a court as "activist" could constitute either praise or criticism depending on the moment, place, or issue addressed in its ruling.

In order to render this term useful it must be analytically and empirically bounded in accordance to its object of study. As we have explained, we focus on structural court rulings dealing with SERs. In this specific context, we can evaluate the level of judicial activism by using Tushnet's (2009) useful distinction between the rights' content as recognized by the courts and the remedies that courts hand down to fulfill those rights.

On one hand, the courts can adopt strong or weak interpretations of SERs' content. A "strong rights" approach recognizes SERs as justiciable, on par with civil and political rights. In contrast, a court that adopts a "weak rights" approach tends to deny the justiciability of these rights. In the middle we find courts that accept SERs' justiciability but subject them to considerable procedural or substantive restrictions. We thus add an intermediate category – "moderate rights" approach – to Tushnet's dyad.

On the other hand, courts can adopt different types of remedies in light of SERs violations. In Tushnet's typology, the criteria to distinguish between the strong and weak remedies are the breadth of judicial orders and the extent to which orders are compulsory and peremptory. Whereas strong remedies involve precise, outcome-oriented orders, weak remedies tend to leave implementation entirely in the hands of government agencies. Moderate remedies, in turn, outline procedures and broad goals, as well as criteria and deadlines for assessing progress, but leave decisions on means and policies to government.

Missing from Tushnet's typology is a third component – monitoring – which is factually and analytically distinct from remedies. Regardless of the strength of their decisions' rights and remedies, courts face the choice of whether to retain supervisory jurisdiction over their implementation. We thus add this dimension to our conceptualization of judicial activism, and distinguish between strong, moderate, and weak monitoring. Strong monitoring can take different forms, from the appointment of commissioners to supervise in detail the implementation of a structural ruling over several years and report back to the Court (as in the above-mentioned landmark right to food case in India), to the creation of a special monitoring chamber within the Court responsible for supervising enforcement (as in the T25 case). What these and other variants of strong monitoring have in common is the Court's willingness to actively engage in the implementation process to foster government compliance based on specific deadlines and benchmarks, oftentimes issuing new decisions in light of progress and setbacks and encouraging discussion among actors in the case. In contrast, other courts adopt moderate forms of monitoring, such as demands for compliance reports that are not meant to lead to additional pressure from the Court, while yet others choose not to keep jurisdiction over the case (weak monitoring). The second ruling that we use as a comparative reference point – the South African Constitutional Court's decision in the *Grootboom* case, on the right to housing – illustrates the working of weak monitoring. Indeed, when the South African Human Rights Commission submitted a detailed report on challenges for the implementation of the ruling, the Court refused to entertain it, claiming that it did not have supervisory jurisdiction over the case (Berger 2008: 77).

This threefold characterization not only allows us to specify the meaning of judicial activism, but also to distinguish degrees and varieties of activism. Since our chief concern is to compare the impact of different types judicial interventions in structural SER cases, we choose to set the activism bar relatively low, and focus on contrasting the approaches of activist courts thus defined. For our purposes, the key variable in determining whether a court can be deemed activist is the strength that it gives to the content of SERs. We thus deem a court to be activist if it follows at least a moderate-rights approach – that is, one that recognizes the justiciability of SERs even as it sets procedural or substantive constraints to judicial enforcement. Above and beyond this threshold, we distinguish among different levels of activism, depending not only on the strength of the Court's conception of rights, but also on the strength of remedies and monitoring.

Courts that most clearly overcome our threshold are those that follow a strong rights approach, by adopting a "minimum core" conception of SERs. In this view, judges have the competence to demand that government guarantee at least a minimal ("core") level of material well-being. The CCC explicitly took this approach in T25 and in most of its other SER jurisprudence. Less consistently and explicitly, this approach has also informed the Indian Supreme Court's jurisprudence in the right to food case and other decisions (Birchfield and Corsi 2010; Chitalkar and Gauri forthcoming).

In terms of the conception of rights, the least activist tribunal in this sample is the South African Constitutional Court, which, despite being provided with the clearest textual basis in the constitution for a strong rights approach, has instead opted for a moderate-rights perspective that "weakened these rights significantly through its consistent refusal to specify their content and through the adoption of a vague jurisprudential approach founded in the notion of 'reasonableness'" of state action in fulfilling SERs (Bilchitz 2013: 68).

Yet, perhaps precisely because its weak-rights approach is closer to that of courts in the United States and most of the Global North, it has dominated the comparative law literature.[8]

We will use this threefold framework to analyze the workings and effects of different degrees of judicial activism, in a range of cases that goes from mildly activist courts that combine moderate rights and weak or moderate remedies and monitoring, to highly activist courts that use strong rights, remedies, and monitoring. We will also use the typology to characterize qualitatively different forms of activist rulings, from court imposed, monologic decisions to dialogic rulings that open up participatory monitoring processes.

As new constitutions in the Global South routinely include SERs in their bills of rights and couple them with judicial review mechanisms, we observe a proliferation of activist courts thus understood. However, the category of the Global South is too broad and internally diverse for the type of empirically grounded analysis of judicial activism that we undertake. In fact, judicial activism on SERs is taking place predominantly in middle-income countries (as opposed to lower-income countries) within the Global South (Peerenboom and Ginsburg 2013). Middle-income countries such as Colombia, India, and South Africa are, by definition, in a gray zone. As with the middle classes within domestic societies, they find themselves in an intermediate ground between precariousness and opulence. Their essence is one of contrasts, as shown by the disparate geography of their large cities, from Bogotá to Delhi to Johannesburg.

Economic contrasts go hand-in-hand with institutional contrasts. The institutions of middle-income countries are hybrids: in them coexist elements of weakness and strength, incapacity and capacity. On some occasions, there is disparity between different institutions – for example, between an authoritarian government captured by private interests, on the one hand, and an independent judiciary that protects citizens' rights, on the other. In others, the asymmetry is found within a single institution, like a tax collecting agency or police force that is efficient in the cities, but absent or incapable of fulfilling its mission in the rest of the country.

This dual economic and institutional contrast makes these countries particularly fertile ground for the judicialization of conflicts regarding SERs (Rodríguez-Garavito 2013). Among the economic variables that favor judicialization, income level and distribution stand out. By definition,

[8] As Alston notes, "rarely have the developments in the field of comparative constitutional law been so dominated by the jurisprudence not only of a single country but in this case of a single court" (Alston 2008: ix).

middle-income countries have more resources than low-income countries, but have a distribution of wealth just as or more unequal than the latter.

The aforementioned institutional asymmetry increases the probability that these demands turn into litigation. Governmental agencies are not sufficiently strong to adequately and regularly resolve citizen petitions, but (in contrast to institutions in low-income countries) do tend to be sufficiently strong and accountable to fulfill judicial orders. When courts are independent and have adequate institutional capacity, litigation offers a particularly promising route to demand the fulfillment of SERs (Gauri and Brinks 2008).

This combination of factors is particularly notable in the more well-off middle-income countries – that is, those referred to as upper-middle-income countries (Peerenboom and Ginsburg 2013). Thus, in order to avoid the risk of overgeneralization associated with the use of exceedingly broad categories, our analysis and arguments in this book focus on Global South countries with both higher incomes within that category and a democratic political system committed to the rule of law. We have in mind, above all, those democratic upper-middle-income countries in which courts have been particularly active in the protection of SERs, such as South Africa, India, Brazil, Colombia, Argentina, and Costa Rica.

Within this category, Colombia is, by far, the most prolific country in SER litigation, as shown by comparative studies on the judicialization of the right to health (Mœstad et al. 2011; Lamprea 2015; Yamin and Gloppen 2011). It is also the country with the most activist Constitutional Court in that category (Rodríguez-Garavito 2013; Bilchitz 2013; Landau 2012).

1.4. METHODOLOGY: LEARNING FROM AN EXTREME CASE

From a methodological point of view, focusing on the Colombian jurisprudence – and on the most ambitious structural case within it (T25) – allows us to observe, as though under a magnifying glass, the effects of courts' interventions in structural distributive issues. Our choice of a paradigmatic ruling on SERs in Latin America is thus explicitly guided by a qualitative sampling logic. Indeed, T25 constitutes what Goertz and Mahoney (2012: 185) have called a "substantively important case" – that is, "an ideal type or well-known exemplar of a phenomenon," which in this case is judicial activism on SERs in the Global South.

T25 has three traits that make it a substantively important case in this universe. First, the ruling has a particularly broad scope. It is a paradigmatic instance of a structural ruling because of the beneficiary population's size, the gravity of the rights violations and radical deprivation that it aims to resolve, the numerous state and social actors involved, and the ambition and duration of the judgment remedies' implementation process, a process which continues even after ten years. As noted, the CCC adopted a strong rights approach in dealing with these challenges, by ordering the government to take immediate action to guarantee the "minimum core" of IDPs' rights.

Second, T25 constitutes the most explicit and systematic Latin American judicial attempt to implement a structural ruling. As we will see, during the ten-year period analyzed in this book (January 2004–April 2014), the CCC maintained jurisdiction over the case in order to compel compliance through 289 follow-up decisions and 20 public hearings to evaluate the government's progress. It is thus a clear instance of strong monitoring.

The third relevant characteristic is the type of remedies the Court handed down in T25. Instead of establishing in detail the precise measures that public authorities must adopt to attend to the IDP population – as it has done in other rulings criticized by many economists and lawyers[9] – the CCC issued procedural orders that contemplate state and civil society involvement in the creation and implementation of programs to confront the humanitarian crisis generated by forced displacement. By ordering policy design and calling periodic public hearings to discuss it, the Court established a gradual, dialogue-based implementation procedure for the ruling. As we will see, the combination of these types of moderate remedies with strong rights and strong monitoring through follow-up mechanisms creates spaces for deliberation which can lead to novel and potentially democratizing alternatives for judicial protection of SERs.

By using a detailed case study of a landmark case to shed new light on issues of courts and social change, our research inserts itself into the tradition of similar studies in the United States, such as those focused on *Brown v. Board of Education* (Minow 2010; Rosenberg 1991). As it engages with rich U.S. socio-legal literature on legal mobilization and constitutional adjudication, it also aims to facilitate South–North dialogues within comparative constitutional studies.

We triangulated several research methods in constructing the case study. First, we conducted eighty-nine semi-structured interviews, lasting one hour on average, with key actors in the case, including state officials, representatives of international agencies involved in the judgment's implementation (such as

9 The most well-known case, and also the most criticized, was judgment C-700 of 1999, in which the Court declared the housing finance system (UPAC, by its Spanish abbreviation) unconstitutional and ordered that it be replaced by a new system, set out in detail by the Court. For critical evaluations of the activism of these judgments from different perspectives, see Clavijo (2001), Kalmanovitz (2001), and Uprimny (2000).

the United Nations Refugee Agency, UNHCR), members of NGOs that have been active in driving the case, leaders of IDPs' organizations and grassroots organizations that work on the issue, and CCC's justices and law clerks involved in this case throughout the years. We also conducted eleven interviews in South Africa with advocates and scholars who are actors in or experts on SER litigation in that country, as well as with five interviews with experts from India, including one of the commissioners in the right to food case.

Second, we participated in or observed various follow-up fora on the decision. These include public hearings held at the Constitutional Court, expert commissions established to produce technical information for the Court, and coalition meetings of civil society organizations that follow and/or participate in the case.

Third, we analyzed the CCC's copious documentation in following up on the case, as well as numerous governmental agencies' and civil society organizations' reports and publications responding to the Court's requests for information during the ten years of follow-up subsequent to the judgment.

Fourth, we analyzed statistics and indicators generated by different actors in the case to measure evolution of the displaced population's situation, in light of the indicators established by the Court in T25 and subsequent orders. Especially useful for this quantitative research were the data from national polls verifying the level of effective enjoyment of SERs by IDPs, done in 2007, 2008, and 2010 by the civil society's Monitoring Commission on Public Policy on Forced Displacement (Monitoring Commission 2008, 2008b, 2010).

Finally, given our interest in examining the judgment's symbolic and indirect effects alongside its instrumental and direct effects, we carried out a media coverage study on forced displacement articles published between 2000 and 2013 in the two most widely circulated national print media sources (*El Tiempo* newspaper and *Semana* magazine). This selection allows us to compare the volume and content of press coverage per year before and after the decision. Thus, this analysis permits evaluation of T25's possible impact on how the media and those who shape public opinion address the issue of displacement.

1.5. THE EFFECTS, PROCEDURE, AND JUSTIFICATION OF JUDICIAL ACTIVISM: THE ARGUMENTS OF THE BOOK

With this analytical focus and object of study in mind, we use the remainder of this chapter to outline the three central arguments of the book: one relating to the *effects* of courts' intervention in structural SERs cases, another relating to the appropriate *procedure* for said intervention, and a third about the *justification* of this intervention. In laying out our arguments, we engage with the different bodies of literature that have tackled these questions. As noted, we approach the literature from a socio-legal perspective by making our empirical data and other socio-legal studies bear on debates that have thus far been dominated by comparative law or constitutional theory.

We claim that in order to capture the full range of *effects* of court decisions, impact studies need to widen conventional theoretical and methodological fields of vision. In addition to direct material effects of judicial remedies – those effects that follow immediately from the *enforcement* of the court order – attention should be paid to the broader impact, which includes equally important indirect and symbolic effects. Based on case study evidence, we posit that the potential range of relevant effects includes, beyond direct effects, the reframing of socioeconomic issues as human rights problems, the strengthening of state institutional capacities to deal with such problems, the forming of advocacy coalitions to participate in the implementation process, and the promoting of public deliberation and a collective search for solutions on the complex distributional issues underlying structural cases on SERs. These constitute indirect and symbolic effects.

With regard to court-controlled *procedures* that may enhance a given ruling's overall impact, two central factors are the type of remedies and the existence and nature of the Court's monitoring. We argue that impact is likely to be higher when courts engage in *dialogic activism*, which we characterize as a combination of strong rights, moderate remedies, and strong monitoring. Dialogic rulings set broad goals and clear implementation paths through deadlines and progress reports, while leaving substantive decisions and detailed outcomes to government agencies. Remedies of this nature are not only compatible with the separation-of-powers principle but also can bolster the overall efficacy of a given decision. Further, a dialogic approach to SERs cases encourages participatory follow-up mechanisms – public hearings, court-appointed monitoring commissions, and invitations to civil society and government agencies to submit relevant information and participate in court-sponsored discussions – which both deepen democratic deliberation and enhance the impact of court interventions.

As for the *justification* for dialogic judicial interventions in structural SERs case, we respond to the criticism that they encroach on the powers of democratically elected officials in the executive and the legislature, and are therefore unjustified in a democracy, by citing frequent cases in which bureaucracies and the political systems of contemporary democracies develop structural impasses that frustrate the realization of constitutional rights. In these circumstances of institutional blockage – which lead to serious deficiencies, or even the complete absence of public policies to address urgent social problems – we posit that courts are the appropriate institutions to remove obstacles impeding the proper state functioning and promote rights protection. From a conception of democracy that emphasizes the importance of public deliberation and horizontal control among the organs of public power, we argue that this type of judicial intervention strengthens democracy rather than erodes it. We illustrate this argument with evidence from T25, in which the Court issued the judgment precisely in order to overcome the bureaucratic impasse that prevented the government from addressing IDPs' humanitarian emergency. The evidence shows how the intervention of the Court complemented, rather than replaced, the role of the Colombian government and Congress.

To elaborate these arguments, we organize the rest of this introductory chapter into two sections. In the first, we delineate our analytical framework and typology of effects of rulings. In briefly illustrating the typology with evidence from T25, we outline the empirical chapters of the book (Chapters 3–7). In the second part, we outline the arguments about the justification and impact of dialogic judicial activism, which we develop in Chapter 8.

1.6. THE BLIND SPOT IN THE DEBATE OVER THE JUSTICIABILITY OF SERS: THE IMPACT OF RULINGS

1.6.1. The Effects of SERs Rulings: An Analytical Framework

The well-established interdisciplinary literature on courts and social transformations offers a useful conceptual and methodological framework to assess the effects of the recent wave of litigation and judicial activism on SERs. The literature has explored the impact of prominent judicial decisions on a variety of topics, including gender equality in the job market (McCann 1994), racial discrimination (Rosenberg 1991), and prison overcrowding (Feeley and Rubin 1998). From different perspectives, these studies have theorized and empirically evaluated the outcomes of the "rights revolution" (Epp 1998) and the corresponding "juristocracy" (Hirschl 2004) embodied by judges' growing intervention in fundamental political and social questions.

Judicial impact studies can be classified into two groups, depending on the type of effects on which the studies focus. On the one hand, some authors concentrate their attention on judicial decisions' direct and palpable effects. Adopting a neorealist perspective, which views law as a set of norms that shapes human conduct, they apply a strict causality test to measure the impact of judicial interventions: a judgment is effective if it has produced an observable change in the conduct of those it directly targets (McCann 1994: 290). For example, the question of determining T25's effects would be resolved by analyzing its impact on the conduct of government authorities in charge of public policy on forced displacement and, ultimately, by evaluating its consequences for the IDPs.

The seminal work of this approach is that of Rosenberg on the effects of the *Brown v. Board of Education* decision from the U.S. Supreme Court (Rosenberg 1991). Contrary to the conventional view on *Brown*, which saw the decision as revolutionizing race relations in the United States and contributing to the birth of the civil rights movement in the 1960s, Rosenberg's empirical study concluded that the judgment had little effect and that the faith placed in courts as mechanisms for social change was a "hollow hope." In his view, the political mobilization of the 1960s and the resulting antidiscrimination legislation (and not the structural judicial decision) achieved racial desegregation.

On the other hand, authors inspired by a constructivist conception of the relationship between law and society have criticized Rosenberg and the neorealists for focusing only on judgments' direct, material effects (Bourdieu 1987). According to these critics, law and judicial decisions generate social transformation not only when they induce changes in the conduct of the groups and individuals directly involved in the case, but also when they produce indirect transformations in social relations or when they alter social actors' perceptions and legitimize the litigants' worldview (Bourdieu 1987). Returning to the example of T25, beyond its direct, material effects, the decision has generated equally important indirect or symbolic effects. For example, it has contributed to changing public perception of the urgency and gravity of forced displacement in Colombia, as well as legitimized the claims and reinforced the negotiating power of human rights NGOs and international human rights agencies that had been pressuring the Colombian government to do more for IDPs.

The preeminent work employing the constructivist approach is McCann's study on the effects of the legal strategies used by the feminist movement in fighting for wage equality in the United States (1994). McCann's findings suggest that litigation and judicial activism's indirect effects may be more important than the direct effects focused on by neorealists (1994). Thus, "[a]lthough judicial victories often do not translate automatically into desired social change, they can help to redefine the terms of both immediate and long-term struggles among social groups" (McCann 1994: 285).

These conceptual differences go hand-in-hand with methodological disagreements. Neorealists' epistemological positivism implies a nearly exclusive emphasis on quantitative research techniques aimed to measure direct material effects. This is evident in impact studies inspired by the law and economics movement, whose conclusions tend to share Rosenberg's skepticism, as illustrated by the economic literature on the CCC's activism (Clavijo 2001; Kalmanovitz 2001).

In contrast, the constructivist approach widens the range of research strategies to include qualitative techniques that capture a given decision's indirect and symbolic effects; constructivists place these on equal footing with quantitative techniques such as analyses of social indicators and measurement of press coverage before and after the decision. One such technique is the use of in-depth interviews with public officials, activists, and members of the beneficiary population. These interviews examine the decision's impact on those individuals' perceptions of their situations and the strategies used to affect their situations. To clarify and highlight the differences between these two perspectives, we have constructed a typology of the effects under consideration.

On the one hand, as shown by the horizontal axis of Table 1.1, rulings can have direct or indirect effects. Direct effects include court-mandated actions that affect participants in the case, be they the litigants, the beneficiaries, or the state agencies that are the target of the Court's orders. Indirect effects include all kinds of consequences that, without being stipulated in the Court's orders, nonetheless derive from the decision. They affect not only the parties to the case, but also other social actors.

TABLE 1.1. *Types and Examples of Effects of Judicial Decisions*

	Direct	Indirect
Material	Designing public policy, as ordered by the ruling	Forming coalitions of activists to influence the issue under consideration
Symbolic	Defining and perceiving the problem as a rights violation	Transforming public opinion about the problem's urgency and gravity

On the other hand, as represented by the table's vertical axis, judicial decisions can generate material or symbolic effects (García-Villegas 2014). The former category entails tangible changes in the conduct of groups or individuals. Symbolic effects consist of changes in ideas, perceptions, and collective social constructs relating to the litigation's subject matter. In sociological terms, they imply cultural or ideological alterations with respect to the problem posed by the case (Swidler 1986). For instance, when courts attract media coverage, their interventions may shape the understanding that both the media and the public have of the issue under consideration.

As the table portrays, the intersection of these two classifications gives rise to four types of effects: direct material effects (formulation of a policy ordered by the Court); indirect material effects (intervention of new actors in the debate); direct symbolic effects (reframing of media coverage); and indirect symbolic effects (the transformation of public opinion on the matter).

With this typology in mind, let us return to the contrast between the neorealist and constructivist approaches. While neorealists center on direct material effects – that is, on the ruling's *enforcement* (Rosenberg 1991) – constructivists consider all four types (Bourdieu 1987). This explains why a judgment can be seen as ineffective by neorealists and as effective by constructivists, to the extent that what the latter see as impact includes a broader set of effects.

In this vein, a neorealist analysis would conclude that virtually all landmark cases in SER jurisprudence have had little impact. Consider, for instance, the well-known South African Constitutional Court ruling on the right to housing in the *Grootboom* case. The fact that the plaintiff, Irene Grootboom, sadly died in a shack while waiting for a decent house eight years after winning the case would suggest that the ruling was in vain, as its expected direct material effects failed to materialize (Joubert 2008). This conclusion, however, ignores important outcomes of the case. For instance, it misses the multiple indirect material and symbolic effects produced by the *Grootboom* ruling, like the flood of similar litigation whereby communities in different parts of South Africa managed to fend off eviction to the creation of emergency housing policies (Langford 2013).

Our study of the impact of T25 is informed by the theory and methods of constructivism. As the following section shows, our case study suggests that indirect and symbolic effects may have legal and social consequences that are just as profound as the decision's direct material effects.

TABLE 1.2. *Distribution of Ruling T25's Effects across Direct–Indirect, Material–Symbolic Typology*

	Direct		Indirect
	Unlocking		
Material	Policy	Participatory	
			Socioeconomic
Symbolic			
			Reframing

1.6.2. *The Effects of SER Rulings: The Case of T25*

As will be detailed in Chapter 2, the CCC dictated three main orders in T25. First, it mandated that the government formulate a coherent plan of action to tackle the IDPs' humanitarian emergency and to overcome the unconstitutional state of affairs. Second, it mandated the administration to calculate the budget that was needed to implement such a plan of action and to explore all possible avenues to actually invest the amount calculated on programs for IDPs. Third, it instructed the government to guarantee the protection of at least the survival-level content ("minimum core") of the most basic rights – food, education, health care, land, and housing. The Court directed these three orders to all relevant public agencies, including national governmental entities and local authorities.

After ten years, what effects have these and subsequent orders had? Interviews with key actors, content analysis of press coverage, participatory observation of court-sponsored meetings and hearings, and data from the extensive paper trail left by this case substantiate the existence of five major effects, as represented in Table 1.2. The following sections will provide short descriptions of each of the effects identified in the table and establish the structure of the book by identifying the chapters that further elaborate them.

1.6.2.1. Unlocking Effect

As we will see in Chapter 3, T25's immediate effect was to shake up state bureaucracies in charge of attending to the displaced population. By mandating the government to draft a coherent policy to protect the rights of IDPs, and by setting deadlines for progress, the CCC used SERs as "destabilization rights" (Unger 1987) – leverage points for breaking institutional inertia and prompting the government into action. Thus, in terms of the above typology, this was a direct material impact of the ruling.

Several interviewees highlighted this effect. For instance, the attorney in charge of IDP issues at the Ombudsman's Office explained how the impending deadlines to report back to the Court served as an effective nudge for the relevant government agencies. He recalled that "in interagency preparatory meetings prior to follow-up meetings with the Court, national and local law enforcement officials would state that they had to hurry because they were going before the Court or because they would miss the Court's deadline."[10] As we will see, the Court kept the pressure on the government through follow-up orders and meetings, which further nudged the government into action. Periodic orders from the Court, which opened the process for contempt complaints against government officials – as well as critical reports from the Attorney General, the Comptroller, and the Ombudsman on the failures of implementation – have kept the pressure on the government to fulfill its obligations.[11]

Further, the structural policy failures underlying the IDPs' humanitarian emergency stemmed not only from the inaction of relevant institutions, but also from the lack of coordination among them. In instructing those institutions to collaborate on the design, financing, and implementation of a unified policy on IDPs, the CCC promoted this type of coordination among agencies directly targeted by the decision and among agencies indirectly related to the case. Hence, as represented in Table 1.2, this was a direct material effect.

In the words of a Ministry of Education official, "the ruling told us to put our own house in order. And it allowed us in government to solve who does what, and to determine which tasks need to be carried out collaboratively by everyone."[12] Although far from perfect, the result is a functioning inter-agency coordination committee that meets regularly and reports back to the Court.[13]

Moreover, T25 had a direct impact on the government's allocation of funds for programs for IDPs due to the Court's second order. Indeed, the ruling prompted the administration to triple the budget allocated to these programs

[10] Interview with Hernando Toro, Ombudsman's Office, Coordinator of the Office of Displacement Assistance, January 22, 2009.

[11] *El Tiempo*, "The Year of IDPs," April 8, 2007.

[12] Interview with Yaneth Guevara, Ministry of Education, February 2009.

[13] Interview with Luis Domingo Gómez, Minister of Environment, Housing, and Development, January 2009.

in 2004 and has had a steady upward effect on the budget since that time (Conpes document 3400 of 2005). The 2014 national budget for IDP programs, albeit still insufficient, was almost ten times that of 2004 (National Planning Department and Ministry of Finance 2014; see also Chapter 3)

1.6.2.2. Policy Effect

As Chapter 4 explains, T25 has had a sizable impact on the design of a long-term national policy on IDPs, as well as on the establishment of mechanisms to implement, fund, and monitor IDPs' programs. Indeed, one year after the judgment, in direct response to the Court's first order, the government issued the National Plan for Comprehensive Care for People Displaced by Violence (Decree 250 of 2005). Thus, given the focus on concrete changes in government policy, this effect is solidly categorized as a direct, material consequence of the Court's ruling.

1.6.1.3. Participatory Effect

As explained in Chapter 5, the CCC has encouraged engagement by, and dialogue among, state agencies and civil society organizations through hearings and periodic petitions for information, thus promoting the type of dialogic judicial activism that we argue can enhance the impact of SER rulings.

This follow-up process to T25 has opened up judicial proceedings and policy making to a broad range of governmental and non-governmental actors. This key material effect has been partly the direct product of the ruling and partly an indirect, unexpected consequence of it. From the beginning, the CCC's orders directly involved not only the core government agencies responsible for IDPs, but also all others with related responsibilities at the international, national, and local levels.

Interestingly, an indirect outcome of the judgment was the formation of civil society organizations and coalitions to participate in the monitoring process. NGOs such as the Consultancy for Human Rights and Displacement (Codhes), the Center for Law, Justice, and Society (Dejusticia), and *Viva la Ciudadanía* joined efforts with grassroots organizations, sectors of the Catholic Church, and academia to found a coalition specifically geared to contribute to the implementation of T25: the Monitoring Commission on Public Policy on Forced Displacement (henceforth, Monitoring Commission). In a striking boomerang effect, the CCC subsequently acknowledged the Commission as party to the follow-up procedures and relied heavily on the data and recommendations that the Commission submitted.[14] Thus, although it was not officially appointed as such by the CCC, the Commission has, in practice, played a role similar to that of the monitoring committees set up by the Indian Supreme Court to oversee the implementation of its decision (Chitalkar and Gauri forthcoming). Thus, the participatory effect straddles the direct and indirect threshold as some of its aspects resulted from explicit orders from the Court while others developed unexpectedly.

1.6.2.4. Reframing Effect

Symbolic reshaping extends beyond the right-holders targeted by the ruling. Through T25 and the follow-up process, the CCC has helped to reframe the issue of forced displacement – once considered a side effect of armed conflict – as a human rights problem requiring immediate action. This is an indirect consequence of the ruling as it concerns a group of actors much broader than the IDPs, ranging from the media to international human rights agencies to the public at large.

As explained in Chapter 6, content analysis of press coverage on forced displacement gives some indication about the operation of this effect. Whereas in the period prior to the judgment (2000–2003), the press covered displacement mostly through the frame of "armed conflict," in the subsequent period (2004–2013), legal categories have come to dominate press coverage of the issue. Indeed, forced displacement is discussed mostly in pieces whose dominant frame is "human rights violations" or "lack of compliance with the law."

1.6.2.5. Socioeconomic Effect

Every SER ruling targets specific sectors of the population as beneficiaries, be it homeless citizens vindicating their right to decent housing, as in *Grootboom*, or impoverished sectors of the population suffering from hunger and malnutrition, as in the right-to-food structural case in India. A key question, therefore, is how a given ruling has affected the conditions of that specific social sector. In this case, has T25 contributed to the amelioration of Colombian IDPs' socioeconomic situation?

[14] Although the Court has not issued an official declaration making the Commission a party, it has effectively acknowledged it as a party. See, e.g., Colombian Constitutional Court, Decision 109 of 2007; Colombian Constitutional Court, Decision 8 of 2009.

In Chapter 7, we consider this question, which pertains to an indirect material effect of T25, as changes in the situation of IDPs do not stem directly from the Court's orders, but rather are mediated by the workings of the institutional reforms mandated by the Court. There is no definitive answer to it, as attempts to answer are riddled with methodological difficulties. Specifically, one of the defining traits of systemic policy failures is a lack of reliable data on the conditions of the victimized population. Indeed, this was one of the reasons why the CCC declared an unconstitutional state of affairs in T25. Thus, we lack a baseline for making comparisons with the IDPs' socioeconomic situation after the decision. However, since the abovementioned civil society Monitoring Commission collects quality survey data, it is at least possible to have a sense of the evolution of the conditions of the IDPs after the judgment. The latest figures show that the situation has changed little: although access to education and health care has dramatically improved, benefiting nearly 80 percent of IDPs, conditions with regards to all other SERs continue to be unsatisfactory.

As suggested by the location of this type of impact in Table 1.2, court decisions can also have symbolic effects on the beneficiary social sector, as their members and organizations adopt the language of the law to frame their future claims. Interviews and participant observation with leaders of the IDP population made this evident, as they peppered their discourse with allusions to the technical language of the Court. Terms such as *tutela* (constitutional writ of protection), *auto* (follow-up injunction), and *audiencia* (hearing) often become intertwined with personal stories of uprooting and radical deprivation.[15]

1.7. AN EMPIRICAL CASE FOR DIALOGIC JUDICIAL ACTIVISM

Beyond the specifics of T25, the empirical analysis of its effects illustrates a general point: judicial activism with regard to SERs may have consequential impacts that go well beyond the direct and material consequences stipulated in court orders. These impacts become visible with the aid of an expanded analytical and methodological toolkit.

This is not to suggest, of course, that structural rulings on SERs in general, and T25 in particular, produce the whole range of effects, nor that when they do have an impact it is substantial. Indeed, the results of T25 have been mixed, as the subsequent chapters will show. While some of its effects (such as the

[15] Interview with Eusebio Mosquera, founding member of the Colombian Association of Displaced Afro-Colombians. Geneva, August 17, 2009; interview with Anonymous.

unlocking and reframing effects) have been profound, others (such as the policy and socioeconomic effects) have been moderate.

Nonetheless, the breadth and depth of T25's effects remain striking when compared to those of other structural rulings by the CCC and other tribunals. What accounts for this variation? In Chapter 8, we argue that institutional mechanisms associated with dialogic judicial activism provide useful clues to answer this question.

Inspired by decisions such as T25 in Colombia, *PUCL* in India, and *Riachuelo* in Argentina, a growing literature in comparative constitutionalism has extolled rulings that, in addition to protecting SERs, promote democratic deliberation. Proponents of this type of dialogic activism aim for an intermediate path between judicial restraint and juristocracy (Hogg and Bushell 1997). While defending the justiciability of SERs, they criticize rulings that, by imposing detailed policies and programs, encroach upon the purview of the executive and legislative branches and close off opportunities for public debate on the underlying socioeconomic issues (Dixon 2007). In their view, instead of playing the classical adjudicator role, courts should exercise "judging by nudging" (Klein 2008), by serving as promoters of deliberation and communicative action among state and social actors (Gauri and Brinks 2012) and fostering reasoned engagement around alternative solutions to pressing distributional dilemmas (Chandrachud 2009; Shankar 2013).

Thus far, the case for dialogic activism has rested on democratic theory and constitutional law. In response to the classic objection against judicial activism – that it allegedly lacks democratic legitimacy and violates the separation-of-powers principle – constitutional scholars and theorists of deliberative democracy have cogently demonstrated the democratic credentials of judicial interventions that elicit collaboration among the different branches of power and promote deliberation on public issues (Abramovich 2005; Gargarella 2006). These and other contributions have made a case for dialogic activism on the grounds that it deepens democratic legitimacy in constitutional regimes committed to decent standards of economic well-being.

In Chapter 8, we want to make a different yet complementary case for dialogic activism. By drawing lessons from the study of T25 and comparing it with similar rulings in Colombia and elsewhere, we want to make an *empirical* case for this approach (Rodríguez-Garavito 2011a). We thus address the two classical objections to judicial activism – that judges are not elected and thus lack democratic legitimacy, and that courts lack the requisite institutional capacity to deal with complex socioeconomic issues and enforce their rulings

(Rosenberg 1991) – by locating the debate in "actually existing democracies," as illustrated by the institutional contexts in which structural cases on SERs occur.

In response to the criticism of the undemocratic origins of judges, we use the evidence from the case study and similar rulings to question the idealized and limited conception of democracy that underlies the views of proponents of judicial passivism. Indeed, those advocating for judges' passivity assume that, unlike the judiciary, other branches of government are democratically legitimated and are invariably subject to democratic accountability mechanisms.

Policy and institutional practice, however, call into question this assumption. This idealized vision of elected bodies can be countered just by looking at the evidence of influence-peddling scandals (legal and illegal) in national parliaments around the world, or attempts by presidentialist governments to manipulate constitutional rules for personal gain. The legitimacy of actually existing democracies is far more complex and problematic than critics suggest.

Practical difficulties are compounded by problems of institutional design. As O'Donnell (1999) has argued, traditional channels of accountability – "vertical" voting mechanisms, whereby voters control elected officials – are too sporadic and subject to manipulation to ensure, by themselves, the validity of democratic order and constitutional rights. For the maintenance of democracy and the rule of law, "horizontal" accountability mechanisms are equally important. These mechanisms create accountability and control *among* state entities themselves, such as judicial review of executive and legislative actions by the courts.

This horizontal dimension of democracy requires the courts to take precisely the type of action that critics condemn, including judicial intervention to protect rights against actions or omissions of the government or legislature. Considering the complex bureaucracies that make up contemporary democratic states, government transparency and accountability cannot be guaranteed through election mechanisms alone. As Sabel and Simon cogently claim, "[p]ublic law litigation rejects the notion that accountability can be assumed from the fact that an agency is nested in a larger administrative structure formally headed by an elected official. Such an assumption would turn separation-of-powers doctrine into empty formalism" (Sabel and Simon 2004: 1094).

Our case study provides empirical ammunition for this response to the critics, as well as for the revision of canonical views of the doctrine of separations of powers in comparative constitutionalism. We show that, in actually existing democracies, there are recurrent institutional deadlocks and policies that impede the realization of rights. While they are common in the Global North (Sabel and Simon 2004), they are particularly frequent and consequential for the enjoyment of basic SERs in the Global South. In these situations, the judiciary often appears to be the only state organ with the independence and power to break the institutional blockage. If judicial activism occurs under the appropriate circumstances and through appropriate mechanisms, its effects, instead of being undemocratic, can energize and promote democracy. The study of T25 and similar rulings reveals innovative institutional practices in the Global South that address the legitimacy objection and hold out the prospect for a revision of canonical conceptions of the principle of separation of powers, in the South and the North alike.

Regarding the question of capacity, evidence from our case study requires that we rethink its terms: capacity for what? The judicial incapacity argument of authors such as Rosenberg makes two controversial assumptions. First, they have in mind the type of judicial activism that marked U.S. jurisprudence in the 1950s through the 1980s, characterized by strong remedies – that is, by rulings mandating very detailed policy and institutional reforms. In this sense, they refer to courts' lack of capacity to implement such reforms. As shown by many judicial interventions seeking to reform the dysfunctional U.S. prison system, judges not only said that there was a structural violation of prisoners' rights, but they also sought to address it through direct and detailed orders on matters as specific as the number of guards that should be hired and the prison facilities' design details (Feeley and Rubin 1998). This is the same type of judicial activism seen in some of the CCC rulings of the 1990s, such as the aforementioned Judgment C-700 of 1999,[16] which not only declared the system of housing finance to be unconstitutional, but also instructed Congress to legislate a replacement system based on a set of detailed parameters.

Second, in pointing out the inability of judges to enforce their decisions, critics take for granted that this type of judicial activism predominantly utilizes judgment-monitoring processes that often place the courts alone in tackling impermeable bureaucracies resistant to change. It is an adversarial process, where the courts and relevant state institutions are usually the only participants. Under these conditions, it is not surprising that the capacity of judges was insufficient to, by themselves, enforce their judgments. However, it is this

[16] See note 8, this chapter.

heroic capacity that authors such as Rosenberg seem to take for granted in criticizing judicial activism.

Our empirical study shows that, indeed, the transformations generated by detailed top-down court orders are much less ambitious than those envisioned by the courts, largely because of resistance from vested interests and because of the legal and technical limitations on courts' capacity to deal with structural social problems. However, evidence of the limited effects of monologic activism does not undermine judicial activism per se, as defenders of judicial restraint would have it. Nor do these effects call into question the justiciability of SERs at large. Nonetheless, these effects do call for a reconstruction of the theory and practice of court interventions in structural socioeconomic issues, in order to address the above-mentioned objections through dialogic activism. This is the task we undertake in Chapter 8.

However, dialogic activism has problems of its own. In recapping our argument in Chapter 9, we point to some of the dilemmas that dialogic courts such as the CCC and the Indian Supreme Court currently face. Prominent among them are institutional burnout, difficulties for measuring progress, and increasing citizen demands for courts to get involved in dealing with massive violations of SERs. These dilemmas point to new avenues for research and public debate.

To understand the potential and dilemmas of activist courts, it is necessary to understand the complex and urgent socioeconomic challenges that they seek to address. In the next chapter, we begin our case study by going back to 2004, to the moment when the CCC, faced with thousands of petitions from victims of forced displacement like Danelly Estupiñán, decided to step in.

2

The Case Study: Forced Internal Displacement and the Intervention of the Colombian Constitutional Court

By definition, the study of the impact of judicial activism involves contrasting the situation before judicial intervention with the situation after. Thus, in this chapter, we open the case study of T25 with a panoramic description of the state of the problem and public policies on forced displacement in Colombia prior to the judgment. Against that background, the subsequent section explains the nature of the Court's intervention, and the last section presents the main actors involved in the case. In the following chapters we analyze the effects of the ruling and the implementation process.

2.1. THE EXPLOSION OF FORCED DISPLACEMENT AND THE EMERGENCE OF A PUBLIC POLICY

2.1.1. *Evolution of Displacement*

In the context of the Colombian armed conflict, forced displacement is not a new phenomenon. Between 1946 and 1966, a period known as *La Violencia* (1948–1953), about two million people were forcibly displaced and never returned (Roldán 2003). Between 1984 and 1995, approximately 600,000 people were victims of displacement (Episcopal Conference of Colombia 1995).

In the second half of the nineties, with the escalation of the armed conflict, internal displacement increased significantly (UNHCR 2007: 13). The most severe displacement occurred between 2000 and 2002 (see Figure 2.1), a period that coincided with the expansion of right-wing paramilitary groups and the collapse of the peace talks with the Revolutionary Armed Forces of Colombia (FARC for its Spanish name), the largest and oldest leftist guerrilla group (Monitoring Commission 2008; Ibáñez 2008: 10). As newspapers reported at the time, "2002 was a dismal year for forced displacement in Colombia.

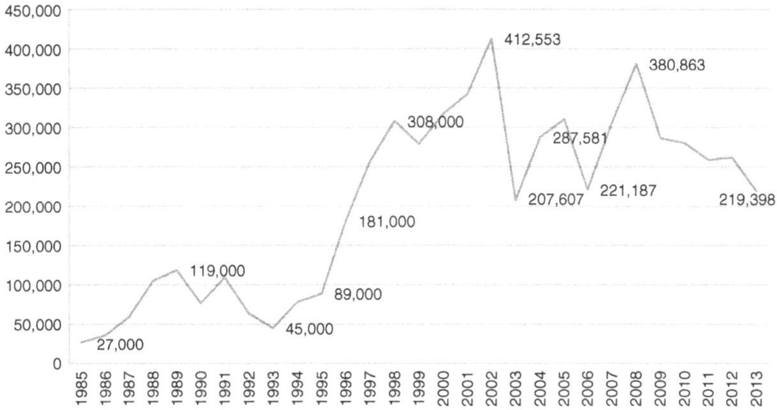

FIGURE 2.1 Evolution of Forced Displacement in Colombia: The Number of Displaced Persons per Year (1985–2013)
Source: Codhes (2014).

During those 12 months, marked by the end of the peace process with the FARC and the transition from the Pastrana administration to the Administration of Alvaro Uribe, 85 percent of the country's municipalities saw some percentage of their population flee for reasons related to armed conflict."[1]

Forced displacement has a number of conflict-related causes. According to the most recent survey carried out with a representative sample of IDPs, the main reasons for leaving are direct threats, murder of relatives and neighbors, massacres, and armed combat (Monitoring Commission 2010: 34).

Contrary to what happened in other countries with large-scale forced displacement (e.g., Sudan, Rwanda, and Syria), where people move en masse to take refuge in special camps which are often across national borders, displacements in Colombia are mainly individual and within the national territory (Ibáñez 2008: 13). However, mass displacements intensified with the escalation of the armed conflict in the nineties (Conpes document 2924 of 1997: 6).[2] At the end of 1996, a mass exodus began in various parts of the

[1] *El Tiempo*, "Colombia Reached Record Rate of Displacement," April 29, 2003

[2] According to Colombian law, "massive displacement means displacement of ten or more households, or fifty or more people. Household means home or group of people, relatives or not, that lives under one roof and shares food and have been affected by forced displacement because of violence" (Decree 2569 of 2000, article 12).

country, particularly in the northern and western states of Antioquia, César, and Chocó. As in the case of individual displacements, the worst of the mass displacements took place between 2000 and 2002.

2.1.2. *Denial of the Problem and the Absence of a State Policy*

Until the mid-nineties, the gravity and magnitude of forced displacement contrasted with the political position of governments, which, without recognizing the contribution of the armed conflict, attributed the problem to economic reasons or natural disasters. This denial of the problem went hand-in-hand with the lack of public policies. As the government recognized in 1995, "faced with the situation before us, the state has been acting in a temporary, deficient and dispersed manner" (Conpes document 2804 of 1995: 4).

After his visit to Colombia in 1994, the Representative of the UN Secretary-General on Internally Displaced Persons, Francis M. Deng, said that "the Government of Colombia does not have any statistics on the number of IDPs, however some government officials, in conversations with the representative, emphasized that the problem was very serious" (Human Rights Commission 1995: paragraph 10). He also stressed that, until that moment, there did not seem to be any methodologically acceptable attempt to calculate the number of internally displaced persons (Human Rights Commission 1995: paragraph 15).

Due to this vacuum on the part of the state, civil society and international organizations such as the Catholic Church, the International Committee of the Red Cross, and the Consultancy for Human Rights and Displacement (Codhes for its Spanish name) provided humanitarian aid and support to the displaced population. For example, the Presidential Council for Human Rights implemented some isolated government projects (Human Rights Commission 1995: paragraph 86), but there were no such programs in several parts of the country (Human Rights Commission 1995: paragraph 59). In short, there was neither an articulated public policy nor a coordinated set of institutions to address the humanitarian crisis caused by forced displacement.

Only in 1995 did the national government recognize that internal displacement was closely linked to the violence, was an urgent humanitarian issue that needed to be incorporated into the public agenda, and would require the development of a policy proposal. It did so through a high-level national policy document that approved the National Program for the Integral Assistance to the Population Displaced by Violence (hereinafter the Program) (Conpes document 2804 of 1995).[3]

The Program identified a range of strategies to address the problem, which included the following: displacement prevention programs; immediate assistance to the emergency; socioeconomic consolidation and stabilization; outreach and research; and social provisions in the areas of education, health, housing, and employment. The policy document also ordered the creation of a set of institutions to implement the Program, including the National Council for Integral Assistance to Displaced Population (CNAIPD for its Spanish name), responsible for setting national policy. Although a deadline of five months was set, the Program's entry into operation took several years.

The IDP's humanitarian emergency also drew the attention of the international community which, until then, was only represented by the International Committee of the Red Cross (Human Rights Commission 1995: paragraph 101). In May 1997, the Inter-American Human Rights Institute, with support from the Swedish Government, organized an inter-agency mission to the region of Pavarandó. The inter-agency mission marked the international decision to intervene, support, and participate in the Colombian humanitarian situation.

Two years after designing the Program through the National Council for Social and Economic Policy (Conpes document No. 2804), and despite the magnitude of the problem posed by the worsening situation of violence-motivated internal displacement, there was no genuine public policy on comprehensive care for the displaced population. In the words of the government, the Program presented "difficulties of management and interagency coordination regarding information and [difficulties] of a financial nature." Given this situation, in May 1997, the Government issued another high-level national policy document, titled The National System for the Comprehensive Assistance to the Population Displaced by Violence, in order "to address existing institutional weaknesses that had limited the state's ability to meet the challenge of providing comprehensive care to the population displaced by violence" (Conpes document 2924 of 1997).

To enhance institutional capacity, the new document modified the institutional structure established by the earlier 1995 Conpes document. The new system was composed of public and private entities at the national and territorial levels, each of which undertook specific measures of assistance to

3 The Conpes documents are high-level national policy documents issued by the National Council for Social and Economic Policy, which is the ultimate authority of national planning and acts as the advisory body to the Government on matters relating to the country's economic and social development.

the displaced population. The document declared that the entities' responsibility would be to implement the agenda contained in the 1995 Conpes document. The 1997 Conpes document launched and changed the composition of the CNAIPD, which, in the two years prior, had not convened, and whose duties include approving the National Policy and the National Plan for the Comprehensive Assistance to the Population Displaced by Violence.

These guidelines, however, had a short life. As we shall see, they were replaced by those specified in a law issued by Congress shortly thereafter.

2.1.3. *The Emergence of Legislation on Displacement*

These two high-level policy documents laid the foundation for a public policy on displacement, but the enactment of the National Plan for Comprehensive Assistance to the Population Displaced by Violence (Law 387 of 1997) created the legal framework for comprehensive assistance to the displaced population. This Law was the result of an inter-agency effort by a team made up of the Presidential Office for Displaced Persons, scholars from the National and Javeriana Universities, the Ministry of the Interior, the Ombudsman's Office, and the Catholic Church.

The Law picked up and articulated what had already been established in the Conpes documents from 1995 and 1997. The Executive branch and the Legislature agreed upon the dimensions that the realigned public policy should have, namely: (i) prevention of displacement, (ii) emergency humanitarian assistance, (iii) voluntary return and population resettlement, and (iv) socioeconomic stabilization.

The Law marks a turning point in terms of legal and public policy formulation at the national level. The Legislature, which had hitherto been absent as an actor, entered the field of displacement policy formulation. Additionally, the Law explicitly recognized the rights of the displaced population.

The 1997 Law also represents a turning point in the international sphere because, "at the time of issue, there were few national and international policies to refer to" (UNHCR 2007: 16). In fact, the UN Human Rights Commission adopted the famous Guiding Principles on Internal Displacement, established by Francis M. Deng,[4] only a few months later in February 1998.

To implement the law, the government issued a series of decrees requiring public policies on three dimensions: adoption of a national plan for assistance,

[4] Which is why they are also known as the Deng Principles.

creation of an assistance fund, and the assignment of responsibility for coordination of IDP policy to the then Social Solidarity Network (subsequently known as the Social Action Agency and now the Unit for Victims' Attention and Reparation and the Land Restitution Unit) tasked with the assistance and coordination of IDP policy. However, the implementation of these standards was limited in practice. In 1999, the government acknowledged deep flaws in the system of service provision to IDPs:

> These policies have faced dispersal of powers (19 public entities involved), the lack of a monitoring system, and the absence of a system of performance indicators to define institutional responsibilities and create a framework for accountability. Similarly, the concentration of activities in state institutions has prevented the articulation and supplementing of their actions by non-governmental organizations (NGOs) and international agencies with extensive experience. Finally, work is needed on improving the institutional ability to channel technical and financial efforts more evenly across regions (Conpes document 3057 of 1999).

In the same statement of accountability, the government acknowledged that:

> There is dispersion in the sources that estimate the total number of displaced persons, and deficiencies in population registration, monitoring and early warning mechanisms. These deficiencies are due to the absence of a single standard methodology, and they have led to unofficial estimates that generate confusion and impede having a current and accurate understanding of the problem. There is also the need to create technical bodies responsible for analyzing information and developing mechanisms for communicating in a timely manner to the responsible entities (Conpes document 3057 of 1999).

Given sustained problems, the government issued a third, high-level policy document (Conpes document 3057 of 1999) which presented an action plan to improve the mechanisms and instruments for the prevention, protection, humanitarian assistance, return, relocation, and economic stabilization of the population displaced by violence. Among the measures, it ordered the creation of an Early Warning System coordinated by the Office of the Ombudsman, to enable any person to report information about potential acts of displacement. The objective of this system was to prevent displacement while preparing and mobilizing the population at risk.

Despite the legal framework and the existence of three high-level policy documents to deal with displaced persons, the problem worsened during the early 2000s. According to the NGO Codhes, the cumulative number of IDPs

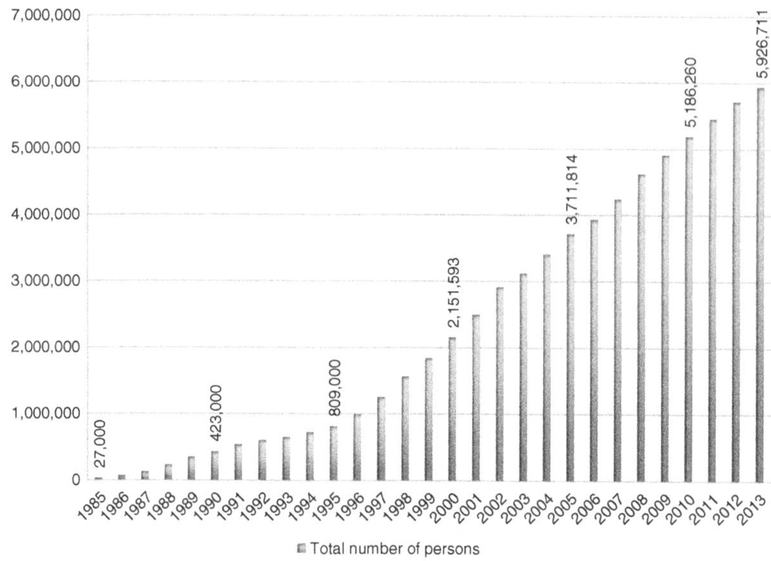

FIGURE 2.2 Evolution of Forced Displacement in Colombia: The Cumulative Number of Displaced Persons per Year (1985–2013)
Source: Codhes (2014).

reached 2.1 million in the year 2000 (see Figure 2.2) and the country witnessed the highest number of displaced persons in a single year with 412,553 in 2002 (see Figure 2.1).

Given the worsening humanitarian crisis and the need to avoid institutional dispersion in the provision of services to the displaced population, authorities initiated institutional changes in the early 2000s to enhance assistance to IDPs. For example, a centralized registration system was put in place[5] and municipal, district, and state committees for the assistance to the displaced populations were created (Decree 2569 of 2000). Additionally, the penal code was amended to criminalize forced displacement, genocide, forced disappearance, and torture (Law 589 of 2000, article 284). Likewise, the government devised mechanisms to protect the land of the displaced population (Decree 2007 of 2001).

[5] The registration system is called the Singular Registry of Displaced Population (RUPD for its Spanish name).

The summary presented of the period between 1995 and 2004 suggests that those years were an embryonic stage for the recognition of the problem and formulation of rules, policies, and institutions in response. The effectiveness of these initial efforts was low and the gap continued to widen between the supply of effective state programs and the demand for prevention and assistance programs for IDPs.

It was at this stage of abundant-but-inefficient regulatory practices that the Constitutional Court came to play the roles of evaluator and coordinator of public policy through a judgment and monitoring process that would alter the perception and treatment of forced displacement. As *Semana* magazine reported at the time of the judgment, "in Colombia the most serious problems are magically resolved with a law. That this law is enforced is another story. But either way, this judgment is revolutionary in that the Constitutional Court ordered the state ... to take seriously the plight of the displaced"[6] We devote the rest of this chapter to this judgment and the implementation process that followed and is still ongoing.

2.2. THE COURT INTERVENES: JUDGMENT T25 OF 2004

2.2.1. *Background: The Status of the Unconstitutional State of Affairs and the Court's Jurisprudence on Displacement*

Before Judgment T25 of 2004 (heretofore T25), the Constitutional Court had handed down seventeen judgments related to forced displacement. In retrospect, the Court appears to have progressively expanded its scope with regard to the issue. While in 1997 the orders were addressed to specific officials and agencies and the solutions contemplated violations of individual rights, between 2000 and 2003 the Constitutional Court proffered several rulings applying to the entire displaced population and made general policy assessments. A quick look at some judgments illustrates this change and demonstrates the novelty of T25.

In the first judgment concerning displacement (T-227 of 1997), the effects of the decision, as is generally the rule in *tutela* judgments, only applied to the plaintiffs. The Court upheld the farmers' rights of freedom, resistance, freedom of movement, and human dignity that had been displaced by paramilitary groups. The Court took into consideration that they had been discriminated against by the then governor of the state of Cundinamarca in addition to 100 different mayors, who accused the displaced farmers of being

6 *Semana*, "The Final Judgment," June 13, 2005.

guerillas and denied them a transitional establishment and the possibility of purchasing land.

Three years later, the Court began to play the role of public policy evaluator that it would systematically develop with T25. In a 2000 ruling (Judgment SU-1150), in addition to taking measures to specifically protect the plaintiffs, the Court ruled on public policy and the political actors responsible for those policies. The Court highlighted the lack of coordination between institutions and the poor development of state policy on forced displacement, as required by Law 387 of 1997. Likewise, in 2003, the Court issued a new ruling (T-602) regarding a *tutela* filed by an elderly victim of displacement, to whom the state had denied health care, housing benefits, and financial support to undertake a farming project. The Court ruled that the state should promote affirmative action and give differential assistance to displaced people. It also defined fundamental concepts, which apply to the entire displaced population, including cessation of IDP status, reparation, and vulnerability. With T25, the Court would adopt an even more activist position.

2.2.2. *Judgment T25 of 2004*

Against this jurisprudential backdrop, in T25 the Court reviewed 108 constitutional writs of protection (*tutelas*) that were filed in 22 cities by 1,150 displaced families with an average of 4 members each.[7] The defendants included a dozen national and local public institutions and officials.[8] The root of the plaintiffs' claims was the failure of the state to meet its duty of care for displaced populations and a failure to effectively respond to their requests. As was made clear in the facts of the judgment, when victims of displacement required assistance to which they were entitled under the Law 387 of 1997, they were met with numerous excuses by authorities.[9]

After an exhaustive evaluation of public policy and the claims of displaced persons, the Court found a number of elements that qualified the humanitarian situation of displaced persons as an "unconstitutional

[7] For a discussion of various aspects of this judgment, see Rodríguez-Garavito 2009b.

[8] Among the defendant institutions and officials were: Social Solidarity Network, Ministry of Finance, Ministry of Social Protection, Ministry of Agriculture, Ministry of Education, National Learning Service (SENA), Colombian Institute of Agrarian Reform (INCORA, today the Colombian Institute of Rural Development, INCODER), and some governors and mayors of areas where the plaintiffs resided.

[9] Among the common responses were: that the entity was not competent because it had only a coordinating role; there was no budget available; humanitarian aid was only for three months and exceptionally extended for another three months; the entity was in liquidation; there was an error in the request; or the housing aid program was suspended due to lack of available budget.

state of affairs."[10] In terms of the elements of judicial activism laid out in Chapter 1, the fact that the Court used the doctrine it had established for condemning and addressing the most serious and massive violations of human rights, which required immediate protection of at least the minimum core of victims' rights, qualifies this ruling as an instance of a strong rights approach.

The Court found that numerous authorities responsible for providing IDPs with assistance and protection repeatedly failed to do so in a timely and effective manner. For example, according to several reports presented to the Court, more than half of those registered as displaced (57 percent) were not receiving emergency humanitarian aid and 80.5 percent of them were not enrolled in income generation programs, which would allow them to live autonomously and with dignity.

Additionally, the Court found poor performance results related to displaced children's access to education. It also established that displaced persons were unaware of their basic rights. The Court likewise highlighted the nearly 50 percent reduction in resources allotted for the comprehensive assistance of the displaced population, going from 130,000 million pesos (US $72m) in 2002 to 70,000 million (US $39m) in 2003. Bearing in mind all of the above, the Court declared the violation of multiple fundamental rights of the plaintiffs in the case and the displaced population in general and, for that reason, declared an "unconstitutional state of affairs" concerning forced displacement.

As noted, T25 was not the Court's first decision declaring an unconstitutional state of affairs. By 2004 this determination had been made on seven occasions, related to varying circumstances such as noncompliance with the state's obligation to register public school teachers in the social security system (Judgment SU-559 of 1997), massive prison overcrowding (Judgment T-153 of 1998), and the failure to pay salaries to municipal civil servants (Judgment T-144, 1999) (Rodríguez-Garavito 2009b).

Faced with the facts of case T25, the Court had four alternative courses of action. The choices included: a judgment that would meet only the demands of the parties in the process; bringing non-parties into the process in order to make a ruling that would apply to all similar future cases; creating a ruling that would apply to third parties that shared common circumstances with the plaintiffs but would not apply to future cases; or declaring an unconstitutional state of affairs, which would mandate the adoption of policies or programs that benefit people who did not bring the case (Botero 2006: 161).

[10] For an analysis of the Court's doctrine of unconstitutional state of affairs, see generally Rodríguez-Garavito (2009b).

Of the four options, the Court chose the last. "We adopted this determination," the Court explained at the time, "because of the situation of widespread and systematic ignorance of the constitutional rights of people displaced by violence, and the structural failures of the State´s response" (Constitutional Court, Press Release, February 6, 2004).

The declaration of an unconstitutional state of affairs had a double meaning. On one hand, the Court established that displaced persons were in a precarious situation due to a structural problem that stemmed from a prolonged failure on the part of the institutions comprising the National System for the Comprehensive Assistance. On the other hand, the unconstitutional state of affairs showed that, in terms of forced displacement, there were few legislative, administrative, and budgetary instruments to avoid the violation of rights. Therefore, the Court found the need for a comprehensive settlement covering all persons immersed in the problem, not only those IDPs who initiated the action.

As we saw in the previous chapter, the Court did not merely state the existence of massive rights violations in general terms. Having learned from the ineffectiveness of previous rulings on unconstitutional states of affairs, the Court retained jurisdiction over the matter and conducted a detailed and continuous monitoring process of the state's performance after judgment T25. To this end, the Court issued numerous specific orders mandating the state to: i) create an action plan to end the unconstitutional state of affairs, ii) strive to ensure the necessary budget to implement the plan, and iii) ensure the basic rights of the displaced population. We now turn to how the Court itself followed up on those orders.

2.3. THE JUDGMENT IN MOTION: PUBLIC HEARINGS, TECHNICAL SESSIONS, FOLLOW-UP DECISIONS, AND THE SPECIAL MONITORING CHAMBER

2.3.1. *The Monitoring Mechanisms*

Unlike previous decisions about unconstitutional states of affairs, in T25 the Constitutional Court did not conclude its work with the enactment of the judgment.[11] The Court retained jurisdiction over the case[12] and unleashed a

[11] In Judgment T-153 of 1998, for example, the Court declared the unconstitutional state of prisons in the country. And even though the current situation in prisons shows that the causes of fundamental rights violations of prisoners persist, the Court has not followed up on its judgment (see Chapter 8).

[12] In accordance with Colombian law, the Constitutional Court "will maintain competency until the right is completely restored or the causes of the threat are eliminated" (Decree 2591 of 1991, article 27).

process of regular monitoring and public participation that continues today, ten years later. In terms of the characterization of judicial activism offered in Chapter 1, it is clear that the persistence and intensity of the follow-up process qualifies it as an instance of strong monitoring.

One of the mechanisms chosen by the Court to track the judgment was the holding of follow-up public hearings (see Chapter 5). About a year after issuing the ruling, the Court requested reports from the core agencies responsible for IDPs, such as the Ministry of the Interior, but also from associations of displaced persons and international agencies such as the UNHCR. On this basis, the Court convened the first public hearing (June 29, 2005), "in order to collect the latest evidence relevant to deciding whether or not there was compliance with the orders of Judgment T25 of 2004 on overcoming the unconstitutional state of affairs, and then to take action as appropriate." The hearing brought in Ministers, the Director of the National Planning Department, and the Attorney General. NGOs, the UNHCR, representatives of the IDP population, and entities that had submitted reports to the Court were also in attendance. After this first experience, the Court continued to use this mechanism and, as of April 2014, had held a total of twenty hearings. The public hearings were open to the public and generally held at the Court's premises in Bogotá.

The second monitoring mechanisms were the technical sessions, both regional and informal, which began in 2010. The regional technical sessions resemble the follow-up hearings as they aim to publicly discuss the fulfilment of the orders handed down in T25. They are held in towns and cities outside Bogotá and the people convened are public officials at the state, district, and municipal levels, in addition to representatives of IDPs' local associations. Seven regional technical sessions were held during 2010 (see decision 314 of 2009). The informal technical sessions are convened to privately discuss a specific issue and only public officials and stakeholders that are expressly invited by the Court are admitted. The Court began holding informal sessions in 2013 and, by April of 2014, a total of twelve informal sessions had taken place.

Due to the extremely demanding nature of the follow-up process (the record is more than 1.5 million pages long), a third mechanism – a Special Monitoring Chamber – was created in 2009 to take responsibility for measuring progress, delays, or setbacks in overcoming the unconstitutional state of affairs, and the adoption of all substantial and procedural decisions related to T25. The Special Chamber is composed of three Justices, one Deputy Judge, and five clerks.

The last monitoring mechanism has been the issuance of follow-up decisions (or injunctions). Between January 2004 and April 2014, the Court handed down 289 decisions to actively monitor the implementation of the orders issued in T25, request reports and precise actions from specific actors, communicate relevant information between actors, set the dates for public hearings and technical sessions, and adopt rights-based indicators to assess progress of the realization of displaced people's rights. A synthesis of the most important decisions handed down in these ten years is presented in Box 2.1.

Box 2.1: Main Follow-Up Decisions of Judgment T25

Decision 176 of 2005: Analyzed the fulfillment of the orders related to the budgetary effort needed to implement the comprehensive assistance policies for IDPs. Solicited the government to design a schedule to specify the timeline and mechanisms for obtaining necessary resources.

Decision 178 of 2005: For the first time, the Court carried out a comprehensive follow-up of each of the issues identified in T25 as causes of the unconstitutional state of affairs. It concluded that the unconstitutional state of affairs remained, and therefore issued orders aimed at ensuring the effective enjoyment of core fundamental rights and overcoming structural flaws.

Decision 109 of 2007: Adopted a battery of indicators to measure progress in the enjoyment of the rights to housing, health, education, food, income generation, identity, and socioeconomic stabilization. It rejected the indicators for the rights to life, physical integrity, freedom, security, repair, participation, and family reunification and ordered the government to present new indicators for these rights.

Decision 116 of 2008: Introduced adjustments to the battery of indicators adopted in Decisions 109 and 233 of 2007. Additionally, adopted new indicators proposed by the government and the Monitoring Commission to measure the rights to minimum subsistence, personal security, participation, restitution, and non-repetition, among others. Proposed its own indicators for the rights to truth and justice.

Decision 92 of 2008: In the first injunction with a differential approach, the Court addressed the issue of displaced women. It identified 12 risks that affect only women, and six instances of public policy that increased the risks. Ordered Social Action Agency to design and implement 13 programs for the protection of their fundamental rights and special measures for the 600 women whose status was established before the Court. It asked the Attorney General to investigate cases of sexual violence documented in the Decision.

Box 2.1: (continued)

Decision 251 of 2008: Addressed the issue of children. Ordered the design and implementation of the "Agenda for Differential Protection of Children and Adolescents against Forced Displacement" and of 15 pilot projects to serve children and adolescent victims of forced displacement. It also ordered the government to take specific actions in relation to each of the 18,000 children and adolescents identified in the injunction.

Decision 4 of 2009: Referred to the issue of indigenous peoples affected by displacement and armed conflict. Ordered the adoption of a "Program to Guarantee the Rights of Indigenous Peoples affected by Displacement" and the formulation and implementation of plans to safeguard the 34 indigenous communities identified by the injunction.

Decision 5 of 2009: Referred to the issue of black communities' victims of displacement. Ordered the creation and implementation of a plan for characterizing collective and ancestral territories inhabited mainly by this population, and a comprehensive plan for the prevention, protection, and assistance of Afro-Colombians.

Decision 6 of 2009: Addressed the issue of displaced persons with disabilities. Required the adoption of the mechanisms needed to overcome the lack of information on this population and the design and implementation of a program with a differential focus, as well as five pilot projects in the field of prevention and comprehensive assistance.

Decision 7 of 2009: Referred to the issue of coordination between local authorities. Ordered the Minister of the Interior and Justice to personally conduct direct coordination between the national government and the local authorities.

Decision 219 of 2011: Conducted a comprehensive evaluation of adopted policies and results attained by the national government in the seven years since ruling T25. The Court reaffirmed the persistence of the "unconstitutional state of affairs" due to the situation of displaced population regarding all rights, except in health coverage of non-ethnic populations, for which the Court declared a conditional cessation of the unconstitutional state of affairs. Additionally, the Court anticipated some of the risks and challenges of the then-recently adopted victims' legislation (Law 1448 of 2011).

Decision 98 of 2013: Ordered the state authorities in charge of the protection of and assistance to female leaders of displaced populations

Box 2.1: (continued)

to fully comply with their constitutional obligations after finding that the risk associated with the leadership and the civic, social, and communitarian work promoted by these women had increased alarmingly since 2009.

Decision 119 of 2013: Evaluated the actions taken by the national government to overcome the unconstitutional state of affairs in matters of registration of the displaced population and ordered the removal of the bureaucratic and conceptual obstacles (article 3 of Law 1448 of 2011) excluding victims that were not a part of the armed conflict from registration. The key order was that the concept of internal displaced person is broader than that of victims of the armed conflict.

2.3.2. *The Evolution of the Monitoring Process*

The monitoring process, by way of orders, has had four phases (see Figure 2.3). The first ran from late 2004 to 2006 and was characterized as a trial of public policy. Therefore, the most important orders of this period evaluated the degree of compliance by authorities according to the ruling's requirements, identified each institution's responsibility on the issue, and issued orders to help enhance the policies.

In line with the dialogical approach to judicial activism discussed in Chapter 1, most remedies at this early stage were moderate, insofar as orders were couched in general terms. They set broad goals and clear implementation paths to overcome bottleneck points in public policy, but left the determination of the specific content to the government agencies. One of the orders of the first set of follow-up decisions (Decision 178 of 2005), which evaluated the performance of several of the requirements of T25, illustrates this general language:

> Second.- ORDER the Director of the Social Solidarity Network, within a period of three (3) months from the communication of this order, to design, deploy and promptly implement all procedures and remedies that are necessary to overcome issues identified in paragraph 1.4. [about] the second ordinal of the operative paragraphs of Judgment T25 of 2004.

The decisions in this first phase are also characterized as documenting and systematizing the failures in the process of public policy formulation and implementation that had contributed to the unconstitutional state of affairs.

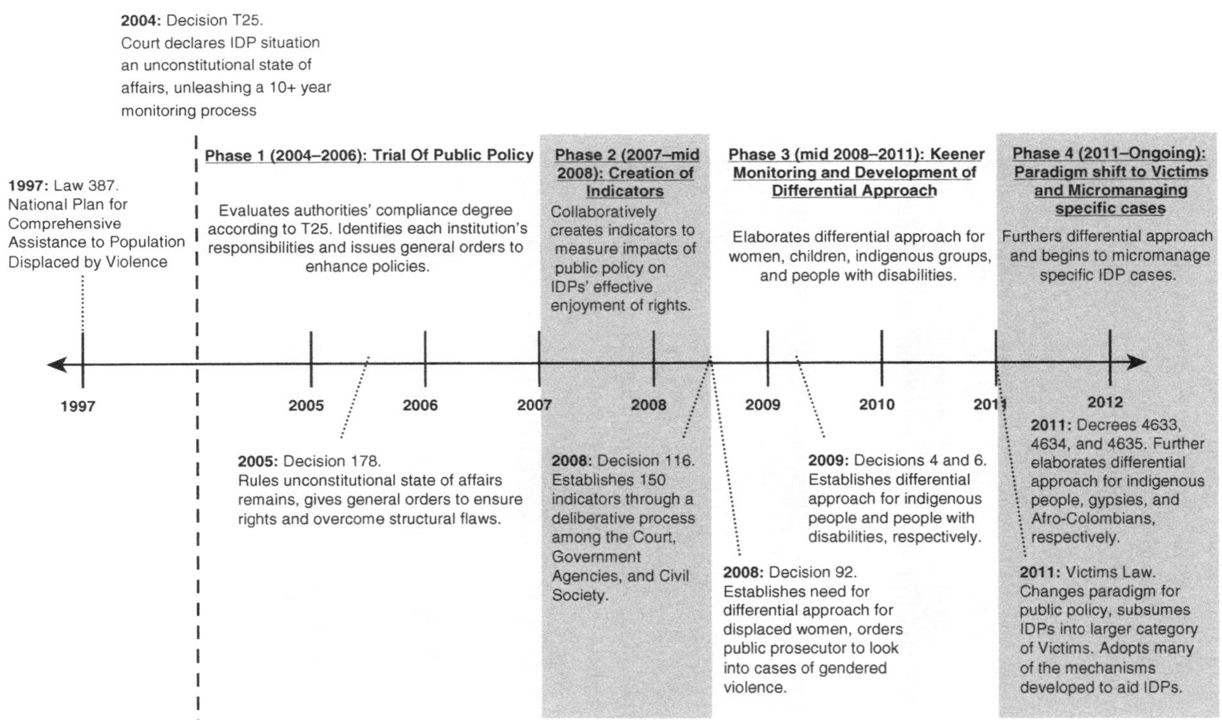

FIGURE 2.3 Timeline of the Monitoring Process of Judgment T25
Source: Authors' design.

As explained in the later chapters regarding such failures, the Court emphasized the flaws in the overall coordination of the displaced population assistance system, the inadequate system of registration and characterization of this population, and the general absence of indicators to measure progress or setbacks in assistance to IDPs.

The continuation of these failures, primarily the one related to the absence of progress indicators, led to a shift toward the second phase of the monitoring process in 2007. Between the beginning of that year and mid-2008, the Court focused on developing outcome indicators to measure progress, stagnation, and decline in the fulfillment of the IDPs' rights. The indicator construction process was led by the National Planning Department, the Social Action Agency, and the Monitoring Commission and commented on by the Attorney General, the Ombudsman's Office, the UNHCR, and other state and non-state actors. The iterative, multi-stakeholder process, which included numerous follow-up court decisions, resulted in the adoption of the first set of 150 outcome indicators for 20 rights (Decision 116 of 2008). However, three years later, after noticing the persistence of flaws on several fronts, the Court resumed the process of indicator creation (Decision 219 of 2011). After several months with multiple follow-up orders, technical sessions, and proposals by governmental and non-governmental agencies, a new set of close to 300 outcome indicators was submitted to the Court.[13] These indicators have provided a shared monitoring framework for all stakeholders in addition to a tool for the Court to fine-tune its follow-up orders based on the evidence of the evolution of policies and the situation of IDPs measured through the indicators. Chapter 4 explores in detail the indicator construction process and focuses on its deliberative and participatory nature.

Given the persistence of public policy failure and the continuation of the humanitarian emergency of the displaced population, the third phase of the process, which began in mid-2008 with a decision on internally displaced women (Decision 92 of 2008), was marked by keener monitoring of government action. On one hand, the orders of this period increased their demands for concrete results and emphasized the urgency of achieving them. In this context, the landmark decision (Decision 8 of 2009) contained an overall assessment of the factors that gave rise to the declaration of the unconstitutional state of affairs, confirmed their persistence (especially on issues like the policies on land and reparations), and reinforced the orders to the government to mitigate it.

[13] At the time of writing the book, the Court was in the process of fine-tuning and selecting a second definitive set.

On the other hand, the Court made its diagnoses and orders more precise through a series of important injunctions on the situation of the most vulnerable groups of IDPs: women, children, indigenous peoples, black communities, and people with disabilities. All these decisions were much more detailed than those made in earlier periods. For example, Decision 92 of 2008, which addressed the issue of protection of fundamental rights of women victims of forced displacement, ordered the creation of 13 programs to meet specific gaps in public policy toward displaced women and girls of all ages. Similarly, in the injunction on indigenous peoples (Decision 4 of 2009), the Court required the adoption of thirty-four ethnic safeguarding plans, one for each of the indigenous peoples at risk of disappearing. Additionally, Decision 6 of 2009 ordered the design and implementation of five pilot projects in the field of prevention and comprehensive assistance for displaced persons with disabilities.

The fourth phase is marked by the passing in 2011 of the Victims and Land Restitution Law (Law 1448), which is commonly referred to as the Victims Law. Signed into law by President Santos in June 2011 in the presence of prominent national and international actors that included the UN's Secretary-General Ban Ki-moon, it is the most ambitious reparations law in Colombia's history (Summers 2011). Inspired by the principles of transitional justice, the law seeks to establish a series of judicial, administrative, social, and economic measures (both individual and collective), to guarantee the rights to truth, justice, and reparations. The law also guarantees non-recurrence of human rights violations and infractions of international humanitarian law resulting from the country's decades-long conflict (article 1). Notably, the legislation aims to return millions of hectares of stolen or abandoned lands to internally displaced Colombians and provide reparations, including financial compensation, to the victims, including IDPs.

The Victims Law represents a profound political, legal, and institutional change. Politically, it acknowledges the existence of an armed conflict, something that the previous government (led by former president Alvaro Uribe) emphatically refused to do. In doing so, the Law legally acknowledges the relevance of international humanitarian law to the Colombian situation and the right of the population to the protections it provides. Institutionally, it implies the implementation of new institutions, programs, and legal procedures for all victims of the armed conflict (not exclusively internally displaced.)

From the perspective of internal displacement, the Law's main change is that it subsumes IDPs in the category of victims (in Colombia, IDPs constitute approximately 82 percent of all victims). IDPs are conceived and assisted as victims of the armed conflict, not as a specific group with its own laws, programs, and government bodies, as had been the case until that moment. The new set of institutions created by the Law for the assistance of victims builds upon the existing institutional framework for the displaced population. For example, the National System of Assistance to the Displaced Population (SNAIPD) was replaced by the National System of Assistance and Reparation to Victims (SNAPIV), which is made up of thirteen additional institutions and special presidential programs (Law 1448 of 2011, article 159). Additionally, the National Council of Assistance to Displaced Population (CNAIPD) was replaced by the Executive Committee for Assistance and Reparation to Victims (Law 1448 of 2011, article 164).[14] Starting in 2012 when the Law went into force, the government no longer established a specific budget for IDPs. Instead, it created a comprehensive budget for victims including IDPs. However, the Law contains a specific section for the assistance of IDPs (Title III, Chapter III) and states that such policy must be complemented by those norms on prevention of displacement and economic stabilization of IDPs. In addition to the Law, and following the Court's guidelines regarding the specific needs of certain groups within the displaced population, several regulatory decrees have been passed, including one for indigenous groups (Decree 4633 of 2011), gypsies (Decree 4634 of 2011), and Afro-Colombians (Decree 4635 of 2011).

The new legal and institutional framework introduced by the Victims Law marked a new phase for the Court. While the law builds on the jurisprudence and guidelines offered by the Court in the follow-up process[15] and on the existing institutional framework for the displaced population, the Special Monitoring Chamber has focused on assuring that the new Law is implemented in accordance with existing jurisprudence and laws, and disentangling particular bottlenecks of the new policy which result in violations of IDPs' rights. One example is Decision 119 of 2013, issued after the Law, in which the Court says that restricting the definition of "internally displaced" to those victims of the armed conflict alone (as the Unit for Victims' Attention and

[14] Likewise, e.g., the National Council of Assistance to Displaced Population (CNAIPD) was replaced by the Executive Committee for Assistance and Reparation to Victims (Law 1448 of 2011, article 164); the functions of the National Roundtable on Strengthening Displaced Persons' Organizations were assumed by the National Roundtable for Victims' Participation; and the Single Registry System for displaced population was replaced by the Single Victims' Registry.

[15] For example, the law considers one of its goals to be "the effective enjoyment of rights" of IDPs, which is the central concept of judgment T25 and recognizes the different needs of different victims, especially women and children, as the Court emphasized in Decision 92.

Reparation was doing) is incompatible with existing jurisprudence and prior laws (Law 387). Hence, it orders the new Registration Unit to register all internally displaced persons, including those that are not victims of the armed conflict. Another emblematic decision of this period is Decision 219, issued four months after the Victims Law. In this decision, informally referred to by the members of the Special Monitoring Chamber as the "splice decision," the Court evaluated, right-by-right, the unconstitutional state of affairs until the adoption of the Law and cautioned the government about the potential setbacks and challenges related to the adoption of the new Law.[16]

The second characteristic of the fourth phase is that the Court went from issuing guidelines for specific groups within the displaced population, as it had done during the third phase, to micro-managing situations. Despite the new Victims Law, the Court continued to receive actions and the situation became specifically dangerous in some areas of the country and for groups within the displaced population. The Court realized that neither general guidelines nor the more concrete decisions for those segments within the displaced population sufficed in addressing these situations and shifted its focus to very concrete cases. For instance, it issued a decision involving IDP women leaders (Decision 98 of 2013), and three others involving two Afro-Colombian communities (Decision A45 of 2012) and two cities (Decision 234 of 2013 and Decision 73 of 2014), each of which is located on the country's Pacific coast, which is an area disproportionately threatened by violence and internal displacement.

In sum, between the first and fourth stages, the Court first went from judging public policy and providing general guidelines in order to enhance public policy to constructing indicators to measure the progress of efforts to overcome the unconstitutional state of affairs. It then helped to design a new policy for particularly vulnerable groups within the displaced population, such as women and children, and finally ended monitoring and micro-managing the situation of IDPs under the new institutional and legal framework introduced by the Victims Law.

2.4. THE CREATION OF THE FIELD OF FORCED DISPLACEMENT: CASE ACTORS AND FIELD STRUCTURE

The ruling and its ten-year monitoring process also helped create social practices and interactions amongst interested social actors. Based on

[16] Interview with Felix Torres, clerk of the Special Monitoring Chamber, March 23, 2014.

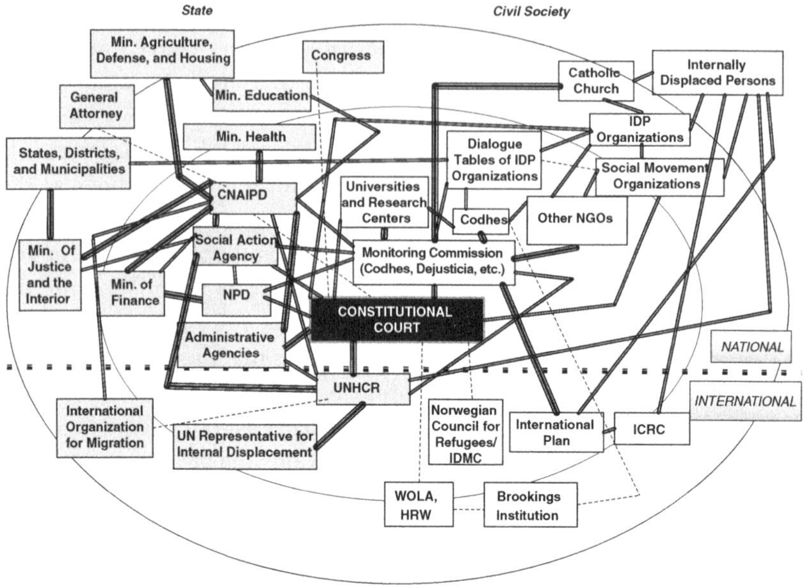

FIGURE 2.4 The Field of Forced Displacement
Source: Authors' design.

Bordieu's concept of social fields (2000), we argue that this interactive arena constitutes a real socio-legal sphere composed of actors, interests, strategies, and discourses revolving around the legal authority issuing the ruling. Although the creation of the "sociolegal field of forced displacement" occurred gradually as the monitoring process evolved, we devote this section to presenting the field at the beginning of the book to provide the reader with a map, presented in Figure 2.4, of the diverse actors, complex structure, and method of operation in order to facilitate the navigation of the following chapters.

In the displacement field, as in all social fields, diverse actors with differing levels of power (economic, social, cultural, and symbolic) interact while defending contrasting positions on the problem's resolution (Bourdieu 2000). The field's contours were first outlined with the issuing of T25, and then acquired more substance as the Court put forth interactive spaces such as public hearings for the delivery of periodic reports before the Court.

With the judicialization of displacement and its submission to constitutional procedures and language, the Court came to occupy the central space of the field, as indicated by the Court's location in Figure 2.4. Additionally, the graph shows that the case has involved a complex network of actors, divided along two axes: 1) state and civil society actors, and 2) national and international actors.

The location of actors in the graph denotes their level of participation in the field (indicated by their central or peripheral location), while frequency of interaction (or proactivity) is represented by the thickness of the lines that link them, as assessed in a comprehensive evaluation performed by the Court seven years into the process (Decision 219 of 2011[17]), before the new institutional framework of the Victims Law entered into force.[18] Reading the graph from left to right illustrates the spectrum of state and civil society actors.

2.4.1. *National State Actors*

The duty to provide assistance to the displaced population was assigned to national bodies – which made up the National System of Assistance to the Displaced Population (SNAIPD, in Spanish, until the entry into force of the Victims Law)[19] – and to subnational bodies (states, districts, and municipalities that the Court and other actors frequently refer to under the term "territorial entities"). This section describes some of the principal actors that comprise SNAIPD and then focuses on territorial entities and other state actors outside of the system, which work in relation to forced displacement.

[17] Decision 219 of 2011 carried out a comprehensive evaluation of IDP public policy, component by component, with the exception of the issues of institutional coordination and policies for specific groups which are addressed in other decisions (e.g., Decision 383 of 2010 on inter-institutional coordination). In the case of the latter issues, evaluation of proactivity and participation level is based on those decisions.

[18] Most institutions were renamed after the adoption of the Victims Law. However, because this book analyzes a time period that fell mostly before such changes, we have chosen to use the institutions' original names.

[19] SNAIPD is made up of 24 institutions: the Presidency; the Presidential Agency for Social Action and International Cooperation (Social Action Agency, which presides over and coordinates SNAIPD); the Ministry of the Interior and Justice; the Ministry of Finance and Public Credit; the Ministry of National Defense; the Ministry of Agriculture and Rural Development; the Ministry of Social Protection; the Ministry of Commerce, Industry, and Tourism; the Ministry of National Education; the Ministry of Environment, Housing, and Territorial Development; the National Planning Department; the Comptroller General's Office; the High Commissioner for Peace; the Vice-Presidency; the Ministry of Foreign Relations; the Ministry of Communication; the Colombian Institute of Family Welfare (ICBF, in Spanish); the National Apprenticeship Service (SENA, in Spanish); the National Television Commission; the Agrarian Bank; the Colombian Institute of Rural Development (Incoder, in Spanish); the Foreign Trade Bank S.A. (Bancoldex, in Spanish); the High Council for Gender Equality; and the Presidential Program for Promoting Respect and Guarantee of Human Rights and Application of International Human Rights Law.

SNAIPD entities are placed in Figure 2.4 according to their participation level and proactivity in the enforcement of judgment T25 and follow-up decisions. As will be discussed in Chapter 7, when we focus on the current situation of the IDP population, the evaluation shows that the policies that have made the most progress originate from the Ministries of Health, Education, and Finance, each of which have played active roles in the follow-up process and overcoming the unconstitutional state of affairs, and have also regularly provided information to the Court. For instance, the Court declared the cessation of the unconstitutional state of affairs in the right to health, given the progress made in relation to health coverage and assistance to the displaced population.[20]

Policies that remain deadlocked are those associated with the Ministries of Agriculture,[21] Defense, the Interior, and Housing, all of which are reluctant actors remaining relatively passive throughout the follow-up process. For example, five years after T25, the Court ordered that the national government should completely reformulate IDP housing policy (Decision 8 of 2009). Two years later, the Court verified that the government had failed to reformulate the policy as ordered and failed to implement the new policy by the set deadline (Decision 219 of 2011), resulting in a deficient housing supply. This explains each group's location in the graph, with the first appearing in the center and the last in the periphery of the displacement field.

Since 2000, coordination of the System was transferred from the High Counsel to the Presidential Agency for Social Action and International Cooperation (known as the Social Action Agency). The Social Action Agency (known as the Unit for Victims' Attention and Reparation since the Victims Law) is responsible for a wide range of activities in coordination with SNAIPD organs, including the training and execution of plans and programs directed to assistance for the displaced population and displacement prevention, registering victims of displacement in the Singular Registry of Displaced Population, and providing emergency humanitarian aid. This makes the Social Action Agency the principal state agent in the field in addition to the interlocutor amongst the majority of public and private actors.

[20] However, the Court found that coverage and assistance to indigenous and Afro-Colombians IDPs was very poor and thus retained the unconstitutional state for affairs for these groups.

[21] The Victims Law is expected to represent a quantitative leap in land policy because one of its objectives is to return millions of hectares to IDPs, and thus, after an initial evaluation of given policy is carried out, the location of the Ministry of Agriculture will most likely be close to the Ministry of Health or other well performing institutions.

There is a cyclical relationship of accountability between the Social Action Agency and the Court: the Social Action Agency reports on its activities, the Court evaluates the reports and issues new orders, and then the Social Action Agency responds with new activities and reports, which the Court evaluates again before issuing new orders. More recently, the Court has also held technical sessions with the Unit for Victims' Attention and Reparation to discuss the implementation of the Victims Law.

Within SNAIPD, a second body plays an important role in the field: the National Council for Integral Assistance to Displaced Population (CNAIPD).[22] Comprised of thirteen SNAIPD entities,[23] it is the advising body and consultant charged with formulating policy and guaranteeing budget allocation for the programs that SNAIPD bodies direct. Notably, there has been a significant budget increase since T25.

The principal ministries and administrative departments with direct responsibility on displacement report to the Council. By the express order of the Court in T25, CNAIPD is also open to displaced persons' organizations, representatives of the governing bodies of these organizations, and international bodies such as the United Nations High Commission for Refugees (UNHCR) and the International Organization for Migration (IOM).

The National Planning Department (DNP for its Spanish name) is another state actor within SNAIPD that has played an active role in this field. The DNP performs three roles: serving as a source of technical government information, calculating a budget attending to the displaced population, and representing the national government in the creation of indicators.

The final, relevant SNAIPD actor is the Ministry of the Interior and Justice (MIJ). The Ministry is the body charged with ensuring coordination between the central government and municipalities, districts, and

[22] Decree 2467 of 2005 ordered the fusion of the Colombian Agency for International Cooperation (ACCI, in Spanish) and the Social Security Network, renaming them the Presidential Agency for Social Action and International Cooperation, better known as Social Action Agency.

[23] CNAIPD is made up of the following institutions: the Presidency; the Presidential Agency for Social Action and International Cooperation (Social Action Agency, which presides over and coordinates CNAIPD); the Ministry of the Interior and Justice; the Ministry of Finance and Public Credit; the Ministry of National Defense; the Ministry of Agriculture and Rural Development; the Ministry of Social Protection; the Ministry of Commerce, Industry, and Tourism; the Ministry of the Environment, Housing, and Territorial Development; the National Planning Department; the Comptroller General's Office; the High Commissioner for Peace; and the Presidential Programme for Promoting Respect and Guarantee of Human Rights and Application of International Human Rights Law.

departments (normally referred to as "territorial entities"). To do so, one of the Ministry's roles is providing accompaniment to territorial entities in the formulation of the principal coordination mechanism for policies and programs on displacement – the Singular Integrated Plans (PIU, in Spanish) – and guaranteeing their implementation. The PIUs coordinate the different SNAIPD bodies, contain the programs and activities that each SNAIPD body will develop at the departmental and municipal level, and establish the resources available for prevention of and attending to forced displacement in each territorial entity. However, the MIJ has fallen short of fulfilling this role, which explains its peripheral location in the graph. In fact, in Decision 177 of 2005, the Court concluded that "this Ministry's compliance is the lowest of all and the results reached are the least satisfying." Five years later the Court declared the persistence of an unconstitutional state of affairs because of the "poor advancement in the correction of the coordination flaws between the National Government and the territorial entities" (Decision 383 of 2010).

The subnational level includes another group of state actors outside of the SNAIPD: municipalities, districts, and departments. In addition to assisting the displaced populations in their respective territories, these actors are responsible for organizing and maintaining active territorial committees for assistance to displaced populations and designing and implementing their respective PIUs. Additional obligations include assigning financial resources for assistance to IDPs, and serving as a bridge between lower territorial entities (municipalities and departments) and higher entities (departmental or national).

Territorial entities are on the periphery of the field map for two reasons. First, they have little interaction with the Court, which is evidenced by the low number of bodies that responded to the requests for basic assessments formulated by the Court in Decision 52 of 2008.[24] Second, the majority of territorial entities have dedicated scarce budgetary and administrative efforts to the issue and to coordination with national entities. As a result of such shortfalls, the Court organized seven Regional Technical Sessions throughout the country, in which governors and mayors discussed with court officials and multiple representatives from the national government

24 With Decision 52 of 2008, the Court requested from governors and mayors of every municipality in the country information on the displaced population's situation in each territorial entity, each territory's need to provide assistance to the displaced population, and the results of efforts undertaken to guarantee the effective enjoyment of rights by the displaced population. Responses to Decision 52 were collected by the Socio-Legal Research Centre at the University of the Andes (Cijus, in Spanish). See Constitutional Court Decision 7 of 2009, which references the report.

the problems faced by the territorial entities in terms of institutional capacities, availability of resources, coordination, and existence of a public policy of assistance.

The Office of the Attorney General also falls in the periphery of the graph. Its duty relating to forced displacement is investigation of the crime. To that end, a special National Unit of Prosecutors against Crimes for Disappearance and Forced Displacement (UNCDES for its Spanish name) was created at the end of 2010. Despite the creation of the new body, existing criminal sentences on this issue are remarkably scarce. According to a 2014 report, the Attorney General's Office has handed down only forty-seven guilty judgments for the crime of displacement.[25]

Despite a lack of affiliation with SNAIPD, a group of administrative control agencies (the Offices of the Inspector General, the Comptroller General, and the Ombudsman) is in the center of the field.[26] In accordance with their constitutional duties, these administrative agencies play an active role in the promotion of displaced individuals' rights, a role strengthened by T25. Following the Court's orders, they established technical mechanisms to monitor the authorities' efforts in providing assistance to the displaced population and have delivered several joint and individual reports on the level of compliance with the ruling.[27] They have also contributed to the creation of indicators for IDPs' rights as discussed in Chapter 4.

Despite being steeped in profound crises of corruption and legitimacy for most of the analyzed period, the last state actor that has participated in the field is the National Congress. This is why, as explained in Chapter 1, the Court has displaced it from a central location in the field. In spite of its semi-peripheral location, Congress has issued important laws on the matter, including Law 387 of 1997 which established the legal bases for prevention, assistance, protection, consolidation, and social and economic stabilization of individuals internally displaced by violence. Additionally, Law 1190 of 2008 modified the functions and coordination of territorial entities. Until 2011, Congress' the position in the graph would have been in the outer circle. However, it was brought closer to the center by the adoption of the Victims Law in 2011.

25 Victims Unit, 2014. "Follow up to Judgment T 25 of 2004. Response to the Order from 11 March 2014." April 2014.

26 The Comptroller General's Office is a special case because, in spite of being an administrative agency, it is also part of SNAIPD.

27 Under the Victims Law they retained this monitoring role, and up to early 2014 had produced two detailed reports on the implementation of the law and the new institutional framework.

2.4.2. *International State Actors*

An additional, important effect of the T25 case was the opening of a legal and institutional space for active participation by intergovernmental bodies, especially the United Nations Refugee Agency (UNHCR). This central actor in the field has participated in three ways: direct aid to the displaced population; evaluations in the follow-up process; and strengthening of state institutions, including providing direct support to the Court (funds, people, and so forth). Among its duties are advising institutions that implement displaced population assistance policies, evaluating results, and identifying problems.

2.4.3. *National Civil Society Actors*

As identified in Chapter 1, a fundamental innovation of the T25 case is the involvement of civil society organizations in the follow-up process, both by the initiative of the organizations themselves and by the express orders of T25 and its many follow-up decisions.[28] This explains the dense presence of such organizations in the displacement field and the participation of two types of NGOs. First, there are organizations that already played an important role in human rights in general (such as the Colombian Commission of Jurists) and displacement in particular (such as Codhes), for whom the ruling opened a space for influence and exchange with the state and other actors in the field.

Second, especially revealing are the new civil society organizations that were created to take part in the follow-up process. The most important actor of this type has been the Monitoring Commission on Public Policy on Forced Displacement (henceforth, Monitoring Commission), a coalition of NGOs, universities, and religious organizations. As its name indicates, the Commission performs a systematic and permanent follow-up of the evolution of policies on displacement and implementation of T25 orders. To do so, the Commission produces analytic reports on those policies with the participation of experts and based on dialogues with agencies such as the United Nations, regulatory agencies, displaced persons organizations, and grassroots organizations. Additionally, it formulates alternative policy proposals, creates outcome indicators to measure the effective enjoyment of rights by displaced persons, and participates in deliberative spaces such as public hearings before the

[28] Decisions 177 and 178 of 2005, 333 of 2006, 116 of 2008, 7 and 8 of 2009, and 383 of 2010 emphasize the importance of guaranteeing the participation of IDPs in the design and implementation of IDP policies and its implementation.

Court and CNAIPD sessions. Pursuant to Court orders, the Commission has also led the National Verification Process for Rights of the Displaced Population through three comprehensive surveys. As Chapter 7 details, the data collected through these surveys constitute the most detailed and reliable information in existence on the issue. Finally, the Commission undertakes public disclosure processes and trains displaced community leaders.

In addition to human rights NGOs, IDPs' organizations have participated in the policy process regarding forced displacement. In large part due to the uprooting and dispersion that defines displacement, the organizational field of the displaced population is highly fragmented and includes a variety of local, departmental, and national associations.[29] It also includes specific organizations for different types of displaced populations, including Afro-Colombians, indigenous peoples, women, and persons with disabilities.

The Colombian Association of Displaced Afro-Colombians (Afrodes) illustrates this field's traits. As evident in Figure 2.4's depiction of the national forced displacement field, Afrodes has participated actively in the follow-up process of T25. For example, together with the international NGO Global Rights and other organizations like the Process of Black Communities, it provided reports that were widely cited in court decisions on displaced Afro-Colombians, especially in Decision 5 of 2009 (Afrodes and Global Rights 2007; Rodríguez-Garavito et al. 2009).

The fragmentation of IDP organizations has been partially mitigated by the effect of the T25 ruling, which ordered the creation of exchange summits between the government and those populations. As a result, the government issued Decree 250 of 2005, establishing the National Roundtable for the Strengthening of Displaced Persons' Organizations (henceforth, National Roundtable), as well as departmental and municipal roundtables, offering spaces for discussion and coordination amongst these organizations. However, in practice, the National Roundtable (and, frequently, departmental and municipal roundtables) has fallen short of carrying though this function due to lack of resources (which the government has a duty to provide) and differences amongst the organizations themselves.[30]

As Chapter 5 discusses, not all civil society organizations enjoy the same level of influence in the field. At the expense of grassroots organizations,

[29] Interview with Eusebio Mosquera, founding member of the Colombian Association of Displaced Afro-Colombians, Geneva, August 2009.

[30] *Id.*

technicalities of the process tend naturally to favor organizations with strong legal bases (such as research centers and organizations with expertise in legal issues). Additionally, as seen in Figure 2.4, the majority of the displaced population, lacking membership in any organization, has remained relatively excluded from the process and occupies a marginal position in the field. However, this trait is common to many other legal fields and has been mitigated to a certain extent by collaboration among human rights NGOs (such as Codhes) and grassroots organizations (such as Afrodes).

2.4.4. *International Civil Society Actors*

Finally, two types of international civil society actors participate in the field. First, certain actors – like the International Committee of the Red Cross (ICRC) and Plan International – focus on attending to the humanitarian crisis of displacement. These actors enjoy a relationship with segments of the displaced population and some, such as Plan, participate in the Monitoring Commission. Second, some international NGOs monitor the patterns of displacement in several countries, produce statistics, and undertake research and seminars on the issue. These include the Washington Office on Latin America (WOLA) – probably the most active organization in working for international solidarity around Colombian forced displacement – and the Norwegian Refugee Council which, through an observatory on internal displacement based in Geneva (the Internal Displacement Monitoring Center, IDMC), contributes to the production of global reports on displacement.

In sum, the analysis conducted in this section demonstrates that the ruling and follow-up processes have created a socio-legal field with actors, procedures, and intervention practices in addition to multiple positions that have been essential to the effectiveness of public policy on the displacement crisis in Colombia.

2.5. CONCLUSIONS

This book focuses on the implementation and impact of structural decisions. We seek to understand the impact of rulings on the state, civil society, social movements, public opinion, and the realization of the rights of those directly involved after they leave the courtroom. However, to do so, it is essential to understand the situation before the cases even entered the courtroom. Accordingly, the first objective of this chapter was to present a general description of the state of the problem of internal displacement and displacement policies before the T25 ruling. The second goal was to describe the ruling and the innovative and participatory monitoring process designed by the Court to guarantee the implementation of its orders. These features entail a judicial intervention characterized by a combination of strong rights, moderate remedies, and strong monitoring. Lastly, we presented the main actors that have participated in the monitoring process and shaped what we call the "field of forced displacement" to give the reader a general sense of the main actors in the case and their interests before proceeding to specific examples.

The 20-year panoramic journey of the state's response to forced displacement leads to the conclusion that, although the issue had been incorporated into the public agenda first by the Executive (Conpes document of 1995) and later by Congress (Law 387 of 1997), the intervention by the Constitutional Court caused a noticeable increase in the visibility and state response to the problem, resulting in the creation of a new field. The following chapters offer an in-depth analysis of the effects produced by this ruling and its follow-up process.

PART II

DIRECT, INDIRECT, MATERIAL, AND SYMBOLIC EFFECTS

3

The Unlocking Effect: Judicial Prodding and Streamlining the Government Bureaucracy

When the Court handed down Judgment T25 in January 2004, the Colombian state had, on paper, instruments to attend to the humanitarian emergency of displacement. As discussed in Chapter 2, Law 387 of 1997 introduced measures for the prevention, assistance, protection, consolidation, and economic stabilization of the displaced population and created the National System for Attention to the Displaced Population (SNAIPD). The United Nations Guiding Principles on Internal Displacement, better known as the Deng Principles, had been recognized by the Constitutional Court as part of the "Constitutional Block of Colombian law."[1]

Yet, as documented by a civil society report at the time, "these norms were not applied in a real and effective manner" (Colombian Commission of Jurists and Colombia Jesuit Service for Refugees 2005: 10). In fact, their practice reflected a state of profound, official passivity and a flagrant lack of institutional coordination in displacement-related activities. Thus, the displacement problem qualified as the type of situation that, as discussed in Chapter 1, justifies judicial intervention in structural cases: situations in which state institutional deadlock results in a massive violation of human rights.

In these contexts, a basic effect of structural rulings consists of the exertion of pressure to unlock the state apparatus. In terms of the theory of "destabilizing rights" (Unger 1987) discussed in Chapter 1, these rulings become mechanisms of the destabilization of bureaucracy stalled by lack of capacity, will, coordination, or budget. Hence, they evoke direct and instrumental effects such as immediate reactions by state entities motivated by judicial orders.

This chapter discusses this type of effect while employing T25 as a case study. It begins by describing the deadlocked situation prior to the ruling and

[1] See, among others, Constitutional Court Judgments 1150 of 2000, Justice Eduardo Cifuentes Muñoz, and T-1635 of 2000, Justice José Gregorio Hernández Galindo.

the Court's efforts to resolve its causes. Against that background, it briefly documents four specific actions and programs that emerged after the ruling, which serve to prove the existence of this effect.

3.1. THE SITUATION PRIOR TO THE RULING AND THE COURT'S ORDERS

Interviews with different actors and the analysis undertaken by the Court in its ruling demonstrate that the institutional deadlock around displacement resulted from three main factors: dispersion of responsibility for the issue, lack of coordination between the agencies in charge of providing assistance to IDPs, and inactivity on the part of state entities. As will be demonstrated in the following section, the immediate effect of the ruling then countered these three factors.

Dispersion resulted from a system of assistance to the displaced population (SNAIPD) that was a true bureaucratic maze of institutions, with overlapping functions and dispersed responsibilities relating to concrete policy results. As the figure of actors in the previous chapter shows (see Figure 2.4), what existed was a veritable alphabet soup of state agencies (the National Planning Department [DNP], Social Action Agency, multiple ministries, and so on) and coordination networks (SNAIPD, etc.). In T25 the Court found deficiencies in the assignment of roles and responsibilities amongst the different institutions comprising SNAIPD. It also reported on duplicate efforts on national and territorial levels. In the Court's terms:

> The assignment of roles and responsibilities among different institutions is blurred. Although SNAIPD and territorial institutions have different roles in accordance with their respective expertise, it remains unclear exactly which duties each institution should undertake and, in many occasions, responsibilities are duplicated.[2]

The dispersion is exemplified by the National Council for Integral Assistance to the Displaced Population (CNAIPD), the body that, on paper, was the seat of decision-making and coordination for the national system of assistance. Instead of facilitating coordination amongst the entities of which it was comprised, the CNAIPD generated a vicious cycle: although it didn't perform adequately, it served as a pretext for its members to relieve themselves of responsibility for the issue and then shift their burden to other institutions

[2] Decision 178 of 2005 (number 3.6. vi.) reiterates that "the lack of clarity in the definition of institutional responsibilities" is one of the institutional flaws that remain a year and a half after the ruling.

(especially the Social Action Agency) while blaming them for the abysmal results of displacement policy.

An official from the Social Action Agency also referred to the imprecise division of responsibility among institutions and resulting duplicated efforts. She attributed this to the need to create a comprehensive response to the population: "For this reason, the Solidarity Network started offering different programs to the displaced population, programs that other institutions had the expertise to deliver."[3]

Given these circumstances, a large part of the ruling's orders consisted either of the reiteration of the legal responsibilities of different institutions or detailed requests to diverse state institutions to assume concrete responsibility for the issue. For example, the ruling reminded the Ministry of the Interior and Justice (MIJ) that it "must encourage governors and mayors to create municipal, district, and departmental committees under Law 387 of 1997 (art. 7)." Likewise, it issued the following order to the DNP:

> Given the importance of obtaining sufficient resources for the policy, as an instrument to overcome this unconstitutional state of affairs, it is fundamental that the Minister of Finance and the Director of the National Planning Department contribute to the budgetary goals required by the assistance policy to the displaced population. Thus, this ruling will be directed specifically to the high officials mentioned so that they may, within the limits of their functions, adopt decisions leading to the correction of this unconstitutional state of affairs.[4]

The ruling handed down similar orders for the rest of the institutions that comprised the SNAIPD. As a result, an official from the MIJ explained in an interview that, "the ruling was the first time that government authorities recognized that they could take responsibility for the issue. Before they thought the displacement problem was only for the Social Action Agency."[5] An official from the Ombudsman's Office shared this view, emphasizing how one of the ruling's effects was "to move the displacement issue from the exclusive purview of Social Action Agency in Bogotá to a responsibility of every state entity, and not just Social Action Agency; one that was the responsibility of territorial entities, also."[6]

3 Interview with Viviana Ferro, subdirector of Assistance to the Displaced Population at Social Action Agency, January 8, 2009.

4 Constitutional Court, Ruling T25 of 2004, Section 10.1.1.

5 Interview with Liliana Guzmán, Coordinator of the Special Protection Program for Displaced Population, MIJ, January 13, 2009.

6 Interview with Hernando Toro, Ombudsman's Office, Coordinator of the Office of Displacement Assistance, January 22, 2009.

In addition to dispersion, a second cause behind the institutional deadlock was the uncoordinated actions of the different agencies in charge of providing assistance. These existed on three levels: 1) among national institutions in charge of the matter; 2) among national and subnational institutions (departmental governments and municipalities); and, 3) among subnational authorities.

There were multiple reasons for the poor government performance. One of the causes for the lack of coordination at all levels was the institutional dispersion described above. Additionally, T25 highlighted the lack of coordination tools and municipal coordination committees, despite the order for their creation by Law 387 of 1997.[7]

Interviews with officials offer abundant evidence of the coordination flaws diagnosed by the Court. For example, an official from what was known as the Ministry of Environment, Housing, and Territorial Development pointed out the lack of linkage amongst different institutions:

> Before [the Court's decisions], due to the government's administrative legacy, the independence of each cabinet ... displacement was handled very disjointedly. So before, when responding to an at-risk population every institutional tool would be applied at once. Each institution would offer assistance by itself, and assistance would come separately.[8]

Against this background, the Court issued a series of specific orders to enhance coordination at various levels. For example, it ordered CNAIPD to adopt a plan of action designed to correct institutional capacity flaws with a precise timeline.[9] Regarding the lack of municipal committees, the ruling held:

> [Territorial] entities [departments, municipalities and districts] must adopt decisions demonstrating a greater commitment, as ordered in ... Law 387 in 1997, which required territorial authorities to organize Committees for Assistance to the Displaced Population. These committees are mandatory in municipalities where forced displacement is present.[10]

Lastly, institutional deadlock stemmed from the very low level of activity of those with responsibility for the issue prior to the ruling. The director of an NGO that works closely with IDPs (Consultancy for Human Rights and Displacement, Codhes) summed up what a majority of interviewees,

[7] Constitutional Court, Ruling T25 of 2004, Section 6.3.1.1.iii.

[8] Interview with Luis Domingo Gómez, Minister of Environment, Housing, and Development, January 2009.

[9] Constitutional Court, Ruling T25, Resolution, Order four.

[10] Id., Order three.

including public officials, reported: "Before T25 ... the government had a marginal conception of its responsibility for displaced individuals. Different institutions provided some responses. [However], these sometimes came more from the voluntary efforts of officials committed to the issue."[11]

One clear symptom and cause of state passivity was the lack of sufficient funds to address internal displacement. In T25 the Court specifically noted that one of the main problems with the policy for the attention of IDPs was the lack of budgetary resources for its implementation.[12] Thus, it ordered the DNP, the Ministry of Finance, and the Social Action Agency to: 1) calculate the necessary budget to fulfil such policy; 2) indicate the means for amassing these resources; and 3) set the relative contributions of national, territorial, and international entities in the amassing of these resources.

In this context of institutional deadlock, an immediate effect of the Court's intervention was the shake-up of the state bureaucracies in charge of attending to the displaced population. As an official from the Ombudsman's Office expressed:

> In a country with so many laws, the ruling has been very interesting as a means to avoid [the notion] that laws are just words on paper, that through the ruling the judges give life to the law's content. It has also been an important mechanism for encouraging the government apparatus. You realize that a lot of officials respond to the displaced population more because they have to abide by the ruling than [because] of their commitment to the rights of the displaced. It's unfortunate, but with this perspective you realize that there's an enormous advantage to the rulings: if officials are spurred by judicial sanctions, and not by honoring rights, at least they're motivated by something.[13]

What does it mean, in concrete terms, for officials to be "motivated" by court orders and for the ruling to "encourage" the government apparatus? The following section documents four types of immediate actions undertaken by the institutions to which the Court directed its ruling: the budgetary increase destined for the displaced population, the reactivation of the coordinating body on displacement policy (CNAIPD) and other coordinating bodies, the collection of basic information, and the creation of urgent programs.

11 Interview with Marco Romero, director of Codhes, December 19 and 23, 2008.

12 Constitutional Court, Ruling T25, Section 6.3.

13 Interview with Hernando Toro, Ombudsman's Office, Coordinator of the Office of Displacement Assistance, January 22, 2009.

3.2. THE UNLOCKING EFFECT: INITIAL REACTIONS AND PROGRAMS

3.2.1. *Calculating Funds Needed to Attend to the Displaced Population*

As noted in Chapter 1, unlike other structural intervention cases of the Court and other courts, the Court's initial intervention in this ruling did not consist of detailed orders. Hence, the Court did not demand an exact cost or budgetary appropriation for a determined amount from the government. Instead, the ruling requested that the administration, within its expertise, calculate the budget required for attending to the displacement emergency and explore all possible avenues to actually invest the amount calculated on programs for IDPs. This is, therefore, a classic case of remitting the problem back to the Executive, wherein the Judiciary attempts to break the deadlock around a public policy without assuming for itself the power to define its details.

The government entities' immediate reaction to the ruling was to postpone compliance. They requested a two-year period to calculate the budget. However, the Court maintained its strict deadline and refused the request, forcing the government to make its first rigorous budgetary calculation for displacement policy.

The exact figure reached was 4.7 trillion pesos (as of 2005), estimated by the DNP in a high-level public policy document (known as the National Council for Social and Economic Policy document, Conpes document), bearing in mind "existing regulation on the displaced population" and "requirements established by the Constitutional Court via Judgment T-025 of 2004," among others (Conpes document 3400 of 2005: 12). According to the government, this was the amount required beyond the then-current expenditures to ensure the minimum protection of the rights of those in the displaced population that were registered with the Social Action Agency at the time (December 2004). The figure of 4.7 trillion pesos is a significant amount, especially considering that in the entire nine year period before the ruling (between 1995 and 2004), the government invested less than one-third of the amount (1.3 trillion pesos of 2005) in the development of a comprehensive policy for the displaced population (Conpes document 3400 of 2005: 6).

The government's immediate budgetary response is a direct reaction to the ruling. Proof of such comes from the Presidential Directive 06 of October 7, 2005, which states:

> Judgment T25 of 2004 and Decisions 176, 177, and 178 of 2005, handed down by the Constitutional Court, contain orders ... to overcome the

unconstitutional state of affairs regarding forced internal displacement. The Court has communicated these orders to the President of the Republic so that he may adopt pertinent decisions.

As a result, it is hereby ordered that the entities that comprise the National Council and the National System of Attention to the Displaced Population at the national level and the public servants that work within these entities and are charged to:

focus resources for assistance to the displaced population within their respective realms of expertise and report these actions to the Coordinator of the National System of Attention to the Displaced Population so concrete, effective measures of protection of the rights of the displaced may be undertaken.

Similarly, the National Budget Law for the fiscal year 2006 incorporated the following article:

> Funds budgeted for the Youth in Action Training Program of the National Apprenticeship Service (SENA) will be directed initially for assistance to the population displaced by violence, in compliance with judgment T25 of 2004, issued by the Honorable Constitutional Court. Once the displaced population is covered, funds will be redirected to other groups.

Finally, the Court imposed further budgetary orders by requiring the MIJ to solicit budgetary and administrative input from states, districts, and municipalities. In response, the Ministry issued special directives directed to the territorial entities (Directives 3 and 4 of 2004). Despite the limited impact of these directives,[14] the responses indicate that the Court's intervention evoked reactions beyond the national level. A clear example of this is the adoption of policies in the capital city. As reported by the media:

> Bogotá became … the first city in the country to adopt a plan that aims to guarantee at least 9 fundamental rights to the 100,000 displaced individuals officially registered. The plan, with a budget of 32 thousand million pesos for the incoming year, is a direct response to ruling T25 of the Constitutional Court handed down on January 22, which ordered the nation and its capital district to undertake action to enforce the violated rights of displaced families. Funds, derived from the 2005 district budget, will be directed to three specific areas: prevention, protection, and humanitarian and socioeconomic stabilization assistance.[15]

[14] In its report to the Court in preparation for the follow-up public hearing held on June 29, 2005, the Ombudsman's Office reported that only a third of the departments (12 of 32) had sent clear and complete information on their programs for assistance to the displaced population.

[15] *El Tiempo*, "32 Trillion to Attend to the Displaced Population," November 21, 2004.

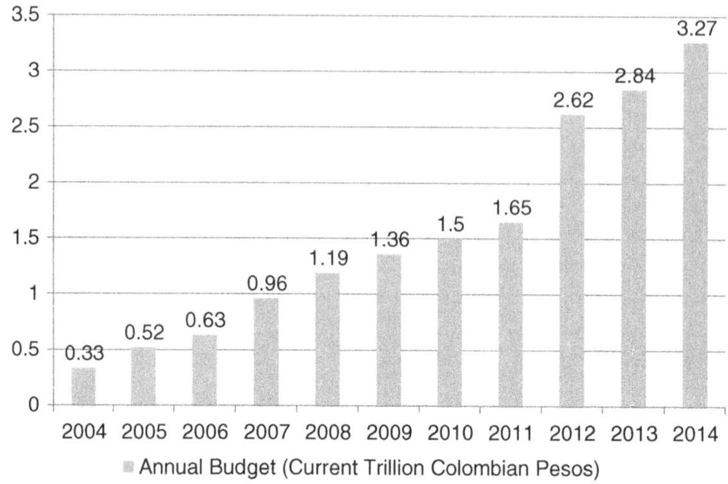

FIGURE 3.1 Total National Government Resources for Internal Displacement Policy (2004–2014)
Source: National Planning Department and Ministry of Finance (2014).

The ruling not only prompted the administration to triple the national budget allocated for programs for IDPs in 2004, but it has also had a steady upward effect on the budget since that time. Figure 3.1 presents the evolution of the national government's budget for programs for IDPs since the year of the ruling, showing a sharp jump after T25 and a ratchet effect since then.

In sum, the budgetary increase for assistance to the displaced population was a tangible, direct effect that resulted from the Court's destabilization of the dormant state apparatus. A second consequence was the attempt to improve coordination among the different institutions responsible for assistance to IDPs through the reactivation and creation of coordinating bodies.

3.2.2. *The Reactivation and Creation of Coordinating Bodies*

When questioned about T25's main impact, several interviewees indicated improvement in the institutional coordination of displacement-related activities, or what we have dubbed a coordination effect. An official from the DNP gave a representative response, saying, "The ruling basically said, 'Get your house in order.'"[16]

An official from the Ministry of Education, an organization linked to displacement policy for over seven years before the ruling, explained the

[16] Interview with María Angélica Alvarado, DNP, January 9, 2009.

Court's orders in the following manner: "It's time to stop. Get your house in order ... And the ruling allowed the government to start saying what everyone's job was, what certain people's jobs were, and what we were going to start responding to in a more timely manner."[17] An official from the Ministry of Social Protection in charge of displacement issues also indicated that the Court "forced every institution to start coordinating its work in the area."[18] Therefore, opinions from interviewed officials suggest the existence of a general coordination effect, due to T25's facilitation of linkage amongst different institutions.

One clear indicator of the state's response to the Court's attempt at streamlining the public administration at the national level is the action undertaken by the CNAIPD shortly after the ruling. As explained above, T25 issued several direct orders to CNAIPD, as the directing organization of SNAIPD charged with formulating public policy for assistance to the displaced population and the guarantee of budgetary availability.

In 2004, after two years of dormancy, the CNAIPD reconvened for the express purpose of complying with T25. From that moment, it assumed leadership of public policy design and coordination among the institutions of the national system and became the authority in charge of following up on the advances made in compliance with the Court's order (UNHCR 2007: 349). For example, to improve coordination and communication amongst the SNAIPD institutions, it created thematic roundtables and technical committees. The United Nations Refugee Agency (UNHCR 2007: 368) lauded the utility of some of these roundtables and committees for the discussion of common problems, adoption of policy, exchange of information amongst different institutions, and system-wide coordination.

With abundant references to both statements issued by CNAIPD in the first two years after the ruling, the influence of the ruling and its follow-up decisions on CNAIPD's actions is recognizable. As indicated in its preamble, Statement 001 of 2005, which defined criteria for responding to requests submitted by the displaced population, was drawn up as a detailed response to the ruling and one of the Court's follow-up orders:

> Considering:
>
> ...
>
> That in section 10.2 of ruling T25, the honorable Court held: "As recounted in the background record of this ruling, suit was brought due to insufficient institutional responses to requests for assistance due under the housing and

[17] Interview with Yaneth Guevara, Ministry of Education, February 2009.

[18] Interview with Susana Helfer, Ministry of Social Protection, January 21, 2009.

> socioeconomic reestablishment programs, as well as to requests for access to health care, education, emergency humanitarian assistance, or for inscription as a displaced individual in the Singular Registration System. Through this suit, plaintiffs hope for a comprehensive and timely response to their requests, leading to the enforcement of their rights";
>
> That in numeral 10 of the ruling's resolutions, the High Court ordered that requests submitted from the displaced population be answered thoroughly, clearly, and exactly, indicating response criteria;
>
> That numeral 9 of Decision 178 of 2005, issued within the same ruling, noted that: "... even when each institution responsible for a part of the components of assistance to the displaced population addresses specific problems, different evaluating entities and organizations identified several common problems, which have delayed the correction of the unconstitutional state of affairs, specifically: ... viii) undue delays in responses to requests submitted by the displaced population."

Beyond the national level, the clearest advance in coordination resulting from the Court's intervention was the creation of municipal, district, and departmental committees. For example, by September 2006, out of the thirty-two states that make up Colombia, the vast majority (twenty-nine) had active territorial committees and included displaced population assistance in their Departmental Development Plans. As indicated by an official at the DNP, "as far as displacement goes, one of the positive effects of the ruling is that, by requesting reports and the creation of committees as ordered by law, it required coordinated efforts."[19]

3.2.3. *The Production of Basic Information on Displacement*

Another immediate effect of the Court's intervention was the initiation of a public administrative effort to produce basic information on displacement. In the ruling's follow-up process, the Court ordered state entities to produce periodic reports. However, the majority of these bodies did not possess reliable, systematic information or statistical systems that would allow them to do so. As an official from the MIJ recognized in an interview for this book, "out of a need to produce reports for the Court, governing bodies established information systems. We needed to create statistics."[20] Similarly, officials from the International Committee of the Red Cross (ICRC) reported that "since T25, more and more information has been produced on how to respond to

[19] Interview with María Angélica Alvarado, DNP, January 9, 2009.

[20] Interview with Liliana Guzmán, Coordinator of the Program for Special Protection to the Displaced Population, MIJ, January 13, 2009.

difficulties and obstacles. Now it is important to see if the situation improves and how this information is applied."[21]

Administrative agencies were also ordered to produce reports. Specifically, T25's execution was assigned to the Ombudsman's Office and the Inspector General's Office. Thus, in the first two years of follow-up, these agencies produced four joint follow-up reports in addition to some individual reports. As the then-representative of the UNHCR in Colombia attested,

> With judgment T25 a new history began to be written. Administrative agencies, which had always been present in the protection of rights of the displaced ... began to establish complementary and technical mechanisms to oversee the work of those authorities responsible for the assistance to the displaced population.[22]

As discussed later (Chapter 5), this immediate reaction translated into the production of regular, detailed information on the evolution of the protection of the displaced population's rights. However, for the purpose of this chapter, highlighting the revival of a dormant state apparatus that, at the time, did not even possess essential data to design and implement informed policies on the humanitarian emergency of displacement, suffices.

3.2.4. *The Creation of the First IDP Programs*

The last indicator that illustrates how the Court's orders served to motivate the state apparatus is the creation of programs or working groups to respond to the ruling. The clearest and most comprehensive example is the creation of the National Assistance Plan for IDPs (Decree 250 of 2005) exactly one year after the ruling. The Plan's main objective was "to establish a general government policy and plan of action for the prevention of and assistance with forced internal displacement in Colombia, permitting the restoration of rights and obligations of Colombians affected by internal displacement."[23] The National Assistance Plan is the principal public policy document on displacement after Law 387 of 1997. In the following chapter, where we present the "public policy effect," we will expand upon the contents of the plan, as it constitutes the backbone of public policies on displacement.

Another example of how the Court's ruling and initial follow-up decisions served to spark the creation of programs occurred within the MIJ. Both T25 and a follow-up decision (Decision 177 of 2005) ordered the Ministry to

[21] Interview with ICRC official who preferred to remain nameless, December 18, 2008.

[22] UNHCR 2007: 18

[23] Decree 250 of 2005, number 2.1.

undertake efforts so that governors and mayors would make the necessary decisions and budgetary adoptions to assure assistance to the displaced population. In response to this order, in September 2006, the Ministry created the Monitoring and Coordination Group to Departments and Municipalities in Care for the Displaced Population. As one of the group's officers reported, "following the order in Decision 177 [of 2005], the Ministry created this group. So now we go to the territories and provide them with technical support in administrative and budgetary matters."[24]

The situation was identical to a later decision that addressed the issue of protection of the right to life and the personal safety of displaced population leaders (Decision 200 of 2007). The Court concluded that the existing program of exclusive protection for leaders of vulnerable populations (among them the displaced) suffered from a series of defects. Specifically, it did not grant the displaced population the priority that it was constitutionally guaranteed, and did not provide for the extension of protective measures to family members of the individuals at risk.[25] To correct this situation, the Court ordered the director of the Ministry's Protection Program to design a specific program to address the existing flaws. In response, the Ministry created the Special Protection Program for Displaced Population to provide protection not only to leaders, but also to any person registered as an IDP who was also at risk.

3.3. CONCLUSIONS

This chapter demonstrates that T25's immediate effect was to shake up state bureaucracies responsible for attending to the IDP population. The Constitutional Court used socioeconomic rights as "destabilization rights" (Unger 1987) to provide the pressure needed for breaking the deadlock surrounding assistance to the displaced population. Such deadlock resulted from dispersion of responsibilities, poor coordination between the agencies in charge assisting IDPs, deficient budget, and sluggishness on the part of state entities. The government, in turn, had budgetary, coordination, information, and preliminary policy reactions.

Under pressure from the Court, relevant institutions made an initial effort to fulfill their obligations or expand their efforts. Consistent with Chapter 1's analysis, the Constitutional Court, rather than usurping the power of the other branches of power to determine the budget or draft policies on

[24] Interview with Clara Yvet Rodríguez, Program for Territorial Entities Coordination, 2008.

[25] Constitutional Court, Decision 200 of 2007, numerals 1 and 2.

displacement, created a lever to activate the national government's action (see also Chapter 8). As an official from the DNP attested:

> The pressure [from the Court] obligated us to work on this quickly. If not for the ruling, I don't think we would have achieved anything near the advances we have. I don't mean to say that we were not assisting the displaced, but I don't think we would have anything close to what we have now.[26]

To be sure, the type of unlocking effect documented in this chapter is only a preliminary reaction of the state apparatus. As with other structural rulings, the effect's duration depends upon the promotion of long-term public policy processes through follow-up decisions involving state and non-state actors. The following chapters use evidence gathered during fieldwork to analyze whether judgment T25 provoked this type of process. The following chapter analyzes the impact of the ruling and subsequent decisions on the basic aspect of the policy cycle: the design and evaluation of public policies.

[26] Interview with María Angélica Alvarado, DNP, January 9, 2009.

4

The Policy Effect: Design and Evaluation of Public Policies Through Judicial Incentives

As discussed in Chapter 1, the majority of studies on courts and social change have focused on the direct, instrumental effects of rulings – those that imply a tangible change to public policy and the conduct of the public authorities to whom the Court's orders are directed (Rosenberg 1991). Although, as previously argued, this emphasis ignores other central effects of judicial activism such as those documented in the following chapters, it rightly highlights evaluation of the concrete impact that courts have on the solutions to problems over which they preside. Ultimately, in terms of our typology in Chapter 1, if a ruling has only symbolic or indirect effects, but no direct influence on public policy and the situation of the affected population, qualifying the ruling as a successful judicial intervention for the promotion of SERs would be difficult. This chapter analyzes the first of these direct effects: T25's impact on public policy on displacement – the so-called policy effect. Chapter 7 will study the impact on the situation of the displaced population itself.

We begin by describing the hybrid, rights-policy tool kit that the Court employed to influence public policy, which consists of a combination of language and strategies of Constitutional and human rights law and economic and public policy. We devote the rest of the chapter to illustrating the two phases of the policy cycle in which the Court intervened: the design of public policies on displacement and their evaluation. The second section is devoted to the former. We show that, in order to impact the design of policies, the Court acted both as a guide (offering general guidelines and principles to influence policies adopted by the Executive or Legislative branches), and as a restrained policymaker, ordering precise measures to be adopted for the hardest-hit groups within the IDP population and communities. In the third section we show how the Court intervened in the evaluation of displacement policies by launching a participatory process in which government agencies, civil society, and the Court jointly constructed rights-based indicators to measure progress, stagnation, or setbacks in the policies and situation of IDPs.

4.1. THE RIGHTS-POLICY HYBRID TOOL KIT AND THE POLICY EFFECT

One of the most significant aspects of the ruling and follow-up orders is its conceptual apparatus and language that are a hybrid of: 1) legal tools of constitutional and human rights law, and 2) economic and public policy tools. The former is the basis for the Court's conclusion that a massive violation of rights exists and of the declaration of an unconstitutional state of affairs. The latter leads to the organizational logic, policy analysis, and measurement tools that the Court employs to diagnose structural flaws in public administration and implement the design, execution, and evaluation of new policies, including a long, sophisticated process culminating in the creation of indicators to measure advances and setbacks in the guarantee of IDPs' rights.

Thus, this case is not an example of the imposition of legal over economic and administrative logic, but rather a combination of the two. It reflects the rise of a hybrid project between two professional and ideological camps – one headed by economists and the other by constitutional lawyers – which had previously clashed over other issues throughout the nineties (Rodríguez-Garavito 2011b). While the former advocated a passive role for the Court and subordinated the enforcement of constitutional rights in favor of economic and policy imperatives, the latter defended judicial activism and the subordination of budgetary considerations to the fulfilment of constitutional rights. By taking elements from both camps, judgment T25 and other rulings from the same era marked a shift in this debate and in the Court's jurisprudence (Rodríguez-Garavito 2011a, 2013). We refer to this compromise as a rights-policy hybrid.

The hybrid existed from the moment the Court issued T25. One of the Court's main objectives was to "analyze public policy on assistance to the displaced population [to determine] if the State, by action or omission in the design, implementation, follow-up and evaluation of policy, has contributed in a constitutionally significant manner to the disregard of fundamental rights of displaced persons."[1] Thus, the ruling dedicated one section to examining state responses to the forced displacement crisis,[2] another to analyzing the results of policy implementation,[3] a third to the follow-up and evaluation

1 Constitutional Court, Ruling T25 of 2004, Section 6.

2 Constitutional Court, Ruling T25 of 2004, Section 6.1.

3 Constitutional Court, Ruling T25 of 2004, Section 6.2.

of management of policy execution,[4] and a fourth to studying the lack of economic resources and its implications for policy results.[5]

As explained, the Court found a number of flaws in the public policy cycle (see Chapter 2, Section 2.2). With respect to the design phase, the Court highlighted the absence of an updated plan of action for the National System for Assistance to the Displaced Population's (SNAIPD) operation to provide for a comprehensive overview of policy, and bemoaned the lack of specific goals or indicators to measure the policy's success or failure. Additionally, the Court emphasized the lack of basic elements of public policy, such as precise deadlines and funding sources. It also detected important flaws in the implementation phase, observing that SNAIPD institutions had not created special programs for the displaced population despite their mandatory nature according to existing laws and policy documents. In the last phase of the cycle, reserved for follow-up and policy evaluation, the main problems included the lack of an information system, which was essential for an up-to-date registry of the total number of IDPs, and the lack of policy evaluation systems to detect errors in and obstacles to design and implementation.

By declaring that these systemic flaws amounted to an unconstitutional state of affairs, the Court's ruling dictated a series of principles and guidelines for the formation of new policy on the issue. For example, the Court established the Principle of Coherence in policy, which, according to its ruling, "aims at having coherence between what the state 'promises' and its economic resources and institutional capacity to fulfill its promises, especially if those promises are legal norms."[6] Additionally, in line with economic, social, and cultural rights doctrine, the Court established the criteria of progressive realization of the enforcement of rights,[7] as well as specificity in policy,[8] deriving from the constitutional mandate to guarantee the rights of especially vulnerable subjects.[9]

During the ruling's follow-up process, the guiding thread continued to be the combined logic of human rights and public policy. In subsequent orders the Court dictated additional guidelines for the creation of policy and spoke of

[4] Constitutional Court, Ruling T25 of 2004, Section 6.3.
[5] Constitutional Court, Ruling T25 of 2004, Section 6.3.2.
[6] Constitutional Court, Ruling T25 of 2004, Section 8.3.1.
[7] Constitutional Court, Ruling T25 of 2004, Section 8.1.
[8] For the Court, specificity must be present on three distinct levels, each of equal constitutional importance: i) in relation to constitutionally protected subjects that are part of the displaced population – the elderly, children, women heads of households, ethnic and racial minorities; ii) in relation to regional differences presented by the displacement phenomenon; and iii) in relation to the displaced person's condition as a victim of armed conflict (Decision 218 of 2006, number 5.2.).
[9] Constitutional Court, Ruling T25 of 2004, Section 6.3.1.1.

central policy aspects such as the budget and the importance of specificity[10] (Decision 176 of 2005); the displaced population's due priority within public expenditure (Decision 176 of 2005); the importance of familiarity with regional and local contexts before formulating policy (Decision 177 of 2005 and Decision 218 of 2006); the need for general coordination amongst distinct institutions (Decision 177 of 2005 and Decision 218 of 2006); and the utility of establishing evaluation and follow-up mechanisms, including indicators of effective enjoyment of rights (Decisions 109 and 233 of 2007 and Decision 116 of 2008), among others.

This rights-policy combination had a direct and tangible effect on public policy. According to the first systemic evaluation of the ruling and process undertaken by the United Nations Refugee Agency (UNHCR) four years after T25 was handed down, the period between 2004 and 2007 saw the greatest development in public policy on assistance to the displaced population up to that point (UNHCR 2007: 117). This evaluation coincides with the perceptions of various actors from the displacement field interviewed for this study. The following quote from the director of the Consultancy for Human Rights and Displacement (Codhes) is particularly illustrative:

> A large part of the policies that exist today are thanks to the ruling [T25]. Law 387 was the basis for . . . state recognition of displacement, but obviously the most important quantitative leap in public policy is the ruling . . . Almost every important program today owes its existence to T25, because before it there was only partial humanitarian assistance.[11]

Other actors in the displacement field referred to more specific ways in which the Court modified policymaking. For example, an UNHCR official explained how the Court established timeframes:

> When the Court got involved, it said, "Listen, we need short, medium and long-term goals with defined policies that you know in which direction are headed." This necessarily changes the vision of a policymaker or a policy implementer and the government wasn't prepared for that.[12]

Likewise, others noted how the Court influenced the content of the policies by making a rights-based framework the chief reference for policymaking. As a clerk in charge of the case revealed "this [the Court's intervention] helped

[10] By budget specificity, the Court means that policymakers must identify the precise manner in which funds will be directed to specific aid for the displaced population, to avoid the diversion of funds into general programs for vulnerable groups nationally (Decision 176 of 2005, number 8.2).

[11] Interview with Marco Romero, Director of Codhes, December 19 and 23, 2008.

[12] Interview with Andrés Celis, UNHCR official, January 17, 2008.

change the way we thought about public policy . . . public policy needs to obey constitutional law . . . and its chief function is guaranteeing people's effective enjoyment of rights."[13] The same perception has been visible in the press, as palpable in a 2008 article in *El Tiempo* newspaper, which reported on the "noted advance seen in recent years in the state's response to internal displacement, coordinated by the Social Action Agency. The Constitutional Court's role has been fundamental in ensuring that this response has a rights-based approach."[14]

In sum, the case study clearly shows the existence of an effect on public policy. But how did this effect come about, and by what processes? We argue that the impact was seen in two of the classic phases of public policy: design and evaluation (Kraft and Furlong 2007).[15] The remaining sections of this chapter address this question and examine the ruling and follow-up decisions' impact on each one of these two phases.

4.2. THE COURT AND THE DESIGN OF PUBLIC POLICY: JUDGES AS POLICY GUIDES AND POLICYMAKERS

Regarding public policy design, the Court has played two principal roles over the course of the four phases of the follow-up process described in Chapter 2: policy guide, and restrained policymaker.

As a public policy guide, the Court issues broad orders and dictates guidelines and principles to strengthen or reformulate existing public policy or direct policy implementation. The Court actively played this role in the first stage of the follow-up period (2004–2006) and resumed the part in the last stage (mid-2011 until today) under the new framework of the Victims Law. In the ruling and in a series of follow-up decisions from these periods, the majority of the Court's commands were issued in general terms. The commands ordered the government to take action, without determining the specific content of each policy or the minimum number of programs necessary, as occurred in the third and fourth phases of the follow-up process. The general

[13] Interview with Clara Helena Reales, clerk of the Constitutional Court of Colombia, December 18, 2008.

[14] *El Tiempo*, "Beyond Numbers, People," October 2, 2008.

[15] According to the classic public policy model provided by Jones (1970) and still used in the majority of literature (Kraft and Furlong 2007), the policy cycle has five phases: problem identification and placement on the agenda; policymaking; policy legitimatization; implementation; and, finally, evaluation and policy change. However, some phases are commonly grouped into three principles phases: design or formation; implementation; and evaluation. The Court followed this model with T25 (see Constitutional Court, Ruling T25 of 2004, Section 6.3.1.).

principles touched on aspects related to budgeting, participation of the displaced population, coherence between norms and policy, policy specificity, criteria to be registered as an IDP, criteria to guarantee humanitarian aid, and the state's obligation to progressively realize the guarantee of effective enjoyment of rights and to design policies with a general rights-based approach.

As public policymaker, the Court assumes a more active role, which results in more concrete orders for specific groups and communities. As the follow-up process advanced without satisfactory government response to some of the most urgent policy concerns (such as assistance to segments of the population hardest hit by displacement), the Court assumed a restrained but more active role as policymaker in certain areas during the third phase (mid-2008–2009) and again during the fourth phase. The orders from the third phase were focused on specific groups within the displaced population, such as women, children, people with disabilities, Afro-Colombians, and indigenous peoples. They contained more concrete demands and specified the number and content of programs the government was to adopt. The orders from the fourth phase (which coexisted with the more general orders issued by the Court in its role as policy guide) were focused on specific communities, located in areas of the country that are at a higher risk of displacement (such as the Pacific coast, for example).

The next section analyzes two paradigmatic examples of these roles that show how the Court influenced the design of public policy: the evolution from the formulation of the National Plan of Comprehensive Assistance to the Victims Law, which illustrates the Court's role as policy guide, and the decisions for a specific segment of the IDP population, in which the Court assumed the role of public policymaker.

4.2.1. *The Court as Policy Guide: From the National Plan to the Victims Law*

In the ten years since the Court handed down T25, Colombia's general response to internal displacement shifted from being a dispersed and patchy set of laws and policies, to a national public policy for the assistance of the IDP population, to a comprehensive national law and set of policies for the attention of all victims of the armed conflict that subsumes the displaced population.

A year after ruling T25, the central government issued the National Assistance Plan to the Population Displaced by Violence (herein the National Assistance Plan, Decree 250 of 2005). It became the principal public policy document on displacement after Law 387 of 1997. The Plan's main objective was "to establish a general government policy and plan of action for the prevention of and assistance with forced internal displacement in Colombia, permitting the restoration of rights and obligations of Colombians affected by internal displacement."[16] The essence of the new Plan was to remind SNAIPD bodies of their institutional responsibilities and to frame the state's response within the new, rights-based framework inaugurated by T25.

The new National Assistance Plan was a direct consequence of the Court's role as guide to the public policy field. As a lawyer from the Colombian Commission of Jurists in charge of displacement noted, "with [T25] the Court achieved several things ... including ... formulation of the National Assistance Plan in 2005, which isn't without its own problems; but at least there is a plan, something that needed reviewing."[17]

There are at least three signs indicating that the Plan was a direct consequence of the Court's intervention in policymaking. First, in the follow-up reports submitted to the Court, the Executive branch presented the National Assistance Plan as the express fulfillment of T25's orders, which demanded the adoption of the plan within a set timeframe, but refrained from elaborating specific content.[18]

Second, the deliberative and consultative manner in which the Plan was debated and adopted followed the orders and participatory guidelines provided by the ruling.[19] Accordingly, the preliminary plan adopted in the weeks following the ruling by the National Council for Integral Attention to the Displaced Population (CNAIPD) was, in turn, debated for approximately six months in meetings of displaced population organizations, officials from public institutions, NGOs, civil society, and the international community.[20]

Finally, the Plan's guiding principles reflected standards set by the Court for designing public policy. According to the technical and policy director of the Social Action Agency's Program for Assistance to the Displaced Population:

16 Decree 250 of 2005, number 2.1.

17 Interview with Juan Manuel Bustillo, Colombian Commission of Jurists, December 22, 2008.

18 Reviewing policymaking flaws, T25 ordered the National Council for Integral Attention to the Displaced Population (CNAIPD) "to adopt within the three months following the issuing of this ruling a program of action, with a precise timeline, aimed at correcting, at a minimum, institutional capacity flaws identified in the present ruling" (T25 of 2004, Resolution, Number Four).

19 For example, T25 expressly ordered the body in charge of the national system of assistance to IDPs (CNAIPD) "to offer organizations representing the displaced population the opportunity to effectively participate in the adoption of decisions made to correct the unconstitutional state of affairs and to inform them monthly on advances made" (T25 of 2004, Resolution, Number Two).

20 CNAIPD, Act 4 of January 12, 2005; statement of José Ubernel Arboleda González, Coordinator of the Joint Technical Unit.

"The new Plan ... seeks to unify fundamental elements; first, the Guiding Principles on Internal Displacement frequently mentioned by the United Nations and the Constitutional Court's recommendations in the T25 ruling, which indicated the need to award priority attention to the displaced population relative to other vulnerable populations in the nation.[21] Accordingly, the National Assistance Plan's guiding principles include a "rights-based approach" to "ensure the enforcement and enjoyment of human rights." Additionally, a "differential focus" was adopted, which required that the formulation of the Plan and the activities that ensue proceed in consideration of the characteristics of the population or groups involved, in terms of gender, age, and ethnicity.

Over these ten years, the design of public policy has been a cumulative process in which novel policies build on previous policies and progressively incorporate new procedural and substantive guidelines issued by the Court in follow-up decisions. Consequently, the Court's orders and guidelines, as well as the principles and content of the National Assistance Plan, were then recognized both in the adoption process and the content of the National Development Plans (NDPs) of 2006–2010 and 2011–2014. NDPs are the government's central public policy document, adopted by each president at the beginning of his or her term, which set the national guidelines for growth and development in the country in addition to the processes for their achievement during the four-year term.

As with the National Assistance Plan, the 2006–2010 NDP was also presented for consultation with displaced population organizations. According to UNHCR, "while we lack exact information on which of their contributions were considered in the design of the Plan presented to Congress, the mere existence of this space represents an advance relative to the formation of both prior plans, neither of which explicitly considered this population" (2007: 170). Additionally, the content of both NDPs reflects the reach of the orders and guidelines issued in T25. While the Plan (2002–2006) prior to the ruling had addressed displacement, the subsequent NDPs did so using the Court's framework and established that "the state will guarantee comprehensive assistance to this population with a rights-based approach."[22]

The Court's role as policy guide peaked with the passing of the 2011 Victims Law, which contains measures of reparation and land restitution for victims of the armed conflict. When asked about the relationship of T25 and the Victims Law, a clerk of the Special Monitoring Chamber explained, "the Law is a

[21] CNAIPD, Act 4 of January 12, 2005; statement of Patricia Luna, Technical and Policy Director of Aid Programs for the Displaced Population, formerly a part of the Social Solidarity Network.

[22] Law 1151 of 2007, number 6.2.2.

child of the follow up process."[23] The Court never explicitly ordered the government or Congress to issue a reparations law. Yet, as the previous statement implies, the Victims Law can be considered a product of the substantive and procedural guidelines and principles offered by the Court during the follow-up process for three reasons.

First, the Victims Law explicitly embraces many of the principles, guidelines, and tools that emerged from the seven-year follow-up process. Most tellingly, the law adopts as one of its overarching goals the central concept developed by the Court in this process –"the effective enjoyment of rights" – both for the rights of IDPs in particular (articles 60, 66, and 67) and for victims in general (articles 17, 91, 168, and 172). Tirelessly, the Court has insisted throughout the follow-up process that "the criteria to declare the overcoming of the unconstitutional state of affairs is not the specific budgetary effort, the redesign of public policies, or the issuing of new and better laws, the creation of macro-administrative structure ... but the effective guarantee of the rights of the displaced population" (Decision 219 of 2011). Furthermore, the Law establishes that the criteria to determine whether the situation of vulnerability that results from displacement has ceased will be determined according to the effective enjoyment of rights indicators that have been established through the Court's jurisprudence (article 67.1). As we will see in detail in the third section of this chapter, the effective enjoyment of rights indicators are another emblem of the follow-up process and the "policy effect." In addition to the notion of the effective enjoyment of rights, the Law incorporates other rights and principles developed throughout the follow-up process, such as IDPs' right to truth (articles 23, 61, 149, 153, and 178); the right to collective reparation for victims, including IDPs (articles 151 and 152); and the victims' right to receive rehabilitation and psychosocial attention (article 135), among others.

In addition to the rights and principles of the Law, the three complementary pieces of legislation that contain measures for reparations and land restitution for victims of particularly vulnerable groups within the victims population – Afro-Colombians, Rom (gypsies), and indigenous peoples – are a direct result of the third phase of the monitoring process in which the Court highlighted the need for recognizing and offering special treatment to the most vulnerable groups of IDPs. These groups are women, children, indigenous peoples, black communities, and people with disabilities. Let us take as an example Law Decree 4633 of 2011, which focuses on victims of the armed conflict that identify as indigenous or that belong to indigenous communities. Its section describing its impetus makes specific reference to the follow-up decision of

[23] Interview with Felix Torres, clerk of the Special Monitoring Chamber, March 26, 2014.

ruling T25 that focuses on indigenous groups.[24] Furthermore, its guiding principles include the rights to territory (article 9), to real and effective participation of indigenous peoples in the bodies of the national system of attention to victims (article 26), and to prior consultation (article 27), all which have been developed by the Court through the follow-up decisions regarding IDPs.

Lastly, and directly related to the previous point, the participatory procedure through which the government adopted some of these decrees also exemplifies the Court's influence. As will be developed in the following chapter, since ruling T25 the Court has emphasized the need to guarantee the effective participation of organizations of displaced populations in the discussion, construction, and adoption of public policies that concern them. For example, the government adopted special legislation for indigenous victims of the armed conflict through consultation.

As documented by Rodríguez-Garavito and Orduz (2012), that decree was constructed through a deliberative process of prior consultation in which representatives from indigenous organizations, civil society, academia, and the government discussed the content of the decree for six months. While the adoption of the three specific laws received a lot of criticism – chiefly because the decrees were adopted after the Victims Law was passed – it is arguably a successful example of prior consultation. Notably, it had the participation of representatives of the indigenous groups, was characterized by the flow of information between the parties, and developed counterbalancing mechanisms to stabilize the unbalanced power relationship between government officials and indigenous organizations (Rodríguez-Garavito and Orduz 2012).

With the analysis of the Court's influence on the Victims Law's content, special decrees, and procedures, we conclude the examination of the first seven years following the T25 ruling. During this period, the Court influenced the design of public policies by issuing general orders with substantive and procedural guidelines and principles. Due in part to the Court's guidelines and pressure, Colombia went from having a fragmented set of policies, to a national public policy for the assistance of IDPs, to a comprehensive restoration and compensation legislation for victims of the armed conflict that recognizes the special needs of specifically vulnerable groups.

As the years passed and plans and documents remained partially on paper only, the Court adopted a more interventionist role in the policymaking

[24] In the case of indigenous groups, the cornerstone injunction is Decision 4 of 2009. Then came more specific decisions, which focused on particularly vulnerable indigenous groups: the Hintú and Makaguán tribes (Decision 382 of 2010), the Awá (Decision 174 of 2011), and the Jiw and Nükak (Decision 173 of 2012).

process, substituting general orders and guidelines for concrete orders and policies. This shift first occurred in the third phase of the follow-up process, with the differential focus decisions, and then again in the fourth phase under the Victims Law when the Court saw the need for intervening in communities particularly affected by violence and internal displacement.

4.2.2. *The Court as Policymaker: Policies for Specific Groups and Communities*

The second way the Court influenced the design of public policy was by acting directly as policymaker. As the follow-up process advanced without satisfactory governmental response to some of the most urgent policy concerns (such as assistance to segments of the population hardest hit by displacement), the Court assumed the more active role of policymaker during the third phase (mid-2008–2009), which continued during the fourth phase. In its new role, the Court gave more precise injunctions and explicitly ordered the creation of specific policies for especially vulnerable groups within IDPs and for communities in extremely violent zones of the country with higher risk of displacement, for which the general orders did not suffice. The first part of this section is devoted to the former type of decisions, and the remaining part to the latter.

T25 recorded the absence of what the Court has dubbed a "differential perspective" in policymaking: one that specifically considers the plight of women, children, people with disabilities, Afro-Colombians, and indigenous populations amongst the displaced, as groups affected differently and disproportionately by displacement. According to the ruling, "there are no policy norms regulating access to aid by displaced groups of particular vulnerability, such as women heads of households, children, or ethnic groups. There are no special programs to respond to the specific problems affecting these groups."[25]

In the follow-up decisions of the first phase, the Court insisted on the importance of developing policies for these groups. For example, decisions such as 218 of 2006 emphasized, "the need to adopt a differential, specific approach that recognizes that the effects of displacement vary depending on the age and gender [of the victim]."[26] In fact, this same decision identified the ten most critical areas in need of revision in the assistance policy, including the "lack of specificity in the displaced population assistance policy" and "the lack of protection for indigenous and Afro-colombian groups, especially

[25] Constitutional Court, Ruling T25 of 2004, Section 6.3.1.1.
[26] Constitutional Court, T25 Decision 218 of 2006, number 5.3.1.

affected by internal displacement." Likewise, the decisions of the second phase demanded that the Executive create indicators to measure the results of policy regarding the more vulnerable groups.[27]

However, by 2008, information gathered by the Court through decisions and hearings clearly showed that the government had not complied with its orders. Thus, staring in the middle of 2008, the Court altered its strategy to *directly* formulate detailed displacement public policy guidelines, using five differentially focused decisions addressing the cases of women, minors, indigenous groups, the Afro-Colombian community, and people with disabilities.[28] Additionally, it convened hearings to publicly debate each specific case with participation from these groups. The Court thus assumed a new role, which became clear to the government officials that had to respond to new orders: "the Court gives an order, and if the government doesn't say how it's going to respond, the Court tells it how to respond. One example is follow-up the decision on women [Decision 92 of 2008]. The Court defined policy; imposed policy."[29]

In effect, in the first set of differentially focused decisions, which clearly marks the beginning of a third phase in the follow-up period, the Court itself designed specific policies. Hence, in each of the first five decisions, which focused on particularly vulnerable and disproportionally affected groups within the displaced population, it ordered a specific, minimum number of programs for each group and specified their content.

In the first of these decisions, the Court addressed the protection of fundamental rights for women victims of forced displacement, who make up over half of the displaced population (Decision 92 of 2008).[30] Considering the lack of a gender-focused policy, the Court ordered the Social Action Agency to create thirteen specific programs to fill the policy void around women, female adolescents, and children.[31] It also set the scope of coverage and the rights to be guaranteed by the programs. Likewise, the Court placed coordination for each

[27] See, Constitutional Court, Decisions 109 of 2007 and 218 of 2006.

[28] Although the Court has issued more than one decision to certain groups, here reference is made to the five principle decisions.

[29] Interview with María Angélica Alvarado, DNP, January 9, 2009.

[30] According to results from the Third National Verification Survey, administered by the Monitoring Commission, 52.4 percent of the displaced population is made up of women, a figure higher than the national percentage, at 50.7 percent (Monitoring Commission 2010: 52).

[31] To give an idea of how detailed the orders became, some of the thirteen programs were explicitly called: 1) the Program for the Prevention of Disproportionate Gender-Based Impact due to Displacement, through prevention of extraordinary gender-based risks stemming from the armed conflict; 2) the Program for the Prevention of Sexual Violence Against Displaced Women and for Comprehensive Aid to Victims; 3) the Program for Prevention of Interfamily and Community Violence Against Displaced Women and for Comprehensive Aid

program in the central figure of the Director of Social Action Agency, set a two-week deadline to inaugurate the thirteen programs, and emphasized the importance of guaranteeing participation of organizations that promote the rights of displaced women in the policymaking and implementation processes. Furthermore, it ordered the Attorney General's Office to prioritize the criminal investigation of 183 cases of sexual violence against women in the context of the armed violence. The press reported on the Court's shift:

> The judges gave the [Attorney General's Office] six months to make advances in the investigation of a terrifying group of gender crimes: ... individual and collective rape and sexual abuse, sexual torture, sexual mutilation and subsequent murder of the victims, as well as ferocious, barbaric sexual acts ... Cases like this, involving sexual violence against women and provoking forced displacement, are detailed in a 1,682 page document from the Constitutional Court that hits a nerve in Colombian society, drawing attention to what the Court calls an "ignored crime:" abuse committed by armed actors against Colombian women.[32]

Later, in October 2008, the Court addressed the issue of displaced children less than 18 years of age, a group constituting more than 50 percent of the displaced population (Decision 251 of 2008).[33] Due to the lack of differential focus for this group, the Court ordered the design and implementation of a new SNAIPD program called the "Program for Differential Protection of Forcefully Displaced Children and Adolescents." The program had two central components: prevention of the disproportionate impact of forced displacement on minors, and assistance to this group. The Court also ordered the design and implementation of fifteen pilot programs in different cities throughout the country, geared toward responding to specific risks and pressing problems confronted by minors due to the armed conflict.[34]

to Victims; 4) the Program for Promotion of Health for Displaced Women; 5) the Program for Aid to Displaced Women Heads of Households and for Employment Opportunity and the Prevention of Domestic and Labor Exploitation of the Displaced Women, in addition to eight others.

32 *El Tiempo*, "600 Women Tell Their Emotionally Powerful Stories Before the Court," May 25, 2008.

33 Constitutional Court, Decision 251 of 2008, number II.A.

34 Of the fifteen projects, one is for prevention of forced recruitment of young people, another is for detection of antipersonnel mines and unexploded munitions, and a third is for the prevention of victimization of minors through social pressure programs operated by armed groups outside the law. The other twelve are projects for assistance to displaced children and adolescents, which are to be implemented in the twelve Colombian cities with the greatest number of displaced individuals: Cartagena, Arauca, Sincelejo, Quibdó, Tumaco, Buenaventura, Bucaramanga, Bogotá, Medellín, Policarpa, Florencia, and San José del Guaviare.

As with the previous decision, and in line with its new role, the Court did not limit itself to suggesting programs or projects for SNAIPD to design, but rather specified with precision the minimum requirements for each program[35] and set deadlines for their inauguration (six months for the programs and two months for the pilot projects). It also emphasized the need for participation by displaced population and child advocate organizations.

The Court applied the same logic in its following three decisions: it evaluated national and international obligations to the vulnerable group, evaluated the state response, identified principal flaws, determined programs to be adopted, and specified the content of the programs. In its decision on indigenous victims of displacement (Decision 4 of 2009),[36] the Court ordered the adoption of a "program to guarantee the rights of indigenous peoples affected by displacement," and the formation and implementation of ethnic safeguarding plans for at least thirty-four tribes identified in the decision (Rodríguez-Garavito et al. 2010).

In the decision on displaced Afro-Colombians (who make up close to 17 percent of the displaced population),[37] in addition to providing official documentation of the disproportionate effect of displacement on Afro-Colombians and the government's noncompliance with its obligations to this segment of the displaced population (Rodríguez-Garavito, Alfonso, and Cavelier 2009: 12), the decision specified a number of actions, more varied than in other decisions, to be taken to address the lack of policy specificity for this population.

The last of this sequence of specific decisions addressed displaced persons with disabilities (Decision 6 of 2009). With the aim of developing differentially focused public policy for this specific group, the Court handed down three main commands. First, it ordered different SNAIPD institutions, under the coordination of Social Action Agency, to improve information systems in order to fill in the information gap around displaced people with disabilities.[38] Second, it ordered a group of institutions, also under the coordination of the Social Action Agency, to adopt within six months a "program for the

[35] For the minimum requirements of the Program's two central components, see Constitutional Court, Decision 251 of 2008, number 1.1. and 1.2.

[36] According to II ENV, 6.5 percent of the RUPD-registered population (6.9 percent of the non-registered) identify as indigenous peoples (Monitoring Commission 2008b: 40). The Court reported in the same decision that at least thirty ethnicities are currently in a state of high risk of cultural or physical extermination due to the armed conflict and forced displacement.

[37] According to the II ENV, 16.6 percent of the RUPD-registered population and 17.8 percent of the non-registered population identify as Afro-Colombian (Monitoring Commission 2008b: 40).

[38] For a list of the minimum factors to be considered by these information systems, see Decision 6 of 2009, Resolution, Number Three.

differential protection of persons with disabilities and their families affected by forced displacement," which, as with the program for children, had two components, both prevention and comprehensive assistance. Finally, it ordered the design of five pilot projects on prevention and assistance for displaced persons with disabilities to be implemented in the city of Bogotá and four other states.

As with ruling T25, but on a smaller, proportional scale, some of these decisions for specific groups within the internally displaced population have in turn triggered their own follow-up process. They have been accompanied by regular monitoring from the Special Monitoring Chamber, follow-up decisions, public hearings, technical sessions, and civil society oversight. The clearest example of this small-scale monitoring is the one that has followed the special decision on internally displaced women and sexual violence (Decision 92 of 2008). Similar to the Monitoring Commission on Public Policy on Forced Displacement (Monitoring Commission) for T25, a National Roundtable for the Monitoring of Decision 92 of 2008, composed of twelve women's organizations and human rights research centers, was set up to monitor the degree of compliance with court orders, specifically those related to sexual violence, which are included in a special annex to the decision. In the six years since the special decision on displaced women, the Roundtable has published five comprehensive follow-up reports detailing the progress made by the Offices of the General Attorney and the Inspector General. Its most recent report exposes almost complete impunity for perpetrators of sexual violence against women. In addition, the Court has handed down follow-up orders requesting that the government report back to the Court on the thirteen programs (e.g., Decision 29 of 2012). Likewise, a recent decision ordered special protection and programs for IDP women leaders, as a group within the women IDP population subject to greater risks (Decision 98 of 2013). Furthermore, a public hearing was convened in July of 2009 to discuss progress made on the five specific decisions, including the one on women (Decision 266 of 2009). More recently, and following the Special Monitoring Chamber's general trend, an informal technical session was held in February 2013 to discuss the progress and drawbacks on the policies for IDP women leaders.

Another example of a special decision that has received similar monitoring is the decision on indigenous IDPs (Decision 4 of 2009). This decision has been supplemented by three follow-up decisions, ordering urgent measures to protect specific groups within the indigenous population that are under greater risk (Decisions 382 of 2010, 174 of 2011, and 173 of 2012). Likewise, a public hearing involving IDP indigenous leaders and organizations, the national government, and academia, among others, was held in September 2013 to discuss progress and setbacks in the compliance of Decision 4's orders.

Apart from direct intervention in the design of policies for groups within the IDP population particularly affected by displacement, during the fourth phase of the monitoring process under the new Victims Law, the Court has intervened in the design of public policies for specific communities. It has handed down concrete orders to address the situation of certain communities disproportionately affected by changes in the patterns of violence and displacement in certain regions, for which neither the general orders of the first phase nor the orders for the specific groups sufficed. One example is a decision that ordered specific remedies to warrant the restitution of the collective territories for the Curvaradó and Jiguamiandó Afro-Colombian communities on the country's Pacific coast (Decision 299 of 2012).[39] These decisions deal with communities disproportionately susceptible to violence and internal displacement, for which the Monitoring Chamber identified the need for directly ordering specific public policies to prevent and avoid further violation of IDPs' rights.

In sum, from a public policy viewpoint, in these ten years we see that the general orders and guidelines contained in the follow-up decisions belonging to the first phase were replaced during the third and fourth phases by decisions that commanded the creation of precise programs for vulnerable groups within IDPs and for specific communities, respectively. The combination of general orders and concrete programs had a direct and tangible impact on how displacement policy was designed and the content of that policy. Thus, there is abundant evidence of the policy effect during the first cycle of the policy-making process. The next section analyzes the scope of the effect in the third public policy phase: policy evaluation.

4.3. THE COURT AND THE EVALUATION OF PUBLIC POLICY: THE CONSTRUCTION OF INDICATORS

One basic principle in public policy analysis is the importance of having methods and tools to evaluate the impacts, advances, and setbacks of

[39] Two additional examples are the decision that orders precautionary protection and assistance measures for the at-risk Afro-Colombian communities and victims of forced displacement of the state of Nariño in the country's southern Pacific region (Decision 73 of 2014) and the decisions that focus on the city of Buenaventura, ravaged by criminal gangs formed by former parliamentary groups (Decisions A45 of 2012 and 299 of 2012).

government policy. However, in T25, the Court indicated that one of the obstacles that obstructed policy implementation was "the lack of monitoring mechanisms for the management of distinct SNAIPD institutions," and the "impossibility of evaluating the timeliness of institutions responsible for program execution."[40] In particular, there were no criteria or mechanisms for measuring policy management that allowed for periodic, rigorous monitoring of policy results.

To fill this void, the Court encouraged, with particular emphasis between 2006 and mid-2008 and again between 2011 and 2013, an indicator-creation process involving the national government and civil society actors. The Court's aim was to develop evaluation mechanisms that would permit permanent measurement of the advances, delays, and reversals in aid programs headed by each SNAIPD institution and the effective enjoyment of rights by the displaced population.

These indicators are the second clear sign of the existence of a "policy effect" (in addition to the impact on the design of policies mentioned in the previous section) in the evaluation phase of the public policy cycle for four reasons. First, they marked a shift in the logic of policy measurement toward evaluation in terms of satisfaction of human rights. As the Codhes director reported: "Colombia is a rule of law state but it never evaluated policy from a rights-based perspective. So it is the first time that we've had public policy evaluation based on rights, with verification tools and indicators, with an entire participatory monitoring process."[41]

Second, measurement favored evaluation by concrete outcomes, rather than by means or processes. According to the authoring justice of the T25 opinion:

> I think the Court applied a lot of pressure. It demanded specific indicators to measure the effective enjoyment of rights by the displaced population. The government had to show how many people were actually being protected at point A, and how that protection improved or increased during the period as a result of compliance with the Court's order in T25.[42]

Third, as will be described in detail below, the process leading to indicator creation was public, deliberative, and experimental. The description of a Social Action Agency official is exemplary of such:

[40] Constitutional Court, Ruling T25 of 2004, Section 6.3.1.1.

[41] Interview with Marco Romero, Director of Codhes, December 19 and 23, 2008.

[42] Interview with Manuel Jose Cepeda, Justice of the Colombian Constitutional Court, May 27, 2014.

> What happened with indicators? We proposed something, and everyone else offered a counterproposal. Everyone else was UNHCR, the Monitoring Commission, and other administrative bodies. So what they counter-proposed, the Court ordered us to do, and we answered them. The process went on like this for the rest of the year. The next year the Court convened another hearing, where they told us that they wanted to start another discussion. And so we had a discussion . . . After that the Court scheduled a meeting where the government and civil society and administrative bodies could meet to create indicators and then hand that work over to them. And we did. For about a month after that we put together review groups to start to debate the different indicators . . . It was a back-and-forth process, and the consensus became the joint document that we presented to the Court.[43]

Finally, indicators are the paradigmatic example of the rights-policy toolbox, as they are an intermediate point between economic and legal logics, between economists and lawyers. Clearly, indicators fit in the quantitative toolbox of economists, but as indicators *of rights*, they also constitute a tool that synthesizes the two approaches.

The indicators designed in this process are outcome indicators because, as their name indicates, they seek to evaluate the policy's final results rather than its process. Each one of the outcome indicators was created as a tool to measure the degree of enforcement of different rights and the impact of aid policy as a means to achieve this (Rodríguez-Garavito 2009b).

Outcome indicators are divided into three categories: effective enjoyment of rights, complementary indicators, and associated sectorial indicators. *Effective enjoyment of rights indicators* are measurement instruments designed to assess, at the household level, aid policy to the displaced population focused on the creation of conditions for overcoming this condition. Its measurement unit is binary, yielding a "yes" when the person or family reports fulfillment of the criteria set for each right and "no" when they report something else (Social Action Agency and National Planning Department 2007: 15).

Complementary indicators are "measurement instruments to assess the state of general progress, setbacks to, or delay of the stabilization process as regards the assistance measures corresponding to each indicator of Effective Enjoyment of Rights" (Presidency of the Republic et al. 2007: 16). Finally, *associated sectorial indicators* are "measurement instruments that reveal information on results obtained by each institution as regards its efforts as part of the sectorial offer" (p. 16).

[43] Interview with Viviana Ferro, sub-director of Assistance to the Displaced Population, Social Action Agency, January 8, 2009.

To demonstrate the central role of indicators in this case, the remainder of this section is dedicated to walking the reader through the eight-year process (2006–2013) that resulted in the adoption of close to 300 outcome indicators to measure advances in public policy in 22 rights (see Table 4.1 for a list of some of the key indicators). The process has had two phases: the first one between 2006 and 2008, which resulted in three key decisions (Decisions 109 of 2007, 233 of 2007, and 116 of 2008) and a first set of 174 indicators for twenty rights; and a second phase between 2011 and 2013 (Decisions 115A of 2012 and of November 1, 2012) in which the first set of indicators was evaluated, updated, and complemented, resulting in the extended set that exists today. Analysis of the issuance and follow-up of these decisions focuses on the participatory and deliberative process by which indicators were created, and the way that they served as a conceptual and terminological bridge between the diverse state and social actors involved in this case.

4.3.1. *Phase 1 (2006–2008): The Adoption Process for the First Set of Indicators*

4.3.1.1. The Initial Dialogue Between the Court and the Government

In the first follow-up decisions, the Court ordered the government to adopt outcome indicators "oriented around the effective enjoyment of rights by the displaced population, which allow determining the dimension of the specific problem and advances, setbacks, or delays in each aid program and component."[44]

The Court insisted on indicators in subsequent decisions. In a decision that identified ten structural flaws that impeded the development of national policy on the displaced population, the Court highlighted "the general absence of significant outcome indicators based on the criteria of *effective enjoyment of rights of the displaced population* in all facets of policy, in spite of advances in certain institutions."[45] This pressure led to a proposal from the Director of the Social Action Agency to the Constitutional Court that included a first set of sectorial indicators from each of the SNAIPD institutions.

The response to this proposal followed the logic of dialogical judicial activism: the Court asked the government to clarify certain aspects related to the outcome indicators, such as the setting of "clear deadlines for compliance by SNAIPD institutions of the actions proposed in the common report."[46]

[44] Constitutional Court, Decision 177 of 2005.

[45] Constitutional Court, Decision 218 of 2006 (emphasis added).

[46] Constitutional Court, Decision 266 of 2006.

TABLE 4.1. *Outcome Indicators Adopted by the Constitutional Court*

RIGHT	EFFECTIVE ENJOYMENT OF RIGHTS INDICATOR			COMPLEMENTARY INDICATORS		SECTORIAL INDICATORS	
	Statement	Formula	Source	Formula	Source	Formula	Source
LIFE	All displaced persons remain alive	Number of forced displacement victims included or dismissed by the RUPD[47] who have been killed / Number of forced displacement victims included or dismissed by the RUPD	National Institute of Legal Medicine and Forensic Sciences Unit for Victims' Attention and Reparation	Number of forced displacement victims included or dismissed by the RUPD who, according to investigations by the Attorney General's Office, have been killed in association with their status as victims of displacement / Number of victims of forced displacement included or dismissed by the RUPD	Unit for Victims' Attention and Reparation Attorney General's Office National Institute of Legal Medicine and Forensic Sciences		
HEALTH	Access to SGSSS[48] – All victims of forced displacement are registered to	Number of forced displacement victims included in or dismissed by the RUPD who	Ministry of Health and Social Protection	Number of forced displacement victims included or dismissed by the RUPD who belong to the contributory	Ministry of Health and Social Protection Single Database of Affiliates (BDUA)	Number of forced displacement victims included in or ceased by the RUPD receiving health care /	Ministry of Health and Social Protection RIPS – Emergency and outpatient hospitalization

[47] RUPD, for its Spanish name, is the registration system called the Singular Registry of Displaced Population.
[48] SGSSS, for its Spanish name, is the General Health and Social Security System.

TABLE 4.1. *(continued)*

RIGHT	EFFECTIVE ENJOYMENT OF RIGHTS INDICATOR			COMPLEMENTARY INDICATORS		SECTORIAL INDICATORS	
	Statement	Formula	Source	Formula	Source	Formula	Source
	SGSSS and receive health care	have SGSSS and receive care when needed / Number of forced displacement victims included in or dismissed by the RUPD		regime or to special regimes		Number of forced displacement victims included or dismissed by the RUPD	
				Number of forced displacement victims included or dismissed by the RUPD with the subsidized system / Number of victims of forced displacement included or dismissed by the RUPD	Ministry of Health and Social Protection	Number of forced displacement victims 12 years or older included or dismissed by the RUPD receiving sexual and reproductive health care / Number of forced displacement victims 12 years or older included or dismissed by the RUPD	Ministry of Health and Social Protection PEDT (Resolution 4505 of 2012)

Access to vaccination – All children victims of forced displacement are completely vaccinated	Number of child forced displacement victims ages 0 to 5 included or dismissed by the RUPD with full vaccination/ Number of child forced displacement victims ages 0 to 5 included in or ceased by the RUPD	Ministry of Health and Social Protection	Number of children between 12 and 23 months old included or dismissed by the RUPD with three doses of preventative vaccines (DPT, HB, and Hib) / Number of children between 12 and 23 months old included or dismissed by the RUPD	Ministry of Health and Social Protection
			Number of children included or dismissed by the RUPD that have two boosters of Polio and DPT and one of MMR (measles, mumps, and rubella) / Number of children 0 to 5 years old included or dismissed by the RUPD	Ministry of Health and Social Protection
			Number of children between 12 and 23 months old included or	Ministry of Health and Social Protection

TABLE 4.1. *(continued)*

	EFFECTIVE ENJOYMENT OF RIGHTS INDICATOR			COMPLEMENTARY INDICATORS		SECTORIAL INDICATORS	
RIGHT	Statement	Formula	Source	Formula	Source	Formula	Source
				dismissed by the RUPD with a dose of MMR (measles, mumps, and rubella) / Number of children between 12 and 23 months old included or dismissed by the RUPD			
RETURNS AND RELOCATIONS	All households affected by forced displacement with the intention of returning or relocating, who have requested the help of the government, and have achieved it or received such help	Number of households victims of forced displacement included or dismissed by the RUPD that have sought government support to return or relocate, and have achieved it or received such help / Number of households	Department for Social Prosperity Unit for Victims' Attention and Reparation	Number of forced displacement victims included or dismissed by the RUPD returned or relocated voluntarily with safety and dignity / Number of victims of forced displacement included or dismissed by the RUPD returned or relocated	Department for Social Prosperity Unit for Victims' Attention and Reparation	Number of return and relocation processes that include prevention and protection / Number of return and relocation processes	Department for Social Prosperity Unit for Victims' Attention and Reparation

	including victims of forced displacement included or dismissed by the RUPD, that have sought government support to return or relocate					
			Voluntariness: number of households victims of forced displacement included or dismissed by the RUPD who returned voluntarily / Number of households victims of forced displacement included or dismissed by the RUPD returned or relocated	Department for Social Prosperity Unit for Victims' Attention and Reparation	Number of households victim of forced displacement included or dismissed by the RUPD relocated or accompanied in return with food security projects / Number of households victims of forced displacement included or dismissed by the RUPD returned or relocated	Department for Social Prosperity Unit for Victims' Attention and Reparation

TABLE 4.1. *(continued)*

		EFFECTIVE ENJOYMENT OF RIGHTS INDICATOR		PRIMARY INDICATORS		SECONDARY INDICATORS	
RIGHT	COMMUNITY	Statement	Formula	Component	Formula	Component	Formula
Territory	INDIGENOUS	All displaced indigenous peoples have the right to territory to ensure their physical and cultural survival	Number of forcibly displaced indigenous peoples that legally access the territory appropriate for their physical and cultural survival / Number of displaced indigenous peoples	Access to territory	Number of forcibly displaced indigenous peoples accessing the relevant territory to ensure their physical and cultural survival / Number of forcibly displaced indigenous peoples	Indigenous territory ("resguardo")	Number of forcibly displaced indigenous peoples living in a shelter to ensure their physical and cultural survival / Number of forcibly displaced indigenous peoples
						Sacred Sites	Number of forcibly displaced indigenous peoples accessing their sacred sites / Number of forcibly

			displaced indigenous peoples
Legal security	Number of forcibly displaced indigenous peoples with legal security to inhabit their collective territories / Number of forcibly displaced indigenous peoples	Titling	Number of forcibly displaced indigenous peoples that have title over their collective territories / Number of forcibly displaced indigenous peoples
		Regularization of land	Number of forcibly displaced indigenous peoples that benefit from a land regularization process / Number of forcibly displaced indigenous peoples

TABLE 4.1. *(continued)*

		EFFECTIVE ENJOYMENT OF RIGHTS INDICATOR		PRIMARY INDICATORS		SECONDARY INDICATORS	
RIGHT	COMMUNITY	Statement	Formula	Component	Formula	Component	Formula
				Appropriateness of the territory	Number of forcibly displaced indigenous peoples inhabiting adequate territories for their physical and cultural survival / Number of forcibly displaced indigenous peoples	Resources, uses, and customs	Number of forcibly displaced indigenous peoples living in territories that permit the use of resources necessary for the development of their customs / Number of forcibly displaced indigenous peoples

In response, the government sent a report detailing the timeline it would follow to comply with its proposed actions and announced that the requested outcome indicators would be created by the end of March 2007.[49] This report also evoked responses from public and civic institutions, which became part of the deliberative and participatory indicator-creation process. Specifically, the Inspector General's Office, the Comptroller General's Office, and the Monitoring Commission on Public Policy on Forced Displacement joined the debate. From this point forward, these institutions would become important actors in the forced displacement field, acting as key participants of the indicator process and fostering a dialogical dynamic that is characteristic throughout.

4.3.1.2. The Arrival of New Actors to the Deliberative Process: Indicators as a Rights-Policy Hybrid

To promote participation of a wider group of actors, the Court designed a methodology to work on and exchange technical documents on the design and use of indicators (Decision 337 of 2006), which resulted in a plethora of indicators. More than 500 indicators were submitted to the Court in December 2006 by the Ombudsman's Office, the Inspector General, UNHCR, the Monitoring Commission, and the national government, represented by the Social Action Agency.

Because several of the documents presented by the Social Action Agency referred to the work undertaken in indicator creation by the National Planning Department (DNP), the Court, serving as the articulator of the field of social displacement, asked DNP's director to submit the list of indicators designed by the institution up to that moment. Shortly thereafter, the DNP presented nine additional indicators of effective enjoyment of rights. At that point in time, the government had presented a total of 116 indicators.

The DNP is an iconic, public institution in the realm of economic technocracy, but its entry into the displacement field marked its integration into a process controlled by legal language and logic, specifically the Court's "rights-based approach." As discussed, indicators offered a point of contact between economic and legal logics, as attested to by a DNP official:

> An institution like National Planning is used to creating public policy for aid to vulnerable groups in a different way ... It was hard to wrap our heads around "measuring with an effective enjoyment of rights perspective" ... What we finally understood was that the Court wasn't interested in knowing

[49] Constitutional Court, Decision 109 of 2007, number 8.

> whether or not [educational] opportunity was being offered, but instead whether that person was regularly attending school or actually living in a decent home.[50]

Encouraged by the process' dynamism and the abundance of indicators, other actors joined the debate characterized by a two-way feedback process. For example, in January 2007, the government reported on the pertinence and utility of indicators proposed by the Comptroller General's Office, the Inspector General's Office, the Monitoring Commission, and the UNHCR. The Colombian Commission of Jurists and the Monitoring Commission, in turn, offered comments on the indicators proposed by the government.

The proliferation of indicators led the Court to call a public hearing to clarify conceptual and technical points of the difference between the proposed indicators and consider the adoption of a definitive set of outcome indicators. At the first hearing on indicators, held on March 2007, the Director of the Social Action Agency, the Minister of the Interior and Justice, and the director of the DNP presented a common set of indicators to measure the effective enjoyment of the rights to housing, education, adequate food, income generation, and others. Public hearings and informal sessions, which offered perfect sites to discuss, adjust, and enhance indicators, became an emblem of the indicator process.

After a new round of exchanges and debates, the Court rejected some indicators, requested that the government improve others, and adopted the first set of outcome indicators for six rights of IDPs (Decision 109 of 2007).[51] In line with the guidelines offered in the previous set of decisions concerning the most vulnerable groups within IDPs, the Court also ordered the government to adopt indicators with a differential approach that would take into consideration the special circumstances of these segments of the displaced population. As we will see, this would remain a pending task until the second phase, beginning in 2010.

4.3.1.3. The Adoption of the First Definitive Set of Indicators

After the adoption of the first set of indicators (Decision 109 of 2007), actors engaged in another round of exchanges. This led to an intermediate decision

[50] Interview with María Angélica Alvarado, DNP January 9, 2009.

[51] The Court adopted indicators for the right to housing, health, education, adequate food, income generation, identity, and socioeconomic stabilization. Each of the rights had effective enjoyment of rights, and complementary and associated sectorial indicators.

that adjusted existing indicators and added new ones (Decision 233 of 2007),[52] later culminating in the adoption of the first final set of 174 indicators considered sufficient, pertinent, and adequate to measure the progress, deadlock, or setbacks in the unconstitutional state of affairs and the effective enjoyment of 20 IDPs' rights (Decision 116 of 2008.)

The participatory process that led to the definitive set of indicators was characterized by (i) the government and the Monitoring Commission's first attempts to test the indicators and provide an initial baseline; (ii) a sequence of multi-actor public hearings;[53] and (iii) closed technical sessions between the government,[54] the Monitoring Commission, and the Court[55] to fine-tune, discard, and create new indicators.

In the decision that adopted the final set, two gaps stood out in the government-presented indicators. First, there were inadequacies in rights related to transitional justice (e.g., the rights to truth and to justice), and, second, the government found itself unable to design policies that recognized the special needs of the most vulnerable segments of the IDP population. Additionally, the decision confirmed that, despite the technical sessions, disagreements persisted between the Monitoring Commission and the government around certain indicators.[56]

Against the background of flaws that persisted in the government's indicators and the government and the Monitoring Commission's inability to reach

52 This decision adopted outcome indicators, of the three types, for three more rights: right to life, to integrity, and to liberty.

53 The public hearings were held during the month of February 2008. In the first of these, for example, the government presented results from its first evaluation of the state of rights of IDPs using the recently created indicators. At the second one, the UNHCR submitted indicators to measure the degree of coordination among national and local institutions. The Monitoring Commission also presented a list of 372 new indicators, addressing flaws in the old set detected by the Court in Decision 233.

54 The technical sessions took place at the National Planning department at the end of February, with a smaller group of actors. They were set up as private working sessions to speed-up the indicator adoption process. As a result of these sessions, on March 12 the government presented a document containing conclusions reached and comments on the three indicators that had generated the greatest debate: outcome indicators for the right to income generation, adequate food, and reparations.

55 As a result of the technical sessions between the government and the Monitoring Commission, the number of indicators was reduced. Also during this period, and as a result of the Court's emphasis on the need to adopt specific indicators to measure the degree of effective enjoyment of rights by women and children, two NGOs – Plan International and Sisma – submitted outcome indicators for rights of displaced children and of women, respectively

56 For example, as for the indicator on income generation, disagreement arose between the national government, which had proposed the extreme poverty line as the proper evaluating parameter, and the Monitoring Commission, which supported the poverty line as the proper parameter.

an agreement over certain indicators, the Court adopted a more interventionist role. For example, with regard to the income generation indicator, the Court felt that an income-level goal below the poverty line did not guarantee the effective enjoyment of rights or decent, autonomous subsistence. Thus, the Court addressed the difference by determining that the government-adopted indicator was only appropriate for measuring one stage on the path toward assuring that displaced individuals live above the poverty line, as suggested by the Monitoring Commission. Furthermore, to address the deficiencies mentioned, the Court decided to supplement its own indicators for the rights to truth and justice.

With the full set of indicators adopted by the Court, the government and the Monitoring Commission carried out the first complete measure for a sample of 8,053 households in 71 municipalities and calculated the first comprehensive baseline. The results were presented before the Court in October of 2008. Two years later the government carried out the second study, with 9,500 households in 103 municipalities, with the objective of comparing the results with the baseline. The issue of indicators would remain dormant in the Court until the Court conducted a seven-year policy evaluation in the second half of 2011 with the enactment of the Victims Law, where it identified serious measurement flaws and prompted a new phase of indicator construction.

4.3.2. *Phase 2 (2011–today): The Adoption Process of Indicators for Ethnic Groups and Indicators Adjusted for the Victims Law*

After three years of silence regarding indicators, the Court resumed the issue in the "splice decision," in which it carried out a comprehensive review of the seven years of policies since T25 and anticipated opportunities and risks with the enactment of the Victims Law. The Court unearthed deep flaws regarding under-registry of IDPs, information systems, and characterization of the displaced population. Embracing the participatory logic that has characterized the indicator construction process, the Court "deemed [it] pertinent to reestablish the technical dialogue between the administrative agencies, the Monitoring Commission, the UNHCR, and the national government to evaluate the technical observations submitted and to adopt the necessary changes." Accordingly, the Court summoned a public hearing to revise, complement, and adjust the outcome indicators employed to date, on the basis of which to continue evaluating the progress, stagnation, or setbacks in the cessation of the unconstitutional state of affairs (Decision 219 of 2011).

The new decision and the idea of an upcoming public hearing triggered a second period of multilateral exchanges and debates between the government, the Court, and civil society. The objective of this new phase was the elaboration of indicators for certain rights that did not have any indicators or the adjustment of some indicators to take into account the new institutional framework introduced by the Victims Law. Emphasis was placed on the rights to truth, justice, reparations, income generation, life, participation, and indicators for the most vulnerable sectors of the IDP population. This phase is ongoing because the Court has yet to discard, fine-tune, or complement the proposed indicators and hand down a decision with a definitive set of indicators.

The second phase of the indicator construction process is characterized by: (i) over a dozen technical sessions held between the DNP, the Unit for Victims' Attention and Reparation, and the Monitoring Commission, to which traditional actors such as UNHCR and the Comptroller and Ombudsman's Offices were invited; (ii) parallel multi-actor technical sessions held at the Court to discuss the progress made in the latter sessions and the indicators gradually submitted; and (iii) the creation of indicators for the collective and individual rights of ethnic groups and for the right to participation.

Following the "splice decision," the DNP, the Unit for Victims' Attention and Reparation, and the Monitoring Commission put together a technical team to resume the indicator-creation process. They held sixteen sessions over a seven-month period, each one devoted to the discussion of indicators for one or two rights.[57] The conclusions of these sessions were in turn discussed with a broader group of actors at public hearings and technical sessions convened by the Court. Besides the usual government actors that had participated in the hearing of the first phase (i.e., the UNHCR, the Monitoring Commission, the Comptroller General, and Ombudsman's Offices, among others), the novelty of these court sessions was that they were attended by representatives of several states and municipalities, revealing a more active participation of territorial entities which, as described in Chapter 2, have been relatively absent in the general follow-up process.[58] Furthermore, in January 2013 the City of Medellín presented one of the first reports implementing the new indicators (Office of the Mayor of Medellín 2013).

[57] The sessions started on November 24, 2011, with the discussion over the indicators for the right to identity, return, and reunification ended on June 12, 2012, with the session for the indicators for the right to income generation.

[58] Issues raised by the territorial entities included the difficulty of measuring some indicators, the fact that some information is not comparable, and the high number of indicators.

In June and October of 2012, the DNP, the Unit for Victims' Attention and Reparation, and the Monitoring Commission presented a set of 283 outcome indicators[59] for 24 rights and 4 sets of indicators for special segments of the IDP population (women, children, disabled persons, and seniors) (Decision of November 1, 2012). In comparison to the previous set of indicators adopted in 2008, this new set includes indicators for four new rights and one additional vulnerable group (senior citizens). The June report that accompanied the indicators explicitly acknowledged that indicators for the right to participation and for Afro-Colombian and indigenous groups were missing, contending that these required adjustments that would take into consideration the recent Victims Law and decrees for indigenous groups, Afro-Colombians, and gypsies.

Starting in October 2012, the government led a process for the creation of the indicators for these vulnerable groups. As a result, it handed over outcome indicators for collective rights of Afro-Colombian and indigenous peoples, such as the right to autonomy and self-government, cultural identity, prior consultation, and the right to territory (see Table 4.1 for the latter). In addition, indicators for the individual rights of these peoples consist of the same indicators for the 24 rights of IDPs and the 4 for the vulnerable segments of the displaced population (women, children, people with disabilities, and the elderly), but with specific reference to Afro-Colombians and indigenous peoples. These new indicators doubled the existing list. In short, the participatory public process coordinated by the Court has resulted in close to 400 outcome indicators. As mentioned above, at the time of finishing this book the Special Monitoring Commission had not issued a ruling adopting a second, definitive set of indicators.

The outcome of this two-phase, systemic effort to create indicators is partly reproduced in Table 4.1, which shows outcome indicators of four rights selected for their representation of the broad array of rights, complex strategies, time horizons, and institutions involved in the realization of the rights and their measurement. The right to life is the most basic right, without which the rest are not even relevant; the right to health is a core socioeconomic right and one which has been used actively by the Court to evaluate the unconstitutional state of affairs; the right to return and relocation is particularly connected to victims of forced displacement and its realization is more long-term; and the right to territory is an example of a collective right for indigenous groups, which is one of the vulnerable segments of the population for which

[59] Within these outcome indicators, 28 indicators were for effective enjoyment of rights, 77 were complementary, and 178 sectorial.

the Court has issued numerous orders. This chart thus constitutes the culminating point of a seven-year, ongoing process that is reconstructed in detail in this section and noteworthy not only for its novelty in the Colombian and global context, but also for embodying the traits of experimental and dialogic judicial activism highlighted in Chapter 1. In effect, instead of defining public policy details and indicators for implementation from the beginning, the Court initiated a process in which, gradually and through acquired experience, instruments for measuring advances in the guarantee of rights were submitted, evaluated, and revised. These instruments arose from an exchange among state and civil society actors that presented proposals and counterproposals which the Court then evaluated as the process advanced.

The result has been a sophisticated public policy-monitoring mechanism that has served as a common reference for actors in the field. From the civil society perspective, for example, the Director of Codhes attested that "the indicators gave the Court a measuring tool that allows them to more clearly and objectively determine compliance levels."[60] From the government's perspective, the DNP official quoted before concluded after the first phase of the indicator construction process that:

> We went from 117 crazy indicators that didn't match up with each other at all, on the number of forms, phone calls, and the sort, to a concrete set of effective enjoyment [of rights indicators] that, although still open to criticism, were an important step. And a large part of that is because of the dynamic generated around this ruling.[61]

The indicators also served as a basis for the systematic gathering of information on the displaced population. At the Court's request, the Monitoring Commission has undertaken three surveys to verify the situation of the displaced population, first in 2007, then in 2008, and lastly in 2010. In the three situations, indicators for the effective enjoyment of rights were the central referents for the collection and organization of data. The results of these surveys offer the most complete view of the displaced population situation, which is addressed in Chapter 7, and have been the basis upon which the Court has evaluated the government's progress with regards to the Court's orders.

The implementation of indicators has not been without problems. As we discuss in Chapter 8, the length and complexity of the list of indicators has

60 Interview with Marco Romero, Director of Codhes, December 19 and 23, 2008.
61 Interview with María Angélica Alvarado, DNP January 9, 2009.

made it difficult for the Court to assess progress as the follow-up process has unfolded. This was evident during a focus group session with members of the Court's Special Monitoring Chamber, who shared with us the challenges of applying indicators to make sense of and evaluate the vast amount of information that the Court receives from government and civil society alike.[62]

4.4. CONCLUSIONS

This chapter aimed to illustrate the direct material impacts of judicial activism that we have dubbed the "policy effect." As we have demonstrated, T25 and the monitoring process have significantly influenced the design of national policy on IDPs, the evaluation of such policy through indicators, and the evolution of the unconstitutional state of affairs. The impact on public policy resulted from two roles played by the Court. First, the role of guide, which consisted of offering guidelines, setting broad goals, and outlining design and implementation procedures for IDP policy. Second, the Court played the role of restrained policymaker, which consisted of handing down more precise orders and defining specific policies to be adopted for the most vulnerable groups and communities within the displaced population. The Court influenced the evaluation phase of IDP policies by fostering a collaborative process for developing outcome indicators to measure the fulfillment of IDPs' rights. Although the application of the resulting long and complex list of indicators has become a challenge for the Court, the process that led to the indicators enhanced the participation of a broad array of governmental and non-governmental agencies, thus contributing to another potential effect of the dialogical activism: the participatory effect. We turn to this effect in the following chapter.

[62] Focus group with members of Colombian Constitutional Court's Special Monitoring Chamber, November 25, 2013.

5

The Participatory Effect: Dialogic Judicial Activism, Public Deliberation, and Problem-Solving

As discussed in Chapter 1, one of the classic objections to judicial intervention in public policy is the idea that unelected judges can usurp decision-making power from democratic institutions such as Congress and popularly elected governments. In response to this criticism, as discussed previously, contemporary courts have elaborated participatory spaces in the follow-up to their decisions. Some examples of this trend are the commissioners which implement orders from the Supreme Court of India and the public monitoring hearings held by Argentine courts in structural cases (see Chapter 8). This chapter contends that structural rulings can foster and deepen, rather than inhibit, democratic deliberation and public accountability for authorities by encouraging post-judgment participatory mechanisms that enable ongoing stakeholder involvement and facilitate effective accountability. We have dubbed this potential impact of dialogic judicial activism the "participatory effect" of structural cases.

What are the scope and limitations of the participatory effect in the specific case of forced displacement in Colombia? This chapter addresses that question based on evidence of the extent of participation by various state and non-state actors that, as described in Chapter 2, comprise the socio-legal field of displacement.

We divide the chapter into two sections. In the first section, we study the scope of the participatory effect. We distinguish between the participatory effect promoted through public hearings and monitoring decisions directly stemming from the Court, on the one hand, and the participation mediated by state and non-state institutions, on the other. In examining these effects, we highlight the opportunities for participation that ruling T25 has opened for diverse civil society actors that have, in turn, become central figures in the debate over policies on displacement. In the second section, we discuss limitations of the participatory effect, identifying the specialized legal logic and language that dominates this process as obstacles to participation.

5.1. THE PARTICIPATORY EFFECT: DIALOGUE WITH THE COURT AND BEYOND

5.1.1. *Dialogue with the Court*

The follow-up process to T25 has opened judicial proceedings and policy-making to a broad range of state and non-state actors. This key material effect has largely been the result of the Court's efforts to actively monitor the implementation of its orders through three types of participatory mechanisms – follow-up decisions, public hearings, and technical sessions – which have opened direct channels and spaces of dialogue with the Court. From the beginning, the Court's orders involved not only the core government agencies responsible for IDPs such as the Ministry of the Interior and Justice (MIJ) and the Social Action Agency (the agency in charge of antipoverty programs which was in charge of IDP policy), but also all other government and non-government actors with related responsibilities at the international, national, and local levels. The Court's position in the center of the field of forced displacement (see Chapter 2, Figure 2.4) is both a cause and a consequence of this dialogical exercise: the Court occupies this position because of the central role it has played in triggering the participatory process and, because of this, became the field's facilitator.

In the ten years after T25 (January 2004 to April 2014), the Constitutional Court handed down 289 follow-up decisions to closely monitor the implementation of the orders issued in T25 and the ensuing decisions, each with diverse objectives. Some are procedural and request information from specific actors[1] or communicate relevant information.[2] Others simply set the date of public hearings or technical sessions.[3] A third type of decision addresses issues

[1] See, among others, Decision 68 of 2008, in which the Court invited academic and specialized organizations to make proposals on the most critical and complex areas of assistance to the displaced population. See Rodríguez-Garavito (2009a) for a sample of one of the studies produced in response to this Decision. See also Decision of March 11, 2014, in which the Court requests information and progress reports from the Victims Unit.

[2] See, for example, Decision 36 of 2009, in which the Court included the Attorney General's Report on cases of sexual violence reported in Decision 92 of 2008. See, also, Decision of November 1, 2012 in which the Court distributed the outcome indicators created jointly by the National Planning Department, the Victims Unit, and the Monitoring Commission to other stakeholders for their feedback.

[3] See, among others, Decisions 27 and 101 of 2007 and 2, 11, and 53 of 2008.

of noncompliance among state officials or contracted employees.[4] The fourth adopts rights-based indicators to assess the evolvement of the realization of displaced people's rights, as explained in the previous chapter.

In fact, a large number of decisions have been dedicated to the substantive work of evaluating compliance with the Court's commands and requesting specific actions.[5] In these evaluations, the Court has encouraged the participation of diverse actors in two ways. First, it has requested information, progress reports, and technical concepts from state institutions, NGOs, and research centers, which have served as a basic input in the Court's analyses. Second, based on these analyses, the Court has issued new orders to actors that, as we will see below, have encouraged those actors' continuous participation in the monitoring process. These decisions have triggered an iterative process in which the Court issues remedies or asks for information from state and non-state actors, the institutions respond through progress reports, and the Court in turn replies through follow-up decisions. Other institutions also provide feedback to the reports of government agencies and the Court distributes these reports to the rest of the actors.

In addition to follow-up decisions, the chief participation and deliberation mechanisms used by the Court are public hearings and technical sessions which are regional or informal. Public hearings[6] are a public accountability mechanism for the government and a space for debate on the results of and obstacles to displacement policies in light of the orders of ruling T25 and the follow-up decisions. Court justices, government delegates, NGO and international organization representatives, leaders of organizations of IDPs, and the general public and public media attend these. The issues discussed vary. Some do a general accountability in which each institution presents its results on IDP issues and compliance

4 See, among others, Decisions 333, 334, and 335 of 2006, and 58 of 2007.

5 See, among others, the five decisions in which the Court analyzed the particular, disproportionate risks experienced by certain vulnerable groups within the displaced population, such as women (Decision 92 of 2008), children (Decision 251 of 2008), indigenous peoples (Decision 4 of 2009), Afrodescendents (Decision 5 of 2009), and displaced persons with disabilities (Decision 8 of 2009).

6 The name of public follow-up sessions has varied. In certain cases, the Court has referred to them as "public hearings," while in others, it spoke of "public information hearings," "accountability hearings," and even "technical information sessions," which are not to be confused with the technical sessions described ahead. The main difference between hearings and technical information sessions is that the latter are generally not attended by representatives of the displaced population, as was the case with the sessions held in 2008 to discuss the issue of effective enjoyment of rights indicators to be used to measure advances in displacement public policy.

with T25, as in the first public hearing, which took place in June 2005, while others focus on key aspects or groups of the follow-up process, as in the most recent hearing, held in September 2013, on internally displaced indigenous peoples. By the closing of this study (April 2014), twenty public hearings have been held at the Court's premises.

Technical sessions, both regional and informal, result from the Court's own learning process and innovation strategy. Beginning in 2010, as the Court found the need to discuss some issues more privately, public hearings were gradually substituted by technical sessions. Like public hearings, these are a space for debate among multiple stakeholders, but are usually smaller, not open to all stakeholders or the media, and focused on more specific topics. As explained in Chapter 2, regional technical sessions resemble the public follow-up hearings in that their objective is to publicly discuss the fulfillment of the orders handed down in T25. The main difference is that they are held in towns and cities outside Bogotá and the people convened are public officials at the state, district, and municipal levels in addition to associations of displaced persons working in the regions. Seven regional technical sessions were held during 2010 in which the main topic discussed was the poor coordination between the national and local governments (see decision 314 of 2009).

Informal technical sessions are different from public hearings. The Court convenes them to privately discuss a specific issue only with specific, previously invited public officials and stakeholders (see, for example, Decisions 8 of 2013 and 145 of 2013). The Court began holding informal sessions in 2013 and, by April of 2014, a total of twelve informal sessions had taken place. One example of an informal technical session was convened by the Court to discuss the progress made in the prevention and protection of the human rights defenders. Another technical session focused on IDP women (Decision 8 of 2013). The Court convened several national government agencies, the Attorney General's Office, the Comptroller General's Office, civil society organizations, representatives of IDP women, the United Nations Refugee Agency (UNHCR), the League of Displaced Women, Amnesty International, Human Rights Watch, and the Norwegian Council for Refugees.

The hearings and technical sessions shaped judicial proceedings and the design and evaluation processes of public policy on forced displacement by making them more participatory and horizontal. First, they opened up the follow-up process to a wider group of national and international actors, including representatives of organizations of IDPs, academia, national and international NGOs, and international organizations such as the

UNHCR, as is shown Chapter 2 (Figure 2.4). Second, they increased publicity about and transparency of the process and the issue of forced displacement. Third, they fostered dialogue between actors who, prior to the ruling, were working in an uncoordinated fashion or rarely interacted because of their differing levels of power. Interviewees mentioned all three of these effects. The sub-director of Assistance to the Displaced Population of Social Action Agency reported:

> The hearings changed the space of the debate because before it didn't exist. What was the relationship like before? It was the typical relationship with a court. Courts [talk] through rulings and decisions and these are answered in writing, without what we lawyers refer to as direct review of the evidence by a judge. Instead, I simply answer in writing what you ask me. Then, because of the dynamic the Constitutional Court inaugurated through hearings, the whole tenor changed. Now there is open debate, where the Court departs from the role of judge a bit to play the role of guarantor of rights and give its opinion within the debate.[7]

As the previous chapter recalls, perhaps the best example of the iterative, multi-stakeholder participatory process promoted by the Court using the three types of participatory mechanisms was the adoption of outcome indicators of displacement policy. Since the details of the content of those indicators were already presented in the previous chapter, for the purposes of this chapter it is enough to recall that they were the product of dialogue regarding proposals from both the government and the Monitoring Commission on Public Policy on Forced Displacement (Monitoring Commission) with the Court serving as an active mediator. It was a gradual and iterative process, in which the Court would ask for new proposals, accept some of the ones presented, and once again request alternative indicators. In sum, this dialogic process, which included multiple follow-up decisions, hearings, and technical sessions, allowed the central actors of the field to cumulatively construct mechanisms to measure compliance with judgment T25.

The clerk in charge of the Court's follow-up process explained it in the following terms:

> It took three years to decide on [the first set of] indicators, from the date of ruling T25. [State institutions] would tell us they did have [indicators], others would say they did not. But they reported on how many flutes they had delivered [to the Ministry of Culture´s music education program], or how many bulletproof vests they had delivered, but no one knew if they were really

7 Interview with Viviana Ferro, Subdirector of Assistance to the Displaced Population at Social Action Agency, January 8, 2009.

> advancing or not, if they had made an effort where one needed to be made, or how much was left to do. So the indicators issue ended up transforming the relationship with the Court.[8]

As Chapters 1 and 8 explain, the Colombian Court, like other activist constitutional courts, sought to answer objections to the legitimacy of its intervention in public policies through public deliberation. As the director of the Consultancy for Human Rights and Displacement (Codhes) affirmed, "T25 is a ruling that has gained great national and international legitimacy . . . through its results and through the great advances made in participation and debate processes."[9] A similar perception exists in relevant public institutions, as demonstrated by the opinion of the former sub-director of Assistance to the Displaced Population of Social Action Agency:

> We gained a space for dialogue and democratic policymaking for victims. No other public policy has a space where one table seats a displaced person, a civil society representative, a government representative, and a representative of the judicial branch to debate whether or not enough budgetary resources are being directed to the population.[10]

However, as we will see in the following section, the participatory effect resulting from the monitoring process has not only been the result of hearings, sessions, and decisions originating from the Court. Civil society actors beyond the Court, who have developed their own spaces of dialogue and strategies to actively engage in the follow-up process, have enhanced participation and debate in judicial proceedings and policymaking.

5.1.2. *Dialogue Beyond the Court: State and Non-State Actors*

The ruling and follow-up process have also had a participatory effect on state and non-state actors. An analysis of the former requires returning briefly to two institutions mentioned in Chapter 3 on the coordinating effect prompted by Court: the National Council for Integral Attention to Displaced Population (CNAIPD), and the territorial committees.

As discussed, in response to T25, CNAIPD reconvened after two years of dormancy. In the first five years after the ruling, CNAIPD convened twenty-one meetings, attended by an average of forty-eight people including

8 Interview with Clara Helena Reales, Constitutional Court Clerk, Chambers of Justice Manuel José Cepeda, December 18, 2008.

9 Interview with Marco Romero, Director of Codhes, December 19 and 23, 2008.

10 Interview with Viviana Ferro, Subdirector of Assistance to the Displaced Population at Social Action Agency, January 8, 2009.

representatives of the majority of CNAIPD institutions, as well as state actors, social actors, and international organizations. To facilitate the discussion and the participatory design of public policies, four CNAIPD roundtables were created,[11] each one for a key item of IDP policy and all including participants from the displaced population.

The other spaces for coordination and deliberation are the local committees for comprehensive assistance to the displaced population, which aim to incite dialogue on public policies at the departmental, district, and municipal levels. These committees facilitate National System for Assistance to the Displaced Population (SNAIPD) management in the subnational context. The committees are comprised of roundtables or thematic commissions which the law obliges to promote citizen participation and inter-institutional coordination through mechanisms such as the formulation of a Singular Integrated Plans (PIU, in Spanish).[12] In sum, while the Court did not create these two coordinating bodies, it managed to revive participation and dialogue in state bodies such as these that, on paper, were participatory and composed of multiple stakeholders.

The ruling and follow-up process have also had a participatory effect on civil society. By creating opportunities for participation such as public hearings or the possibility to provide comments on public policies, the Court encouraged the participation of social organizations interested in the displacement issue and the formation of new coalitions. As an UNHCR official rightly observed:

> There were a number of organizations in the country working on the issue, and the Court's invitations have had a powerful effect, allowing different considerations and perspectives to come together before the Court. Different sectors started to say "I want to participate, too," and started organizing in order to participate.[13]

The clearest examples of alliances formed as a result of the follow-up process are the Monitoring Commission created in November 2005 and the Monitoring Roundtable to Decision 92 (which was the special follow-up decision on displaced women and female victims of sexual violence) in 2008. The rest of the section focuses on these two alliances.

[11] The roundtables were about: 1) protection and prevention, 2) emergency humanitarian assistance, 3) socioeconomic stabilization, and 4) strengthening the organizational process around the displaced population.

[12] PIUs are a formal coordination mechanism employed by territorial committees that include the private sector and civil society to ensure concerted efforts for the prevention and attention to forced displacement among national, departmental, and municipal SNAIPD institutions.

[13] Interview with Andrés Celis, UNHCR official, January 17, 2008.

Chapter 2 explained the origin and membership of the coalition of civil society organizations that form the Monitoring Commission. This chapter focuses on two main features of the Commission. First, its existence results from the follow-up process initiated by the Court, where founding civil society organizations conceived it as a tool to incite compliance with Court decisions and to contribute to proposals aimed to remedy the unconstitutional state of affairs. As explained by Monsignor Henao, director of one of the religious organizations that is part of the Monitoring Commission:

> [The Commission] was born out of the linkage of a group of people who had been working on the displacement issue. What the group does is that, at a certain moment, it convenes given the need to create tools and mechanisms to support the Court in everything it needed, such as very concrete surveys on displacement data, including the measure of the problem in medium-sized cities, in the countryside, in large cities, and in the most affected areas.[14]

Second, the Monitoring Commission is a space for deliberation on the issue. In effect, it periodically convenes NGOs (such as Viva la Ciudadanía and Codhes), segments of the Catholic Church (Pastoral Social), research centers (Center for Law, Justice and Society), academic institutions (the Law School of the University of the Andes), as well as experts and activists, in a continuous process of discussion, which has resulted in contributions central not only to the follow-up process before the Court, but to the public debate in general.

As a result, the Commission has produced over a dozen reports and a series of documents delivered to the Constitutional Court that comment on policy proposals presented by the government and provide original data on different topics, from the problem of land stolen from the displaced to the situation confronted by particularly vulnerable members of the displaced population. Additionally, at the Court's request, the Commission, in collaboration with the National University, undertook three National Verification Surveys to measure the level of fulfillment of the IDPs' rights (see Chapter 7). Based on these studies, the Commission has become one of the most dynamic actors in the participatory spaces described above. With the new Victims Law, the Monitoring Commission, like many civil society organizations and government agencies, has felt the need to gradually shift its work from focusing exclusively on IDPs to focusing on the victims in general.

Another example of a participatory space that emerged as a result of the Court's orders and the monitoring process is the Monitoring Roundtable to

14 Interview with Monsignor Héctor Fabio Henao, Director of Pastoral Social, December 18, 2008.

Decision 92 – Reserved Annex (from now on, the Roundtable to Decision 92). In Decision 92 the Court addressed the issue of displaced women by identifying risks that particularly affect women and ordering the creation of thirteen programs for the protection of their fundamental rights. Among these risks, the Court highlighted sexual violence and concluded that "sexual violence against women is a common, extended, systematic and invisible practice in the context of the Colombian armed conflict" (Section III.1.1.1). Consequently, in an annex to the Decision (commonly referred to as the Reserved Annex), the Court ordered the Attorney General's Office to investigate 183 alleged cases of sexual violence against women committed in the context of the armed conflict, for which the Court had information that was documented in the Annex. Furthermore, it invited the General Inspector's Office to carry out strict oversight of these processes. Likewise, the Court invited NGO Codhes to participate in the follow-up process to this decision and to the Annex.

As a result of this invitation, and based on the experience of the Monitoring Commission, Codhes summoned 11 civil society organizations[15] to form a roundtable to monitor the level of compliance of the orders directed to the Attorney General's Office regarding the 183 female victims of sexual violence. Since 2008, the "Roundtable to Decision 92," with the support of the UNHCR and UN Women, has published five reports on the level of compliance of the orders issued to the Attorney General's Office and the Inspector General's Office and participated in multiple public hearings and technical sessions on the matter.[16] It generally concluded that impunity continues to be the norm in most cases and, therefore, that the court orders have been largely unobserved (Guzmán and Cabrera 2013).

The formation and interventions of the Monitoring Commission and the Monitoring Roundtable on sexual violence reveal two important characteristics of the participatory effect produced by the Court's intervention. First, the participatory effect regarding civil society is both a direct product of the ruling and monitoring process and an indirect, unexpected consequence of it. While the Court expressly invited non-state actors to participate in the follow-up process (e.g., Codhes and the UNHCR), the formation of the civil society coalitions to participate in the monitoring process is an indirect outcome of

[15] The organizations include: Alianza Iniciativa de Mujeres Colombianas por la Paz; Dejusticia; Colectivo de Abogados José Alvear Restrepo; the Colombian Commission of Jurists; Codhes; Corporación Casa de la Mujer; Corporación Sisma Mujer; and the League of Displaced Women; among others.

[16] See, e.g., the fifth report published in October 2013 (Guzman and Cabrera 2013).

the opening up of judicial proceedings. By joining efforts, NGOs such as Codhes, Dejusticia, and Viva la Ciudadanía, grassroots organizations, sectors of the Catholic Church, and academia spontaneously formed a coalition to contribute to the implementation of T25. Additionally, Codhes led the initiative to start the Monitoring Roundtable on sexual violence. However, in a striking boomerang effect, the Court then acknowledged both alliances as parties to the monitoring process and relied heavily on the data and recommendations that both coalitions submitted.[17]

The second characteristic of the participatory effect is that it has triggered the participatory, public discussion of issues related to, but not limited to, displacement. The clearest case is the issue of sexual violence against women. The 183 cases prioritized by the Court were not all cases of internally displaced women. They were cases of sexual violence that took place in the context of violence, which also causes displacement. In that sense, the monitoring process has served as an umbrella under which actors have found a space to discuss issues related to displacement or the armed conflict.

In sum, this section analyzed how the Court initiated a novel follow-up process that opened channels and spaces for direct dialogue while provoking debates on displacement and related issues in diverse public spheres. By creating opportunities and mechanisms to participate and requiring the participation of specific actors, the Court adopted the type of experimental judicial activism discussed in Chapter 1 in which courts, rather than determining the details of public policy, involve multiple voices in the collective exploration of solutions to complex problems like displacement.

However, as sharp readers will recognize, the less-mentioned actors in this section are displaced persons and their social organizations. This is because the results of their participation are mixed. Our fieldwork shows that the inclusion of this population in the discussion and adoption of the policies that directly affect them increased but continues to be the main drawback of the participatory effect. The following section discusses this issue.

5.2. LIMITATIONS OF THE PARTICIPATORY EFFECT: THE CHALLENGES OF IDPS' PARTICIPATION

Since the creation of the first policies and laws on displacement in the middle of the nineties, criticism on the lack of effective participation by victims and

[17] The Court has not issued an official declaration making the Commission or the Roundtable a party, but it has effectively acknowledged them as parties by convening them to public hearings and technical sessions and issuing them special orders and invitations. See, e.g., Decision 109 of 2007, which is one of the decisions of the indicator construction process.

calls to guarantee it have proliferated. For example, Law 387 in 1997 created participation mechanisms for victims within CNAIPD and the territorial committees. However, in practice, these laws were rarely applied despite the fact that the UN Guiding Principles on Internal Displacement called for the participation of the displaced population, and they were summarily incorporated into Constitutional Court jurisprudence.

Various court decisions, including judgment T25 and numerous follow-up decisions, addressed this gap.[18] For example, the ruling demanded that "decisions made relative to remedying the unconstitutional state of affairs be presented to representative organizations of the displaced population, giving them the opportunity to effectively participate," and clarified that "this implies, at a minimum, anticipatory awareness of decisions to be enforced, as well as opportunity to make observations that will be duly considered and will receive responses."[19]

The effect of such decisions was visible in the two types of spaces analyzed in the preceding section, including direct dialogue with the Court and other opportunities for debate on policies concerning displacement within the state, such as the CNAIPD and the territorial committees.

The Court called representative organizations of the displaced population to the vast majority of its hearings and actively solicited information from some of them that it later gathered in several fundamental follow-up decisions. For example, in the first monitoring hearing held, three organizations of IDPs participated: the National Roundtable on Strengthening Displaced Persons' Organization (National Roundtable), the Departmental Roundtable of the State of Nariño, and the Bogotá Working Roundtable on Internal Displacement. In a document sent to the Court before this hearing, the Bogotá Working Roundtable highlighted the importance of this space:

> We would like to thank the honorable Court for extending an invitation to participate in such an important hearing. We understand this to be a truly

[18] The Constitutional Court's decisions that deal with the issue of participation of IDPs are: Decisions 177 of 2005 and 178 of 2005 (declare that all coordinating bodies should guarantee the participation of organizations of IDPs); Decision 333 of 2006 (heightens the state's obligation to help the Organizations of Displaced Persons overcome the obstacles that impede them to engage in dialogues with the state); Decisions 116 of 2008 and 7 and 8 of 2009 (emphasize the need to develop a participation strategy for IDPs); Decision 383 of 2010 (on the importance of having IDP organizations participate in policymaking and on the specific need to train IDP leaders) and lastly, decision 219 of 2011 (which conducts a review of all reports and actions taken by the government since 2004 to guarantee participation of IDPs and declares a low level of compliance with the order).

[19] Constitutional Court, Judgment T25 of 2004.

> democratic act. We also recognize the importance of this hearing and the participation of several civil society actors, including ourselves as direct victims of the sociopolitical conflict afflicting our country and which, regarding the case at hand, we ourselves personally suffer as victims of forced displacement (Bogotá Working Roundtable 2005: 7).

Participation by organizations of IDPs was also evident in hearings held over the particular effects of displacement on more vulnerable groups such as children, persons with disabilities, and the Afro-Colombian and indigenous populations. As a reading of the decisions stemming from these hearings shows, opinions expressed by representatives of victims and the data these organizations presented to the Court provided central sources of information and proposals that the Court considered when issuing new decisions related to these populations.

In its systematic evaluation of public policy on displacement, the UNHCR summed up the participatory impact of these spaces in more general terms:

> The Court's intervention generated positive responses in this area [participation of the displaced population]. Organizations of IDPs now have spaces of dialogue that would have been inconceivable in 2003. High-level state officials have held discussions with the displaced population on public policy and the scope of the state's efforts (UNHCR 2007: 28).

When considering participatory and deliberative spaces promoted by the monitoring decisions beyond the Court, the impact has been felt in a few state agencies. For example, since May 2004, CNAIPD opened its sessions to the displaced population and adopted specific measures (such as Directive 2 of 2005) to promote IDPs' participation. Representatives of the organizations of IDPs attended these sessions regularly.[20] As for territorial committees, two years after the ruling, the displaced population was participating in 21 of the 26 active departmental committees, and in 106 of the 357 committees located in municipalities with the larger number of displaced individuals expelled or received.[21] Additionally, an initiative originating from the displaced population and aided by the National Roundtable resulted in the formation of 8 territorial roundtables on strengthening displaced

[20] The displaced population was represented by members of the National Roundtable on Strengthening Displaced Persons' Organizations, themselves also members of individual associations of IDPs such as Asowomens and Work Organization, Asdecol, and Advicora. Additionally, certain sessions were attended by representatives of the Indigenous Roundtable on Displacement, the National Network of Displaced Women of Colombia, and the United Association of the Displaced (see CNAIPD, Acts 1–21).

[21] CNAIPD, Act 10, July 18, 2006.

population organizations in the capital city and in 7 of the 32 states.[22] Moreover, the representatives of the displaced population were invited to participate in the government committees that decide on which members of vulnerable populations must receive state protection (known as the Committees for the Evaluation of Risks and Recommendation of Measures [CERREM]). As a former advisor to Afrodes explained when referring to the latter, "Winning these spaces in those terrains has allowed greater interaction and incidence. Even if it is for them to say 'no.' Before, they would tell us 'no' in a letter. There was no representative of the population group."[23]

In spite of these scattered advances, our fieldwork and documental analysis reveal profound limitations upon the involvement of displaced populations in the follow-up and policymaking processes. In fact, the participatory effect has had a greater impact on other civil society sectors, such as human rights and research organizations, than among victims of displacement. A 2008 Monitoring Commission report reflects an outlook criticized by representatives of displaced population organizations four years after T25. According to the Commission:

> Only a third of displaced population organizations (OPD, in Spanish) have some type of communication channel with the National Roundtable and less than half are represented in departmental organizational institutions. It is estimated that only 32% of displaced persons belong to an OPD. Indigenous (e.g., the National Indigenous Organization of Colombia, ONIC) and Afrodescendent social organizations (e.g., Process of Black Communities) have no context in which to directly exercise their right to participate in public policy decisions on displacement (Monitoring Commission 2008a: 49).

Against this background the Court continued to exert pressure on the government by suggesting innovative tools to guarantee IDP organizations' right to participation. In 2009, for instance, the Court ordered the government to create a "Participation Protocol" as a procedural tool containing guidelines so that the organizations of displaced persons, through the Roundtables for the Strengthening of Displaced Persons' Organizations, could effectively enjoy the right to participation. It also gave instruction on how local governments and the National System of Assistance to IDPs could provide them with the elements needed to participate effectively in all the policymaking scenarios

22 CNAIPD, Act 10, July 18, 2006. The departments of Sucre, Risaralda, Santander, Antioquia, Valledupar, Bolívar, and Cauca.

23 Interview with Diego Grueso, former advisor to the Colombian Association of Displaced Afro-Colombians (Afrodes), June 25, 2014.

related to IDP policy. However, in its most recent evaluation on this issue (Decision 219 of 2011), the Court revealed that the government had not reported on the concrete results attained with the Protocol. Nor had it used the indicators to report the effective enjoyment of the right to participation, so it was not possible to determine progress or drawbacks on this issue. Therefore, the Court again concluded low fulfillment of its orders and stagnation on the participation issue.

The introduction of the Victims Law in 2011 has not yet fully enhanced the participation of IDP organizations either. In fact, the Court had warned the government about "possible traumatisms that could be generated by the transition from the national system of assistance to the displaced population to the national system of assistance to victims" in several matters, including the participation of the organizations of displaced persons, and ordered it to take the appropriate measures to "ensure the adequate participation of the displaced population in this transition process" (Decision 219 of 2011). Indeed, scholars and activists have characterized the process that led to the Victims Law and its implementation by a lack of participation of IDPs and victims in general. Regarding the former, the fact that the government adopted the Law without a process of consultation, even though a high percentage of victims are from Afro-Colombian and indigenous groups, clearly exemplifies the process' poor participatory nature.[24] As explained in Chapter 4, the government adopted the special decrees for Afro-Colombians, gypsies, and indigenous groups only after the President signed the Law, and only the latter enjoyed a process of prior consultation (Rodríguez-Garavito and Orduz 2012).

Participation has also been weak in the implementation of the law even though the Victims Law contains several mechanisms to guarantee victims' participation.[25] The best example is that the government adopted the Protocol for Effective Participation, which regulates the participation of victims as required by the Law (article 194), only two years after it passed the Law (Resolution 388 of 2013). As a result, the implementation of the Victims Roundtables and other participatory spaces created by the law were delayed

[24] Prior consultation (or *consulta previa*) is the collective right of indigenous (and, in Colombia, Afro-descendant) communities to be consulted prior to the adoption of legislative or administrative measure that might affect them (ILO Convention 169 of 1989).

[25] For instance, Title VIII of the law guarantees the victims' right to participation in the design, implementation, and evaluation of programs and plans on victims policy, through the Participation Roundtables at the national, state, district, and municipal levels (article 193) with presence in the National System for the Assistance and Reparation of Victims (article 161) through two of its institutions: the Special Administrative Unit for the Comprehensive Assistance and Reparation of Victims, and the Committees of Transitional Justice (article 162).

for two years.[26] Moreover, according to the first follow-up report to the Victims Law published by the Comptrollers General's Office, the Inspector General's Office, and the Ombudsman's Office (2012), the new Committees of Transitional Justice, which are in charge of designing the assistance plans for victims at the local level, have not guaranteed the participation of victims' representatives as the law orders because they lacked a procedure to select victims' representatives at the time of the installation of these committees (Comptroller General's Office et al. 2012: 39). The report also revealed that public officials have received training in multiple aspects related to the new law (e.g., International Humanitarian law, the Victims Law and its decrees, the construction of indicators), but no such training on participation mechanisms. Furthermore, another follow-up report by the same group of institutions, which focused on the implementation of the special decrees on indigenous, Afro-Colombian, and gypsy populations, found that the Victims Unit has not regulated the participation procedures for these groups (Monitoring Commission of Administrative Agencies 2013: 35). Overall, while the Participatory Protocol "unlocks the process and opens the doors to a new panorama where victims will be active actors of their reality," effective participation of IDPs is still an unresolved issue. As explained by a former advisor to the Colombian Association of Displaced Afro-Colombians (Afrodes), "what worries many of us is that the expertise gathered in the previous period related to internally displaced, was not transferred."[27]

The displaced population's lack of participation in the follow-up and policymaking processes has diverse and complex roots, some of which are beyond the Court's sphere of influence and, indeed, beyond that of the monitoring process itself. At least three factors stand out. First, the legal response to the displacement issue implies the utilization of specialized language and mechanisms that are accessible to state bureaucracy and civil society organizations but not as much to grassroots organizations. In addition to the specialized knowledge barrier, displaced population organizations have profound logistical limitations that make it difficult for them to keep up with the large quantity of information generated by the Court, the government, and academic and human rights organizations. This is an unintended consequence of the judicialization and dynamism of the follow-up process. Although the construction of a common human rights

[26] Ironically, as the second follow-up report by the Comptroller General's Office, the Inspector General's Office, and the Ombudsman's Office argues, the Participation Protocol was constructed with low participation of victims' organizations (2013: 23).

[27] Interview with Diego Grueso, former advisor to Afrodes, June 25, 2014.

language and quantitative indicators has facilitated exchange between specialized government and non-government actors, such change has come at the cost of constructing an access barrier to victims' organizations.

Second, the usefulness and empowerment of participation spaces created by the monitoring process has been limited. Several interviewees belonging to civil society organizations pointed to a conclusion similar to the one presented by the Colombian Jurists Commission and the Jesuit Service for Refugees in a 2005 report from the United Nations Representative to the Secretary-General:

> For some displaced population organizations, these spaces do not provide true dialogue with the government or an effective means of participation, because they are not informed in advance of what issues will be discussed, they are not given copies of the documents to be discussed, and because there is no opportunity to weigh in on decisions already made. Instead, these spaces have served to legitimize government policy, using the argument that the displaced population was consulted. On many occasions, displaced population organizations were invited to receive information on decisions that had already been made (Colombia Jurists Commission and Jesuit Service for 2005: 12).[28]

The situation had not changed in 2011 when the Court concluded, based on the reports of multiple stakeholders, that "many of the bodies of National System of Assistance to the Displaced Population have considered the participation of social and displaced population organizations as a mere, formal requisite that must be observed to validate already-adopted decisions without having offered real opportunities for effective participation" (Decision 219 of 2011).[29] These flaws are not particular to the T25 case. As studies on deliberative democracy show (Fung and Wright 2003), they are endemic to institutions and political processes that seek to open participatory spaces. Given this issue's centrality in the ruling and follow-up decisions, they constitute a significant limitation of the follow-up process and the policymaking process.

Finally, a unique factor of this case is the target population, whose situation and characteristics give rise to specific difficulties regarding participation. By

[28] This statement was ratified by Juan Manuel Bustillo, researcher at the Colombian Jurists Commission, in an interview on December 22, 2008.

[29] In previous years, the assessment had been identical. The Monitoring Commission concluded that these spaces tended to include displaced population organizations only as "passive sources of information through characterizations, massive events and other passive forms." (Monitoring Commission 2008a: 52). See also the assessment of public policy undertaken by UNHCR (2007: 369).

definition, IDPs are one of the most fragmented populations and one of the hardest hit by massive and grave human rights violations that entail the violent and abrupt rupture of their forms of cohesion and organization (Ibáñez 2009). Physical uprooting leads to the erosion of social ties and collective action, which are difficult to rebuild in sites where the community arrives. The extremely precarious situation of the IDP population, including its leaders (who are under constant threats from the same illegal armed actors that uprooted them in the first place), creates a powerful barrier to the basic operation of the type of dialogue spaces that we have studied in this chapter. For example, these practical difficulties, combined with a lack of adequate funding from the government, have hindered the adequate operation of the National Roundtable on Strengthening Displaced Persons' Organizations, the main participatory space for IDPs in CNAIPD deliberations.

5.3. CONCLUSIONS

Contrary to the predictions of critics of judicial activism, judgment T25 and the follow-up process have spurred and expanded democratic deliberation in multiple state and non-state spheres. Through novel mechanisms such as public hearings, technical sessions, and follow-up decisions, the Court has directly opened judicial proceedings and policymaking to state and civil society actors that have driven public discussion on alternative solutions to the complex problem of displacement. Likewise, by creating opportunities for participation within the follow-up process, the Court has indirectly stimulated the creation of new coalitions of civil society organizations, which have become key parties to the monitoring process. In that sense, the participatory effect fostered by civil society coalitions is partly an indirect consequence of the follow-up process as it did not follow from a specific court order. For that reason we have placed this chapter at the end of the second part of this book, which focuses on direct effects of judicial activism and sets the ground for the study of the indirect effects of the follow-up process in the following chapters.

Thus, this study offers evidence in favor of judicial intervention in structural cases of human rights violations that emerge, at least in part, from systemic flaws in the public policy process. However, as Chapter 1 argues, the T25 case suggests that these interventions enjoy greater legitimacy and efficacy when they facilitate – rather than replace – deliberative democracy. This intervention modality – which we have dubbed "dialogical activism" – implies a gradual and relatively prolonged follow-up process in which the judicial branch assumes the role of promoting deliberation and public accountability. Moreover, it requires judicial decisions that, rather than dictating the details of public policy, offer guidelines and set broad goals for such policy and leave policymaking to government agencies. This has been the process initiated by the Colombian Constitutional Court, through a novel experiment of judicial monitoring which has expanded over ten years and has become the axis on which the debate over forced displacement turns in Colombia.

However, this chapter has also revealed the costs and limits of the participatory effect of judicial activism. Sustaining participatory follow-up processes requires periodic intervention, preparation of public hearings, comparative analysis of information from diverse actors, and, in general, considerable efforts that that demand considerable time and energy from already overburdened courts. In fact, as we will see in Chapters 8 and 9, looming burnout has become a significant challenge for the Court ten years into the follow-up process.

As for limits, our analysis shows that the secondary effect of the judicialization of displacement has provided greater access to public deliberation and the follow-up process for actors with expertise in legal language and human rights terminology at the expense of those directly affected by the process's results – that is, the displaced population. Although this is a common effect of the judicialization of social conflicts (McCann 1994), especially when involving highly vulnerable sectors such as the displaced population, this finding is striking when considering that judgment T25 and its follow-up decisions frequently insisted on the need to include IDPs in the debate over public policy. Despite the fact that the ruling opened participatory spaces for this population, fieldwork shows that these orders have been poorly implemented. In this context, the civil society groups that have been most influential in the process have been academic and human rights organizations with expertise in the technical, legal, and economic terminology that have come to dominate the case.

6

The Reframing Effect: Forced Displacement as a Human Rights Problem

Studies on judicial activism tend to assume that judges intervene to respond to existing social or political problems. This assumption, implicitly and explicitly, is found in legal analyses focused on questions of constitutional technique, as well as in neorealist socio-legal studies centered on the direct impact of rulings on those problems.

As Chapter 1 described, one of the blind spots in these studies is the courts' role in bringing to the public's attention the social problem in which they intervene. This means that, rather than intervening in a landscape wherein relevant actors, institutions, discourses, and perceptions are fixed from the outset, judicial decisions help to define them.

In political sociology terminology (McAdam, Tarrow and Tilly 2001), one of the fundamental effects of judicial interventions is setting a frame for the debate and public policies around the issue. As legal and social movement sociology have shown, framing is a fundamental political process insofar as it shapes how social actors perceive the issue at hand (Snow et al. 1986; McCann 1994).

By framing social problems in legal terms, courts generate a central effect: defining a problem as a human rights issue and designating legal processes as an appropriate mechanism to confront it. We refer to this impact when we argue that judges reframe the discussion: not only do they give it a visibility and urgency that could be lacking, but they do so in legal and human rights terms.

In this chapter we argue that T25 has had precisely this type of reframing effect. Following the typology introduced in Chapter 1, we thus treat it as an indirect, symbolic effect of the process. It is symbolic because it refers to the perceptions on forced displacement; it is indirect in that it concerns a group of actors much broader than the state agencies directly addressed by the Court, from the media to the international community to the public at large.

The argument is developed in two parts. First, we demonstrate that the case contributed to the issue's visibility. Second, we show that the case framed the problem as a human rights issue. In fact, with the ruling and follow-up process, the Court imported an entire human rights conceptual and institutional apparatus and "judicialized" the problem. We mainly use content analysis of press coverage on forced displacement and interviews to understand the operation of this effect.

6.1. MAKING THE PROBLEM VISIBLE

In 2004, when the Court issued judgment T25, forced displacement was relatively absent from the public discussion. In spite of the gravity of the issue and the framework the government had been constructing since 1995 to attend to the affected population, displacement was not central to the agendas of either the state or civil society; nor was there any systematic efforts to collect basic data on the problem (see Chapter 2).

For example, after visiting the country in 1999, United Nations Representative Francis Deng concluded that there was still a lack of "reliable, precise data on the number of internally displaced people in Colombia" (Human Rights Commission 2000: num. 13). Similarly, the clerk participating in the authoring of T25 used the following terms to describe the context during the year preceding the ruling: "We requested information from all [of the actors with knowledge on the issue] in 2003 and everyone agreed on the diagnosis: this is a disaster, no one knows who is attending to [displaced individuals], no one can tell you how many IDPs there are. This cannot continue to be this way."[1]

Thus, before the ruling, there was a gap between references made to the displacement problem in a group of official documents on one side, and the understanding by public officials, the media, NGOs, and other relevant social actors regarding the dimension, urgency, and treatment of the phenomenon on the other.

All interviewees agreed that the ruling has contributed to reducing the visibility gap. An official of the Ministry of Social Protection in charge of the displacement issue explained that "the ruling is fundamental because ... it showed the country the situation of a population that is truly more vulnerable."[2] Officials from the Ministry of Finance also affirmed that "T25 put the

[1] Interview with Clara Helena Reales, clerk of the Court, Colombian Constitutional Court, December 18, 2008.

[2] Interview with Susana Helfer, Ministry of Social Protection, January 21, 2009.

issue on the table for discussion."[3] Additionally, an official from the Ministry of the Interior and Justice (MIJ) in charge of coordinating policies amongst departments and municipalities stressed that "[after T25 of 2004] the issue figured higher on the Ministries' internal agendas."[4] Moreover, a high-ranking official from the Ombudsman's Office noted that "with the ruling the Court has succeed in publicizing a serious problem that other sectors attempted to make invisible."[5]

Similarly, two officials from different institutions involved with the issue of displacement since the passage of Law 387 of 1997 highlighted the ruling's role in creating the problem. According to one of them working at the National Planning Department (DNP), "T25, the follow-up decision, and in general the entire Constitutional Court process succeeded in defining the magnitude of the problem."[6] Additionally, the official from the MIJ reported that T25 "heightened the issue's profile. The issue had been forgotten, left behind ... and it made it an important issue on the agendas of the government, NGOs, and the international community."[7] The cumulative visibility effect is evident in a 2009 editorial from one of the leading national newspapers, which stated that "Five years after the Constitutional Court's ruling T25 ... it calls out attention ... that the tragedy of displacement has become part of the government's agenda."[8]

This quote signals a more general indication of the issue's visibility: its appearance in the media, analyzed in the following section.

6.1.1. *Forced Displacement in the Media*

As other studies on the media effect of structural litigation have shown (Haltom and McCann 2004), an analysis of media coverage offers a useful indicator of the visibility and dominant framing of a public issue. To measure these variables in the case of judgment T25, the period between 2000 and 2013 was analyzed, looking at news media's treatment of the issue.[9] Because an analysis of the

3 Interview with Rutty Paola Ortiz Jara, Office of the Budget, Ministry of Finance, January 23, 2009.
4 Interview with Ángela Nicholls, responsible for the coordination of territorial entities, MIJ, January 14, 2009.
5 Interview with Hernando Toro, Ombudsman's office, Coordinator of the Office for Displacement Assistance, January 22, 2009.
6 Interview with María Angélica Alvarado, DNP, January 9, 2009.
7 Interview with Liliana Gúzman, Coordination of the Special Protection Programme for Displaced Population, MIJ, January 13, 2009.
8 *El Espectador*, "The Displaced Population's Situation," April 25, 2009.
9 Press articles include all information that appears in the written media, i.e., news articles, editorials, and opinion columns.

ruling's impact necessarily implies comparison between what happened before and after the Court's decision, the observation period (January 1, 2000 to December 31, 2013) was chosen so that the data would illustrate both the short- and longer-term impacts of the ruling on media coverage.

The sources used were the virtual press archives of *El Tiempo* newspaper and *Semana* magazine, the country's two main press outlets. They were chosen not only because they are the newspaper and magazine with the largest national circulations, but also because they are the only two print media sources with full virtual archives, guaranteeing systematic coverage of the period under analysis.[10]

The analysis first sought to measure the issue's appearance in the selected media sources by looking at 1) the number of articles on forced displacement in the fourteen years analyzed, and 2) the location of these releases. In the two sources referenced, 1,580 press releases were published between 2000 and 2013, with an average of 113 articles annually.

For the purposes of this study, figures on the evolution of articles are more useful than absolute numbers. This information appears in Figure 6.1.

At first glance, some of the graph's data appear paradoxical. For example, in *El Tiempo*, coverage decreased in the period immediately before the ruling. In fact, a steep decline in coverage by the newspaper occurred between 2003 and

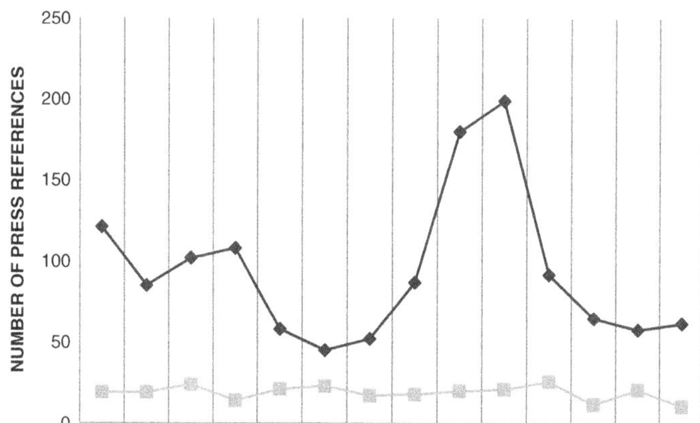

	2000	2001	2002	2003	2004	2005	2006	2007	2008	2009	2010	2011	2012	2013
El Tiempo newspaper	121	85	102	108	58	45	52	87	180	199	92	65	58	62
Semana magazine	19	19	24	14	21	23	17	18	20	21	26	12	21	11

FIGURE 6.1 Evolution of Press Coverage of Forced Displacement, 2000–2013
Source: Authors' calculations.

10 Search categories used included the words "displaced," "displacement," "forced displacement," "victims," "displaced population," "Constitutional Court," and "T-025 ruling/judgment."

2004: while 2003 saw 108 articles, the year in which the ruling was produced saw only 58. The downward trend continued in 2005 and, although it reversed in 2006, it was after 2007 that coverage increased in comparison to the period before the ruling. Thus, there is no evidence that T25, in itself, led to greater coverage in the newspaper with the largest national circulation.

A formal regression analysis controlling for different variables and evaluating this conclusion is beyond the scope of this section. However, the same data from the graph show that the paradox, rather than disproving the thesis of the ruling's symbolic effect, serves to qualify it. For one thing, the downward trend is not present in the other media source analyzed (*Semana*), in which coverage increased in 2004 and remained relatively stable until a decline in the last three years of the studied period. Second, the coverage increase in both sources is especially noteworthy at the middle of the period, when it reached unprecedented levels (200 articles in 2008, and a record of 220 in 2009). This leads to the following hypothesis: just as the follow-up process (and not the ruling by itself) was essential for affecting public policy, the evidence from the graph indicates that the issue gained greater visibility in the media as the Court focused its decisions on more vulnerable groups within the displaced population (the peak in the graph corresponds to Phase 3 of the follow-up decisions discussed in Chapter 2). The ruling's visibility effect, then, appears to be cumulative and mediated by the follow-up mechanisms.

Figure 6.1 also shows a decline in both sources since 2010. This period corresponds to the years immediately before and after the adoption in June of 2011 of the Victims Law (Law 1448 of 2011). The Victims Law addresses all victims of the armed conflict, subsuming the category of internally displaced into the category of victims. Accordingly, as argued in Chapter 2, while the Law represents a victory of the monitoring process in the sense that it adopts many of the principles and guidelines issued by the Court throughout the monitoring process and the new victims' apparatus is built on the existing apparatus for the assistance of IDPs, it also implies that the internally displaced are no longer given the same pride of place. The media reflects this shift. The term "victim" and the issues regarding the Victims Law have become more common in the media, while the internally displaced are downgraded in visibility.

As for the location of the articles, Figure 6.2 shows that, before ruling T25, both sources placed the issue of forced displacement primarily in the "National" section and, in the case of *El Tiempo*, in the "General Information" section as well. However, there is a noticeable increase in the percentage of articles published in the most visible section of *El Tiempo* ("National") after the ruling – from 26.2 percent of the total press articles in *El Tiempo* before the ruling to 53.8 percent of total press articles in *El Tiempo*

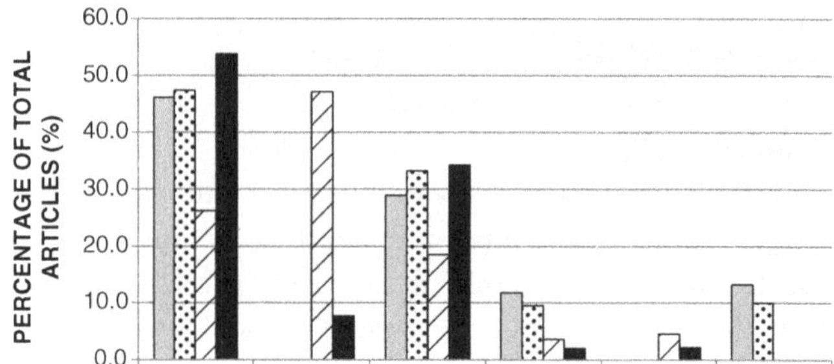

	National Section	General Information	Others	Opinion Column	Editorials	Special Report Section
Before Ruling T25, *Semana* magazine	46.1	0.0	28.9	11.8	0.0	13.2
After Ruling T25, *Semana* magazine	47.4	0.0	33.2	9.5	0.0	10.0
Before Ruling T25, *El Tiempo* Newspaper	26.2	47.1	18.5	3.6	4.6	0.0
After Ruling T25, *El Tiempo* Newspaper	53.8	7.7	34.2	2.0	2.2	0.0

FIGURE 6.2 Location of Articles on Forced Displaced Before and After the Ruling (2000–2013)
Source: Authors' calculations.

after – which shows the issue's gradual shift from one of general interest to one of national importance.

In short, both fieldwork and press analysis suggest that the ruling – and, above all, the follow-up process – are correlated with greater visibility of the issue in the public discourse. The next section addresses a second type of impact postulated by the idea of the reframing concept: the shift in framework or framing used to discuss the issue.

6.2. A FRAMEWORK SHIFT: FORCED DISPLACEMENT AS A HUMAN RIGHTS ISSUE

6.2.1. *IDPs: From Secondary Effects of War to Victims Entitled to Rights*

With the ruling and follow-up process, human rights language and legal procedures began to shape the language used in addition to influencing how the phenomenon was addressed.[11] Thus, urgent social problems such as

[11] T25 was not the first ruling that tried to frame the displacement crisis in legal terms. In particular, Ruling SU-1150 of 2000 had already defined forced displacement as a massive and continuous violation of fundamental rights. However, T25 represented the Court's first systematic and sustained effort to redefine the problem.

malnutrition, reduced access to education and health care, and dangerous living conditions for the displaced population were redefined by the Court in terms of violations of the rights to food, education, health, and decent housing, respectively. Additionally, the Court's orders to governmental bodies, both in the ruling and in subsequent decisions, were formulated in legal terms and for the express purpose of guaranteeing effective fulfillment of rights.[12]

Several interviewees highlighted this redefinition of the framing of the issue. For instance, the director of the Consultancy for Human Rights and Displacement (Codhes, for its Spanish name), stated that:

> The ruling has been very useful for affirming a rights-based perspective. I think that has been the fundamental point, with everything that it implies: transitional justice rights ... humanitarian aid, prevention if so desired, access to social rights, rights related to victims of displacement.[13]

The official we interviewed from the Ombudsmen's Office also contended that "the Court has managed to make displacement as a human rights issue one of the central themes of national public policy."[14]

Similarly, officials from the International Committee of the Red Cross (ICRC) emphasized that, before judgment T25, the same phenomena linked to displacement that were described in social and economic terms were now described in human rights terms. "Whereas before only 'return' was spoken of, now the terms relocation and socioeconomic reestablishment exist," said the interviewed official.[15] This shift was evident in statements from public officials with long-term experience in violent regions of the country, who contended that T25 was "an achievement ... for the recognition of the rights of displaced persons."[16]

Especially noticeable is the borrowing of legal language for use by the state's economic bureaucracy, represented by the DNP. An official from this institution, responsible for the displacement problem since the issuing of Law 387 in 1997, illustrates this change:

> An institution like the National Planning Department is used to designing public policy for vulnerable populations but in a different way [not in terms of rights] ... [However], the General Director, in her speech, at least now

[12] Constitutional Court, Ruling T25 of 2004, Section 9.

[13] Interview with Marco Romero, Director of Codhes, December 19 and 23, 2008.

[14] Interview with Hernando Toro, Ombudsman's office, Coordinator of the Office for Displacement Assistance, January 22, 2009.

[15] Interview with an official from the International Committee of the Red Cross (ICRC) who preferred to remain nameless, December 18, 2008.

[16] Interview with Maida Selene, Coordinator of Assistance to the Displaced Population in the department of Córdoba, January 16, 2009.

> mentions the effective enjoyment [of rights] issue, something that was never mentioned before. [The director of Social Action Agency] also uses it in his speech; it appears as if it isn't such a distant issue anymore.
>
> The other thing, obviously, was the difficulty in measuring things from an effective enjoyment perspective. We ended up realizing that the Court wasn't ultimately interested in [educational or housing] quotas but in whether the individual is actually regularly attending school or has access to decent housing ... And we have at least made a first measurement.[17]

Similarly, and in a highly revealing way, the official at the Social Action Agency summarizes the path toward a human rights framework:

> Four years ago, the displaced population was just people that were standing at the traffic lights. Today, they are people with rights, people to whom the state has an obligation to restore all of their lost rights. That is certainly a change in mentality – and a big one. The visibility of the same displacement problem in Colombia has changed a lot.[18]

In more precise terms, the symbolic shift driven by the Court has transformed the perception of displacement from a secondary effect of the armed conflict into an issue of human rights violations. Consequently, the ruling reconceived the IDP population as victims of these human rights violations. This point is illustrated by testimony of a displaced leader who was questioned by the Court as to whether the conception of displaced persons held by social and state actors had changed:

> Yes, it has changed a lot. Because before ... I knew of people who went looking for work and had doors slammed in their faces, because they were displaced. Not anymore. Now it's changed, and the conception of the word displaced is different. Now it means victim of conflict, because displaced can simply be anyone that moves from one place to another. But if you call that person a victim of conflict, everything changes ... because before displaced was seen as being inferior to homeless.[19]

This effect of the ruling was reflected by Law 975 of 2005, which standardized displacement as a crime. A United Nations Refugee Agency (UNHCR) official explained how the combination of the Court's intervention with the passing of Law 975 contributed to a process that shifted the displaced

[17] Interview with María Angélica Alvarado, DNP, January 9, 2009.

[18] Interview with Viviana Ferro, Subdirector of Assistance to the Displaced Population at the Social Action Agency, January 8, 2009.

[19] Interview with Ana Cecilia Prada, displaced leader, legal representative of Fundagro, January 16, 2009.

population from the category of vulnerable population to that of victims of serious legal and human rights violations:

> [The ruling] paved the way, for example, for other processes. [Displaced individuals] weren't recognized as victims until very recently. So before, if you asked the leaders of the National Roundtable, some of them with a lot of experience in social organizing, about their recognition as victims, they only began to understand about two years ago, after Law 975 [of 2005] etc., but also because they knew that T-025 had already spoken to that as well.[20]

Yet the culmination of this shift in perception to an understanding of displacement and its victims as a human rights issue is the Victims Law of 2011 (Law 1448), passed seven years after T25. As explained in Chapter 2, in line with international standards and guidelines offered by the Constitutional Court in T25 and its follow-up decisions, the Victims Law officially recognized forcibly displaced people as victims of the armed conflict and thus entitled to the rights to truth, justice, reparation, and non-repetition.

The effect, however, has been gradual and partial. For example, another UNHCR official emphasized of the Court's intervention that:

> It helped change the perception of things because up to four years ago Colombia didn't have victims. Now it has victims. But Colombians aren't used to seeing victims or treating them as a victim should be treated. The same goes for governmental bodies. This is an organizational cultural change that has just started ... but for the most part, public institutions don't see them as victims.[21]

The impact has been felt less in the private sector and in the general population. "In society at large," explained an official from the MIJ, "when you talk about social responsibility and displacement and victims, people say, 'What?' Private industry says, 'That doesn't have anything to do with us.'"[22]

Additionally, interviews with leaders of the displaced population demonstrate that daily experiences with discrimination persist based on negative perceptions of victims. For example, a leader residing in Quibdó, Chocó who was displaced from Urabá (a zone in the Colombian Northwest at the heart of the armed conflict) reported that "here rejection comes straight from society at large. They call the bananas that come from Urabá 'displaced,' to offend the displaced persons. All kinds of rights we have are

[20] Interview with Andrea Buchelli, UNHCR official, January 17, 2008.
[21] Interview with Andres Celis, UNHCR official, January 17, 2008.
[22] Interview with Liliana Güzman, Coordination of the Special Protection Programme for Displaced Population, MIJ, January 13, 2009.

violated, just for trying to save our own lives; because that's why we came here; to save our lives."[23]

Further ahead, Chapter 7's examination of the ruling's impact on the displaced population discusses how the symbolic effect has been selective: while displaced organization leaders are well aware of the ruling and define both their situation and the displacement problem in terms of human rights, the ruling and human rights language are still foreign concepts to the vast majority of victims.

The symbolic effect of the ruling – and its echo across national and international organizations –has been considerable. In fact, the increase in visibility of internal displacement became at one point a significant public image problem for the Colombian government, to the extent that the administration of President Álvaro Uribe unfolded a national and international strategy to counteract that perception. The most well-known example of this is the infamous thesis defended by José Obdulio Gaviria – the most influential ideological consultant in the Uribe administration – that postulates that in Colombia there is no displacement, only "migration." This was put forth on a visit to Washington in 2008, undertaken to counteract increasing American concerns over the human rights situation in Colombia: "We don't have displacement, but rather migration, due largely to paramilitary and guerilla conflict ... Those people left for the cities and are there as migrants, in addition to the people that left the country, from upper and middle classes."[24]

Beyond the profound factual misrepresentation and accompanying lack of legal and moral foundation beneath this official position, what is most striking here is the extent to which the perception of displacement had changed, such that the government felt it necessary to contain it. The net effect of this controversy was even greater visibility of the problem and its frequent appearance in the media, as demonstrated by a quote from a 2009 editorial of *El Espectador* newspaper, which indirectly alludes to the government's declarations:

> The image of the "displaced individual" that has materialized in the popular imagination deserves, perhaps, more attention. Displaced families are considered, usually, victims of a natural catastrophe that should be cared for by the state with aid mechanisms. Some even classify them, in a startling display of cynicism, as "migrants," "lawsuit happy," "bums," or "scroungers."[25]

[23] Interview with Alba, displaced women, leader of Adacho. Interview conducted by César Rodríguez-Garavito and Tatiana Alfonso, July 24, 2008, Quibdó, Chocó.
[24] Cambio Magazine, "The Country According to José Obdulio," August 13, 2008.
[25] *El Espectador*, "The Displaced Population's Situation," April 25, 2009.

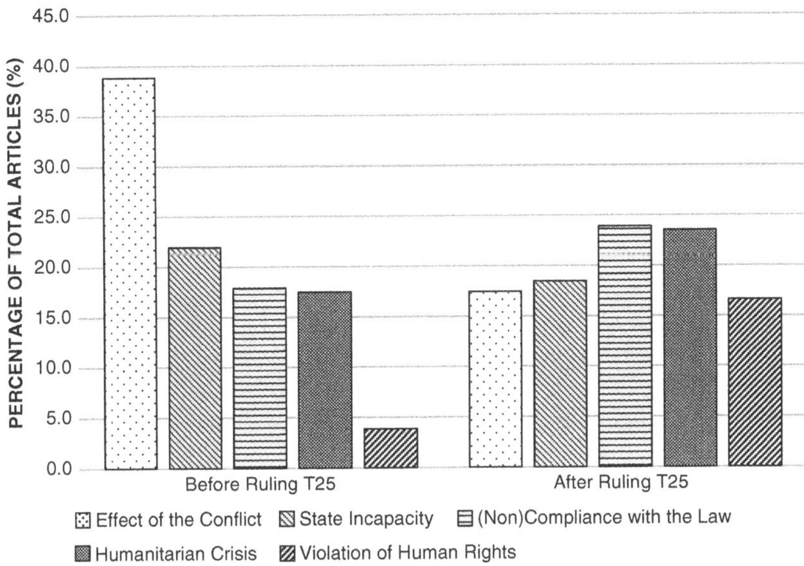

FIGURE 6.3 Framing of Forced Displacement in the Media Before and After the Ruling, 2000–2013
Source: Authors' calculations.

This quote suggests that the redefining of displacement and the displaced also occurred in the media. Evidence of this shift is apparent in the data drawn from the press analysis previously mentioned.

6.2.2. *The Framing of Forced Displacement in the Media*

In media analysis, the concept of framing is a qualitative tool used to identify how editors, columnists, and journalists design and categorize information for their recipients (Haltom and McCann 2004). A review of the press from 2000 to 2013 identifies the five most frequently recurring framing categories as: 1) consequence of the armed conflict; 2) result of state incompetence; 3) failure to comply with judicial decisions (laws and rulings); 4) humanitarian crisis; and 5) violation of human rights.

Figure 6.3 shows an interesting evolution in the importance of these forms of framing. Before the ruling, the media sources analyzed tended to speak of displacement as a consequence of the armed conflict. Thus, displaced individuals were typically portrayed as a type of secondary effect of war. In fact, this was the dominant framework and comprised 38.8 percent of the total articles from this period from both press outlets. The following quote from *El Tiempo*, published in 2000, is an example of the many articles that used this framework during this period:

> Combat between Front 22 of FARC and paramilitary forces in the Lower Magdalena region in Cundinamarca resulted in the displacement of approximately 120 people from the municipality of Caparrapí ... The clashes, sporadically occurring over the past month, intensified on Thursday at six in the morning. From that moment, 500 people that resided in the village escaped in trucks that had been hired by some of the villagers since last Monday, when rumors of possible intensified fighting began to circulate. That same day, members of guerilla forces gave orders for civilians and business owners to abandon the zone.[26]

After the ruling, the news and opinion pieces that framed displacement as the effect of the armed conflict decreased by more than half (from 38.8 percent to 17.5 percent of total articles) and the dominant framework for displacement became a violation of the general legal system, and T25 in particular. While in the previous period this focus appeared in 17.9 percent of articles (alluding to the principal legal instrument of the period, Law 387 of 1997), in the subsequent period violation of the general legal system comprised 23.9 percent of media converge and became the most frequent frame. The press analysis thus supports the hypothesis that "juridicalization" of the displacement issue occurred as a result of the ruling. The following quote from an article published in *Semana* in 2005 offers evidence of such:

> The government has reached an agreement regarding displaced individuals. It has promised 5.1 trillion pesos to aid them. This is only the first step in a long journey ... One day before the deadline to respond to the Court's ultimatum and avoid time behind bars for various ministers, the government earmarked the largest sum ever to attend to the population displaced by violence. This unprecedented increase in investment in the displaced population is the direct result of a January 22, 2004 ruling, in which the Constitutional Court ordered the government to take seriously the drama suffered by these victims of the armed conflict.[27]

Similarly, in 2007, *El Tiempo* stated:

> The Constitutional Court continued to pressure the national government on the displacement issue ... Concretely, they made reference to ruling T-025 of January 2004, wherein they demanded results from the government on the displaced population, reminding them of the several follow-up decisions

[26] *El Tiempo*, "Displaced Civilians of Caparrapí," April 22, 2000.
[27] *Semana*, "Good News, At Last," February 12, 2006.

> issued since then and that the Social Action Agency has still not delivered indicators of the results demanded by the high court . . . which basically seeks to verify the effective enjoyment of rights by the displaced.[28]

As these statements indicate, press coverage since 2004 has tended to address the issue in terms of government fulfillment of obligations imposed by the Constitutional Court, a body that, as discussed earlier, has become the center of the socio-legal field of displacement. Additionally, the above allusion to "effective enjoyment of rights by the displaced" – the language of the Court in T25 and subsequent decisions – demonstrates the expanded presence of human rights in the coverage of the issue. In fact, as seen in the graph, although this focus continues to be secondary, its presence in the press doubled after 2004.

The juridicalization of the issue in the media came hand-in-hand with a noticeable increased focus on displacement as a violation of human rights, which was the language employed by the Court. While before the ruling less than 5 percent of the press articles referred to displacement as a human rights violation, after the ruling more than 15 percent of the articles framed it as such. Thus, the general tendency of portraying forced displacement as a human rights violation instead of a collateral effect of the conflict is represented by a shift described by Rodrigo Uprimny, director of the Center for Law, Justice and Society and a member of the Monitoring Commission on Public Policy on Forced Displacement (Monitoring Commission), in a hearing before the Court:

> One of the greatest contributions that Judgment T-025 and the follow-up decisions made was to show that displaced individuals are not victims of a natural catastrophe or vulnerable people that deserve special attention from the state because of their vulnerability. Rather, they are victims of the heinous crime of displacement and, as such, have a right to reparations and that right is distinct to social rights satisfied through public benefits and humanitarian aid policies.[29]

Finally, it is worth noting that, although the second most frequent framework before the ruling – displacement as a result of lack of state capacity – continued to be used after the decision, the terms used by the press to employ it changed in 2004. While before the decision the issue was described in terms of intrinsic failings of the state apparatus (e.g., the lack of budget), after the ruling it tended to be described in terms of the analysis that the Court has made of those failings. The following contrast illustrates this point. In

[28] *El Tiempo*, "Court Requests Concrete Data on Displaced," February 2, 2007.

[29] Rodrigo Uprimny, Director of Dejusticia and member of the Monitoring Commission, statement at Accountability Hearing, Constitutional Court, July 10, 2009.

April 2000, *El Tiempo* reported that "the displacement problem in Colombia is one of the severest humanitarian crises in the world, according to the UN. However, the government lacks legislation and tools," and specified that:

> There appears to be a lack of sufficient government will or determination to put its laws into practice . . . The principle obstacles to an effective displacement policy are: 1) regulation of Law 387 . . . 2) Budget shortages. The government . . . did not have funding for humanitarian aid until November of last year [1999]. Thus, non-governmental institutions like the International Committee of the Red Cross and Pastoral Social had to assume a large part of the responsibility of emergency care for the displaced. 3) Lack of information . . . 4) Political indifference. The lack of social awareness of the displacement problem becomes an even greater problem when the political class refuses to assume responsibility for confronting it . . . 5) Lack of emergency legislation.[30]

However, in December 2004, *Semana* spoke of the issue in terms of the Court's analysis:

> The Court is concerned that minimum rights of the displaced are not being fulfilled . . . The government has not been able to coordinate organisms responsible for attending to the displaced, including the majority of the ministries, the Ombudsman Office, the Inspector General's Office, and the Attorney General's Office, among others. Officials, in particular those of local government, are uninformed of and ignore, for example, that the displaced population is entitled to preferential treatment, requiring priority care.[31]

In sum, both the press analysis and the interviews conducted show that the Constitutional Court is connected to a shift in the public perception of displacement and the terms used to discuss it. Together with the greater visibility of the issue, this shift constitutes the indirect, symbolic component of the reframing effect.

6.3. CONCLUSIONS

The analysis conducted in this chapter shows that courts not only intervene in social problems but also help to define them. Judicial activism can have an effect on how actors beyond those targeted by the ruling conceive the problem at stake, producing what we have dubbed the "reframing effect." Content analysis of press coverage and interviews with actors in the field of forced displacement reveal how, through T25 and its follow-up process, the Court has

[30] *El Tiempo*, "Band-aids," April 3, 2000.

[31] *Semana*, "Time's Up," December 12, 2004.

helped to reframe the phenomenon of forced displacement, increase its visibility, and transform it into an issue of human rights violations and victims. The media, state agencies, society at large, and the displaced themselves have come to see displacement as a human rights violation, with victims entitled to specific rights and immediate attention, instead of considering it as a collateral effect of Colombia's armed conflict.

7

The Socioeconomic Effect: The Impact on the Situation of Internally Displaced Persons

In April 2009, the editorial page of one of the principal Colombian newspapers read:

> Five years after the Constitutional Court's T25 ruling that declared "an unconstitutional state of affairs" in response to the abysmal assistance received by displaced individuals from the Colombian state, an analysis of the recuperation and the effective enjoyment of fundamental rights [of IDPs], reveals an outlook that, although slightly improved, remains worrisome.[1]

The outlook of an official from the Ministry of the Interior and Justice, responsible for the Special Protection Program for Displaced Population, was equally pessimistic:

> For a large part of the population [the ruling] hasn't been very helpful. That's the saddest thing ... As far as I know, very few people's condition has improved after the ruling. They just repeat the ruling like parrots, or use it as a weapon to attack officials. They only do a partial reading of it.[2]

A displaced leader voiced a similar complaint in an interview in a very different corner of the country – the Villa España neighborhood in the city of Quibdó, inhabited by displaced individuals from Chocó, Colombia's poorest state – concluding:

> I don't think that ruling T25 in favor of the displaced population is being complied with here in our state. It's not being complied with. Real, effective enjoyment of rights isn't being given to displaced individuals. It's not working here. Look around. Look at the school. Everything we've shown you. It's a

[1] *El Espectador*, "The Situation of the Displaced," April 25, 2009.

[2] Interview with Liliana Guzmán, coordinator of the Special Protection Program for Displaced Population, Ministry of the Interior and Justice, January 13, 2009.

> sign that the ruling in favor of the displaced population isn't being complied with. Law 387 is on paper only. As if it were just to hang on the wall. So that one, as an IDP, knows that one has those rights, but is not enjoying them effectively.[3]

These quotes reveal the ambiguity of what we call the "socioeconomic effect:" the impact that the ruling has ultimately had on the target beneficiary population (see Chapter 1). On the one hand, as the following pages show, the material situation of IDPs remains alarming and continues to constitute a humanitarian tragedy on a global scale. On the other hand, the legal language used by the displaced leader from Chocó in the last quote – with allusion to "the effective enjoyment of rights" and "Law 387" – clearly shows the impact T25 has had on the way in which IDPs, or at least their leaders, have appropriated the Court's jurisprudence to demand their rights.

How should we understand this effect? How can we determine if, ultimately, the ruling has helped the displaced population? In light of the available evidence, is the balance truly negative? This chapter addresses these complex questions, which require two analytical and methodological clarifications.

First, in accordance with this book's conceptual framework, it is necessary to distinguish between material and symbolic effects on the displaced population (see Chapter 1). While the former relates to the case's impact on the material reality of the displaced, the latter refers to changes in how displaced individuals and collectives conceive and confront their situation. An appropriate way to measure material effects is by comparing quantitative data on displaced individuals' material situation before and after the ruling, including in areas of basic rights such as nutrition and education. Meanwhile, this chapter evaluates symbolic effects mainly through qualitative methods that explore IDPs' perceptions of the ruling, their familiarity with it, and how it has affected their individual and collective actions.

Second, from a methodological point of view, it is important to bear in mind a particular difficulty that arises when measuring the ruling's material effect. Because this measurement implies, by definition, contrasting the IDP population's material condition before and after the ruling, it requires comparable data from both of these moments. However, systematic data of this sort were collected only after the ruling – or, more precisely, due to the process initiated by it. The most comprehensive and trustworthy data on the subject come from the First, Second, and Third National Verification

[3] Interview with a group of displaced persons living in Villa Espana, Quibdó, Chocó, with César Rodríguez and Tatiana Alfonso, July 25, 2008.

Surveys (I, II, and III ENV, in Spanish), conducted by the Monitoring Commission in 2007, 2008, and 2010, respectively. The I and II ENV resulted from Decisions 109 and 233 of 2007 and 116 of 2008 in which the Court adopted a set of 174 indicators to measure 20 key points on displacement policy (see Chapter 4). To evaluate these points, the Monitoring Commission, in association with the Center for Research on Development (CID, in Spanish) at the National University of Colombia, conducted I ENV between November and December of 2007 and the II ENV between July and August 2008. The surveys covered both the displaced population officially recognized by the state – that is, the population registered in the Singular Registry of the Displaced Population (RUPD, in Spanish)[4] starting in 1999 – as well as the non-registered population.[5] The Monitoring Commission conducted I ENV through interviews with 6,616 households with displaced persons registered in the RUPD, located in urban areas of 50 municipalities in the country. It conducted II ENV through interviews with 8,442 households located in urban zones in 61 municipalities.

Two years later, it carried out III ENV in two phases between July and August of 2010. A total of 10,433 surveys were conducted, in 68 municipalities of the country, constituting the largest survey carried out with IDPs in the country to date (Monitoring Commission 2010: 14). In general, the same methodology as the one implemented in the first two was used, enabling a comparison from 2007 onward. In this chapter, we compare the 2007 data with the 2010 data to cover the widest time span possible – when available and comparable – and, if not, the 2008 data with the 2010 data. Unless otherwise noted, the comparisons highlighted in this chapter are statistically significant to at least the 90 percent significance level. In some cases, the chapter discusses changes in indicators that are not statistically significant, which it mentions explicitly in the text. Table 7.1 presents some selected indicators and the significance, if any, in changes between 2007 and 2010.

4 RUPD is a technical tool created by Decree 2569 of 2000. It registers declarations of displacement made by displaced persons or households. The person or household may be classified as: Included or Registered, Not Included, Excluded, or Removed.

5 The latter population was included because the Commission's analysis demonstrated that RUPD has an "appreciably large" sub-registry (Monitoring Commission 2008b: 17). Thus, institutions such as the Attorney General's Office, the Ombudsman's Office, UNHCR, and the Monitoring Commission itself insisted on including the non-RUPD registered population in II ENV. The survey excluded, however, persons and family groups that had been previously registered with RUPD and later excluded or removed by authorities (Monitoring Commission 2008b: 11).

TABLE 7.1. *Selected Effective Enjoyment of Rights Indicators with Statistical Significance of Differences, 2007–2010*

Right to Health				
Indicators for Access to the General Health and Social Security System				
Type of Affiliation	2007	2008	2010	Statistically Significant Difference[6] 2010–2008 2010–2007
1. Paying	7.5	5.8	7.0	* –
2. Subsidized	71.2	69.4	78.0	*** **
3. Affiliated Subtotal	79.0	75.3	85.0	** *

Right to Education				
Indicators for Internally Displaced Persons aged 5 to 17 Years				
Indicators for the Effective Enjoyment of the Right to Education	2007[7]	2008	2010	Statistically Significant Difference 2010–2008
4. Percentage that attended a formal educational institution	83.6	86.2	87.1	–
5. Percentage with access to free education (not paying registration and tuition)	66.5	65.4	79.3	–
6. Percentage of students not receiving any aid for goods and services necessary for attending school	69.1	83.9	85.8	**

6 In order to calculate the significance of indicators' change among different years, each proportion was taken as a sample mean with its own standard deviation of the same variable at different times. A standard difference of means test was used to calculate the significance of the difference at the 90, 95, and 99 percent significance levels. If the finding is significant we are at least 90 percent confident that the difference between the two years is not zero (i.e., there was a change).

7 Data from 2007 are not strictly comparable to 2008 and 2010 data due to different question wording.

TABLE 7.1. *(continued)*

Right to Adequate Food

Indicators for the Effective Enjoyment of Nutritional Rights

Due to Lack of Food or Money to buy Food in the Week Previous to the Survey:	2007	2008	2010	Statistically Significant Difference 2010–2008 2010–2007
7. Consumed less than they desired	52.1	63.0	61.6	*** ***
8. Complained about feeling hunger	41.8	45.6	47.9	*** ***
9. Skipped a main meal	50.3	50.1	46.5	*** ***
10. One of the above	59.1	67.6	65.2	*** **

Right to Housing

Indicators for the Effective Enjoyment of the Right to Housing

Percentage of Displaced Households who had Housing:	2007	2008	2010	Statistically Significant Difference 2010–2008 2010–2007
11. With stable tenancies, through either a registered writing or a written rental contract	17.4	13.7	21.6	*** *
12. With access to all basic utilities (energy, sewage, garbage collection, running water)	63.2	49.2	54.9	** **
13. Without overcrowding	48.8	57.0	64.6	*** ***
14. All of the above	7.5	5.5	10.5	*** **

Right to Minimum Subsistence and Humanitarian Aid

Indicators for Immediate Assistance or Aid

Component	2007	2008	2010	Statistically Significant Difference 2010–2008 2010–2007
15. Temporary housing	2.7	6.2	5.8	– ***
16. Food	17.1	23.5	26.4	*** ***

TABLE 7.1. *(continued)*

				Statistically Significant Difference 2010–2008	2010–2007
17. One of the above	17.9	30.6	33.8	***	***
18. None	82.1	69.4	66.2	*	***

Indicators for Emergency Humanitarian Aid

Component	2007	2008	2010	Statistically Significant Difference 2010–2008	2010–2007
19. Rent subsidies	30.1	52.2	43.7	***	**
20. Places in schools	6.2	23.8	22.2	**	***
21. Legal assistance		5.1	5.7	–	N/A
22. Protection		3.9	5.0	***	N/A
23. Health insurance	9.6	48.1	47.9	–	***
24. One of the above	60.5	83.2	74.3	**	**
25. None	39.5	16.8	25.7	**	**

The Right to Adequate Income

Indicators for the Effective Enjoyment of the Right to Adequate Income

Indicators that use Poverty Lines as Reference	2007	2008	2010	Statistically Significant Difference 2010–2008	2010–2007
26. Percentage of displaced households that live above the poverty line	2.0	1.4	2.4	**	–
27. Percentage of displaced households that live above the extreme poverty line	26.0	17.4	21.2	*	–

TABLE 7.1. *(continued)*

Employment and informality indicators	2007	2008	2010	Statistically Significant Difference 2010–2008 2010–2007
28. Percentage of displaced individuals that reported themselves as employed	45.2	46.4	43.4	–
29. Percentage of displaced individuals that reported themselves as unemployed	4.8	5.0	3.8	–
30. Percentage of displaced individuals that reported themselves as not actively seeking work	50	48.7	53	–
31. Rate of informality	97.8	96.6	96.5	–

*** Statistically significant at 99% confidence level;
** Statistically significant at 95% confidence level;
* Statistically significant at 90% confidence level;
– No statistically significant difference found.
Sources: Monitoring Commission (2008), Monitoring Commission (2008b), and Monitoring Commission (2010).

However, no comparable data exist from before T25, given that, as discussed, a lack of systematic information on the issue was precisely one of the serious flaws detected by the Court's appraisal. This data asymmetry prevents the drawing of firm conclusions on the direct material effect of T25 on the displaced individual.

Yet this does not mean that no information on the displaced population existed before 2004. In fact, the data available from that era were used by the Court in its appraisal of the issue, and to declare the unconstitutional state of affairs.[8] Thus, while not calculated using the same methodology employed in the I, II, and III ENV, these data do serve to give an idea on the displacement situation at the time of the ruling.

With these caveats in mind, this chapter subsequently analyzes the socioeconomic effect, with an emphasis on its material component. The chapter is divided into three sections. The first section addresses the material component, beginning with an overview of the displaced population's situation

[8] See Constitutional Court, Ruling T25 of 2004, Section 6.

before 2004 and the Constitutional Court's appraisal of it in ruling T25, which formulated a list of fundamental rights that the state was obligated to guarantee. The second section then proceeds to analyze I, II, and III ENV data on the degree of effective enjoyment of these rights by the displaced population. The chapter concludes with a review of fieldwork evidence of the ruling's symbolic effect on displaced persons and organizations.

7.1. THE DISPLACED POPULATION'S SITUATION BEFORE THE RULING AND THE COURT'S ANALYSIS OF RIGHTS

When the Court issued T25, the IDPs' situation was dire. According to a study by the UN World Food Program (WFP) from 2003 which evaluated 1,503 displaced households in 41 municipalities in the country, 92 percent of the displaced population had unmet basic needs (UBN) and 80 percent lived in abject poverty. This meant that the displaced population clearly lived below the bottom 20th percentile of the urban poor, of which only 30 percent had UBN and 39 percent lived in abject poverty (WFP 2003).[9]

The WFP study also found that 63.5 percent of the displaced population had inadequate living conditions, and 49 percent did not have access to basic utilities. These figures were well above the bottom 20th percentile of the urban poor, of which only 7.1 percent had inadequate living conditions and 6 percent lacked basic utilities.

Health conditions among the displaced population were also alarming. In 2003, the mortality rate for the displaced population was six times the national average. Specifically, WFP found that for children less than 12 the mortality rate was 3.32 out of 1,000, while the national average was 2.0. Similarly, for IDPs between 12 and 25 years old, the mortality rate was 24.28 out of 1,000, while the national average was 2.0. Finally, the displaced population older than 25 had a mortality rate of 53.42 per 1,000 – that is, more than 40 percent above the national average (6.8 per 1,000 habitants).

The situation facing under-age IDPs was even more critical. WFP found that 23 percent of children below six years of age fell below the minimum nutrition standards, and thus were underweight for their age, behind in educational progress, visually impaired, and at a greater risk for infant mobility, respiratory, and digestive diseases. It also found that 25 percent of children between 6 and 9 years old and 54 percent of children between 10 and 15 did not attend an educational facility.

9 This report was the main source for the Court's appraisal (see footnote 85 in T25), as well as for the data provided in this section.

As shown in Chapter 2, this outlook led the Court to declare an unconstitutional state of affairs via ruling T25. It did so using the framework of human rights violations. Thus, extreme deficiencies in health and education among the displaced population came to be treated as grave violations of the right to health and the right to education, respectively. But the Court, conscious that the problem's complexity made it impossible to comprehensively confront in one fell swoop, established priorities among the rights to be guaranteed to the displaced.

To do so, the Court used the United Nations Guiding Principles on Internal Forced Displacement from 1998, according to which "there exist certain minimum rights of the displaced population that must be satisfied above all else by the government, because their fulfillment is necessary for the dignified subsistence of persons in this situation."[10] The Court then created a list of nine rights that entailed the minimum benefits the state is obligated to satisfy. Those rights, together with their legal source in the Political Constitution (PC) and the UN Principles, are as follows:[11]

1. The right to life (PC, article 11 and Principle 10).
2. The rights to dignity and physical, psychological, and moral integrity (PC, articles 1 and 12 and Principle 11).
3. The right to family and family unity (PC, articles 42 and 44 and Principle 17), especially in the case of families comprising subjects entitled to special constitutional protection.
4. The right to an adequate standard of living (Principle 18).
5. The right to health (PC, article 49) when health care is urgent and necessary to preserve a person's life and integrity (Principle 19) and for children (PC, articles 44 and 50).
6. The right to protection from discrimination based on displaced status (PC, article 13 and Principle 22).
7. The right to basic education up to fifteen years old (PC, article 67.3 and Principle 23).
8. Those rights relating to the provision of aid for the purpose of self-sufficiency (CP, article 16) through socioeconomic stabilization of displaced persons (Law 387 of 1997 and Principles 1, 3, 4, 11, and 18).
9. The rights to return and reestablishment.

In addition to creating this list, the Court's ruling also ordered all relevant authorities to guarantee at least a minimum amount of protection to the

10 Constitutional Court, Ruling T25 of 2004, Section 9.
11 Constitutional Court, Ruling T25 of 2004, Section 9.

displaced population. Thus, the Court ordered the National Council for Integral Attention to Displaced Population (CNAIPD) to undertake, within six months, efforts to provide all displaced individuals with effective enjoyment of this minimum core of rights and protections that the state is obligated to satisfy.

As explained in Chapter 2, this list of rights became the foundation of the Court's follow-up decisions. Specifically, they became the categories used to create outcome indicators to evaluate the government's response to internal displacement. Hence, the Court has called them "indicators of effective enjoyment of rights." After the ruling, those indicators became categories for the systematic collection of data on the displaced population – specifically I, II, and III ENV – and thus offered an approximation of the ruling's socioeconomic effect. The next section analyzes these evaluations' results based on the list of basic rights constructed by the Court.

7.2. THE DISPLACED POPULATION'S SITUATION AFTER THE RULING

7.2.1. *The Right to Health*

In the T25 follow-up process, the Court adopted three indicators of effective enjoyment of the right to health in an effort to evaluate access to and quality, acceptability, and availability of health care. Those three indicators are: 1) access to the General Health and Social Security System, 2) access to psychosocial care, and 3) access to vaccinations. This section discusses the evidence on the first three indicators.

The first indicator measures registration in the General Health and Social Security System (SGSSS, in Spanish), both for paying and subsidized subscribers. This indicator showed substantial improvements between 2007, when approximately 79 percent of the RUPD population was registration in the public health care system, and 2010, when the percentage increased to 85 percent (Monitoring Commission 2008: table 22; Monitoring Commission 2010: figure 15). However, in both cases, the percentages are lower than the national percentage (88 percent according to the 2010 National Demographic and Health Survey, ENDS) (Profamilia 2010: table 14.1.1). Of those registered in 2010, 7 percent of them were paying subscribers, while 78 percent were subsidized. Such a low level of subscription reveals, on the one hand, that the displaced population lacks the necessary stable income to be paying subscribers. On the other hand, it suggests a high degree of employment in the informal sector, or indeed an exclusion from the entire labor market (Monitoring Commission 2008b: 67). Moreover, one of the principal barriers to access to health care for IDPs is their forceful abandon of their places of residence; those with a subsidized registration (the majority) thus lose access to health care because of laws that make subscription non-transferable.

The second indicator of effective enjoyment of rights is access to psychological care, given the need for this type of attention due to the trauma of displacement. However, analysis of I ENV data reveals that in 2007, only 14.6 percent of the RUPD-registered population requested psychological care, while in 2010, this figure dropped to 4.1 percent (Monitoring Commission 2008: table 24; Monitoring Commission 2010: table 29). This suggests that the displaced population does not have adequate information regarding even the most essential resources available to them.

The third and last of the indicators is access to vaccinations. This indicator measures state efforts in the promotion of health and prevention of disease. In 2010, 82 percent of the RUPD-registered population less than five years old and 79.6 percent of the non-RUPD-registered population less than five years old had received the first dose of the MMR[12] vaccine (Monitoring Commission 2010: table 30).[13]

In sum, although the data show that the rate of the displaced population's effective enjoyment of the right to health still falls below the national average, the panorama has improved considerably in recent years, in particular regarding registration in the subsidized regime. This improvement was recognized by reports of the Monitoring Commission (2010) and interviews with some of its members, such as Monsignor Héctor Fabio Henao, for whom the ruling "has generated more impact on the health care issue."[14] Accordingly, in 2011 when the Court evaluated right-by-right the unconstitutional state of affairs, it declared that "even when structural problems persist that generally affect the health system ... given the Government's commitment to attaining a high level of fulfillment ... it is no longer necessary, except in the case of the right to health of the indigenous and Afrocolombian communities, that the Constitutional Court continue to permanently monitor the government's actions regarding health" (Decision 219 of 2011: numeral 319). In doing so, the Court acknowledged that the government had overcome the unconstitutional state of affairs

12 Provides immunization for measles, mumps, and rubella.

13 I ENV data are not comparable because it asked the question for registered population less than eight years old (Monitoring Commission 2008: 69).

14 Interview with Monsignor Héctor Fabio Henao, Director of Pastoral Social, December 18, 2008.

regarding the right to health of the displaced population (with the exception of the indigenous and Afro-Colombian communities).

7.2.2. *The Right to Education*

Drawing on the development of the right to education in international instruments,[15] in Decisions 109 of 2007 and 116 of 2008 the Constitutional Court adopted a set of indicators to measure the degree of effective enjoyment of the right to education and progress in the fulfillment of that right, as well as a series of complementary and associated sectorial indicators. The following section presents the principal results of an analysis of the four essential components of the right to education, providing an idea of the degree of T25's educational goals fulfillment for IDPs.

With respect to access to education[16] for the displaced population, there has been progress. "Without a doubt there are advances . . . in nominal coverage," affirmed the Monitoring Commission (2008b: 101). The indicator for fulfillment of the right to education in 2010 revealed that 87.1 percent of displaced children and adolescents between 5 and 17 years old registered in RUPD attended a formal educational institution (Monitoring Commission 2010: table 44). Although the figures are not strictly comparable and thus we cannot compute its statistical significance, in 2007 this figure was 83.6 percent (Monitoring Commission 2008: table 26; see Table 7.1). In this sense, the state is complying with its minimal educational obligation toward displaced children, which T25 defines as guaranteeing education by reserving spaces in public or private institutions in the area.

Another indicator that measures access to education is whether or not it is free. Between 2007 and 2010, there was a visible improvement in regard to this issue (see Table 7.1). In 2010, 79.3 percent of the school-age displaced population registered in RUPD that went to school had access to free education, defined as not paying for registration and tuition, while in 2007, the figure was 66.5 percent (Monitoring Commission 2008: table 28; Monitoring Commission 2010: table 39). However, in 2007, and still in 2010, the majority of the students (69.1 percent and 85.8 percent of those registered with RUPD

15 According to General Observation No. 13 of 1999 of the Committee on Economic, Social, and Cultural Rights, the right to education has four components that, as in the case of the right to health, are considered basic attributes: i) availability, ii) accessibility, iii) acceptability, and iv) adaptability.

16 Educational accessibility includes three components: non-discrimination, physical accessibility, and economic accessibility. Committee on Economic, Social, and Cultural Rights, General Observation No. 13 of 1999, paragraph 6; Constitutional Court, Ruling T-1037 of 2007.

that go to school, respectively) had to pay for costs associated with books, supplies, uniforms, or transportation (Monitoring Commission 2008: table 29; Monitoring Commission 2010: table 44). We could not compute the statistical significance of either of these indicators' differences from 2010 to 2007 as the data are not strictly comparable.

The second component of the right to education – adaptability[17] – obligates the state to develop systems to avoid student dropout. II ENV reported that 4.3 percent of displaced persons between 5 and 17 years old registered with RUPD dropped out of school.[18] Females are more likely to drop out (Monitoring Commission 2008b: 99). The III ENV revealed an improvement as only 2.3 percent of students had dropped out at the time of the survey (Monitoring Commission 2010: table 41).

Regarding the last two components of the educational right – adequacy[19] and availability[20] – displaced households interviewed for III ENV identified several recurring problems with secondary schools, including overcrowded classrooms, school safety concerns, a lack of laboratories and computers, a lack of teachers and their frequent absence from work, and inadequate conditions for people with disabilities (Monitoring Commission 2010: 116).

The information presented shows, therefore, that the government has primarily improved education by increasing coverage and free tuition, but has failed to provide adequate access to other necessary goods and services such as transportation and uniforms. In general, the data indicate a positive socioeconomic effect, albeit a moderate one, thanks to T25's influence on the right to education. Nonetheless, in its 2011 evaluation of the unconstitutional state of affairs right-by-right, the Court determined that, unlike for the right to health, the government still had not overcome the unconstitutional state of affairs for the right to education. It cited the lack of consistency in the numbers, the impossibility of strictly comparing the different data, and

[17] Adaptability refers to state measures to ensure education possesses the necessary flexibility to adapt to the needs of changing individuals and communities, responds to the needs of students within their diverse social and cultural settings, and guarantees continued participation in the education system.

[18] I ENV data on school drop-out are available from children between 5 and 11 and it is of 3.4% (Monitoring Commission 2008: 81).

[19] Acceptability requires that the form and substance of education, including curricula and teaching methods, be relevant, culturally appropriate, and high-quality. Committee on Economic, Social, and Cultural Rights, General Observation No. 13 of 1999, paragraph 6; T-1037 ruling of 2007.

[20] Availability implies state obligation to maintain a sufficient number of educational institutions and programs to guarantee inclusion for all persons within its jurisdiction (Committee on Economic, Social, and Cultural Rights, General Observation No. 13 of 1999)

the lack of information about certain measures taken by the government to overcome the structural problems identified in T25 as a justification for its ruling (Decision 219 of 2011: numerals 340–341).

7.2.3. *The Right to Adequate Food*

Following international standards,[21] the Court adopted several indicators for the effective enjoyment of nutritional rights. Of these, four are particularly illustrative and have been used by the Court since 2007: (i) the number of people in the household who consumed less than they desired due to lack of food or money; (ii) they complained about feeling hunger for the same reasons; (iii) skipped one of their main meals for the same reasons and; (iv) one of the above symptoms.

The surveys uncover worrying results regarding the right to adequate food (see Table 7.1). The III ENV of 2010 revealed a worse nutritional situation than the one detected by the I ENV in 2007. In 2010, 65.2 percent of RUPD-registered displaced persons reported some symptom of lack of adequate food in the week before the survey was conducted – 6 percentage points higher than the corresponding figure in 2007 (59.1 percent) (Monitoring Commission 2008: table 35; Monitoring Commission 2010: table 45). The tendency holds for the other indicators. For instance, while in 2007, 41.8 percent complained about hunger, in 2010 the figure rose to 47.9 percent. Critically, close to 50 percent of RUPD-registered IDPs were unable to have three main meals a day. The elderly (above 60 years of age) had the worst nutrition (Monitoring Commission 2010). Increasing food prices[22] and the population's low income helps to partly explain this decline in enjoyment of the right to adequate food between 2007 and 2010.

Although no comparable data exist for before 2004, a comparison between 2007 and 2010 does not offer preliminary evidence of a positive impact of ruling T25 on nutritional indicators. Despite the slight improvement between 2008 and 2010, the latter figures are still worse than those of 2007.

[21] The DESC Committee, in General Observation No. 12, affirmed that the basic content of this right includes that food: be available in sufficient supply and quality to satisfy individual nutritional needs; free from adverse substances; and culturally acceptable. It also implies sustainable access to these foods that does not prejudice the enjoyment of other human rights.

[22] The Consumer Food Price Index increased nearly 54 percent between January and July 2008, compared to the same months in 2007, growing from 8.51 percent in 2007 to 12.77 percent in 2008 (Monitoring Commission 2008b: 107).

7.2.4. *The Right to Housing*

By definition, forced displacement most gravely violates the right to housing as it obligates people to abandon their houses and endure inadequate housing conditions in the places that receive them.[23] In fact, according to displaced households' own rankings of needed aid, adequate housing is at the top of their list of necessities (Monitoring Commission, 2008b: 60).

According to the Court, the effective enjoyment of the right to housing must guarantee, at a minimum, the following seven components: (i) legal security for tenants; (ii) availability and proximity of utilities, facilities, and infrastructures; (iii) affordable and dependable utilities; (iv) habitability; (v) overall affordability; (vi) suitable location; and (vii) cultural adequacy.

The I ENV found that the displaced population lives in extremely precarious conditions. Only 7.5 percent of RUPD-registered households lived in housing that fulfilled the criteria necessary to be considered decent (Monitoring Commission 2008: table 50). The III ENV reveals improvements in the overall protection of this right: 10.5 percent of registered households lived in decent housing (Monitoring Commission 2010: table 58). Despite the improvement, the 2010 figures still indicate that close to 90 percent of IDPs lack decent housing.

Likewise, while some of the individual components of the right to housing also show an improvement, the figures still reveal particularly critical situations (see Table 7.1). For example, in 2010 only 21.6 percent of registered displaced households had stable tenancies, through either a registered writing or a written rental contract (Monitoring Commission 2010: table 58). Additionally, 35 percent of the RUPD-registered population lived in overcrowded conditions (Monitoring Commission 2010: table 58). Finally, only half of the displaced population had access to all basic utilities (Monitoring Commission 2010: table 58).

Against this background, the Monitoring Commission concluded four years after the ruling that "the [housing] situation is one of unthinkable gravity and denotes the extremely vulnerable conditions that characterize the country's displaced population" (2008b: 181). Accordingly, shortly afterwards the Court concluded that the national government should profoundly reformulate its housing policy in favor of the displaced population, given its inability to satisfy the housing demand in the foreseeable future, and set a deadline for the start of the new policy (Decision 8 of 2009). Two years later the Court concluded the government had missed the deadline and thus failed to overcome the unconstitutional state of affairs (Decision 219 of 2011).

[23] Constitutional Court, Ruling T25 of 2004, Section 5.2.

7.2.5. The Right to Minimum Subsistence and Humanitarian Aid

Based on United Nations Principle 18, ruling T25 established the right to minimum subsistence, obligating the state to provide and assure access for displaced persons to essential foods and potable water, basic shelter and housing, adequate clothing, and essential medical and health services. In doing so, the Court applied its doctrine about the state's duty to guarantee at least a "minimum core" of material benefits by virtue of SERs in the national constitution and international treaties.

Additionally, the Court emphasized that the right to minimum subsistence is linked to the right to humanitarian aid,[24] which itself has two components: immediate assistance or aid, offered when displacement occurs, and Emergency Humanitarian Aid (EHA), to which every displaced person has the right upon registering as displaced.[25] The Court considered the relationship between the right to minimum subsistence and the right to humanitarian aid when elaborating indicators for the effective enjoyment of the latter. Thus, among the indicators of effective enjoyment adopted by the Court to measure the right to subsistence, one measures the degree of receipt of Immediate Aid and another measures receipt of Emergency Humanitarian Aid. The other indicators of effective enjoyment directly reference components of the right to minimum subsistence, measuring aid efforts in clothing, essential foods, and essential medical services, among others.

Despite T25's emphasis on the importance of Immediate Aid, the Monitoring Commission reported low coverage in 2007 and 2010, although it improved slightly in this period. In 2010, 66.2 percent of RUPD-registered family groups did not receive any type of Immediate Aid (82.1 percent in 2007), while 33.8 percent (17.9 percent in 2007) received some component of it (see Table 7.1; Monitoring Commission 2008: table 12; Monitoring Commission 2010: table 19). The relative improvement is partly due to increases in two components between 2007 and 2010: the percentage of IDPs granted temporary shelter, and the percentage granted food (see Table 7.1). The coverage level is directly proportionate to the time spent in displacement: the more recent

24 See, Deng Principles No. 24 to 27.

25 To provide this aid in the case of individual displacement, the Social Action Agency signed agreements with governments, cities, and churches. When mass displacement occurs, aid is provided according to rules established in contingency plans drawn up by Territorial Committees, in coordination with the International Committee of the Red Cross and territorial entities. Displaced communities must receive shelter, education, nutrition, and psychosocial assistance. The components of immediate aid are: hygiene articles, beds or mattresses, cooking articles, medical evaluation, medicine, urgent medical care, temporary shelter, and psychosocial evaluation.

the displacement is, the fewer the households that receive aid (Monitoring Commission 2008b: figure 14).

Emergency Humanitarian Aid exhibits larger coverage and relative increase. In 2010, 74.3 percent of RUPD-registered households received some component (60.5 percent in 2007), while 25.7 percent received none (39.5 percent in 2007) (Monitoring Commission 2008: table 13; Monitoring Commission 2010: 70). Of the main components, those that exhibited the greatest improvement – despite none of them covering more than 50 percent of registered IDPs – were rent subsidies, places in schools, and health insurance (see Table 7.1).

In sum, there has been a general increase in the amount of aid provided both in terms of Immediate Aid and Emergency Humanitarian Aid. Nonetheless, these figures suggest that, in spite of the ruling and follow-up decisions, profound gaps continue to exist in the guarantee of basic human rights. Accordingly, in 2013, after evaluating new government reports, the Court concluded that, "regarding the humanitarian aid component there persists administrative, budgetary, and institutional flaws previously identified," and thus declared the persistence of an unconstitutional state of affairs (Decision 99 of 2013).

7.2.6. *The Right to Adequate Income*

According to the Court's diagnosis in 2004, "the impossibility of generating income prevents displaced persons from autonomously satisfying their basic needs in nutrition, housing, health, and education in the case of minors. This prolongs and worsens the vulnerable situation of displaced persons."[26] Six years later, the same diagnosis was still applicable, as the Monitoring Commission concluded that the labor and income generation conditions of the displaced population were "extremely precarious" (Monitoring Commission 2010: 182).

A first group of indicators that provides an idea of the economic situation of the displaced population are the rates of formal employment and informality.[27] The displaced population has very low formal employment levels and the trend has remained similar over the years. Of the working-age,[28] RUPD-registered population, only 43.4 percent declared itself as employed,

[26] Constitutional Court, Ruling T25 of 2004, Section 6.3.2.

[27] Informality is defined as non-registration in a social insurance program, income below the minimum wage, and unpaid work (Monitoring Commission 2010: 182).

[28] That is, persons 12 years or older.

3.8 percent unemployed, and 53 percent as not actively seeking work (Monitoring Commission 2010: figure 43). In 2007, these figures were 45.2 percent, 4.8 percent, and 50 percent, respectively (Monitoring Commission 2008: table 58). With respect to informality, the figure in 2010 was 96.5 percent (97.8 in 2007) (Monitoring Commission 2008: table 70; Monitoring Commission 2010: table 72).

While we were unable to calculate whether the differences were statistically significant, the figures above translate into a marked inferiority of working wages. In fact, when evaluated using the effective enjoyment of rights indicators that have as their reference the poverty and extreme poverty lines, the situation is clearly worrisome. According to the indicator measuring monetary working wages alone, in 2010 97.6 percent of RUPD displaced households lived below the poverty line (98 percent in 2007, difference not statistically significant), and 78.8 percent lived below the extreme poverty line (74 percent in 2007) (Monitoring Commission 2008: table 71; Monitoring Commission 2010: table 73). The latter figure indicates that the majority of the displaced population lives in abject poverty, without the income necessary to guarantee suitable nutrition for all household members (Monitoring Commission 2008b: 150; Monitoring Commission 2010: 183).

The outlook is particularly critical when considering that nearly half of the displaced population was not poor *before* displacement. In fact, before expulsion, 51 percent lived below the poverty line, while in 2010 the figure was closer to 98 percent (Monitoring Commission 2010).

Testimony from displaced leaders also confirms the gravity of the situation. Virgelina Chará spoke of work opportunities for the displaced population after the ruling:

> In that respect, the ruling didn't change anything because private industry won't hire us because of employment discrimination; because they don't know what we used to do; because they think we were displaced because of something we did, not because of the armed conflict; and because they can't hire "that type of person" for their business, and because the work they offer IDPs is as a car washer or maid.[29]

Thus, with regard to employment opportunities and the right to adequate income, we find little evidence of a tangible socioeconomic effect due to the ruling and its first seven years of follow-up.

[29] Interview with Virgelina Chará, displaced leader, director of Asowomens and Work Organization, January 15, 2009.

7.2.7. *The Rights to Truth, Justice, Reparations, and Return to Dispossessed Lands*

The last indicator of the possible social impact of T25 on the displaced population relates to justice and compensation for the crimes of which they have been victims. The most comprehensive information available on this subject relates to the dispossession of land and other assets. According to II ENV, 96.5 percent of displaced households had some type of asset, either goods and chattels or real estate, before displacement (Monitoring Commission 2008b: 161) and when asked if they had abandoned some type of asset because of displacement, 94.6 percent of interviewed household responded affirmatively (Monitoring Commission 2008b: 168). According to III ENV, 42.4 percent of displaced households lost rural real estate and 74.7 percent lost chattels and animals (Monitoring Commission 2010: 190).

Since 1998, a total of 5.5 million hectares have been abandoned or dispossessed, not counting properties larger than 100 hectares or collective properties belonging to Afro-Colombian and indigenous populations (Monitoring Commission 2009: 12). The largest percentage of abandoned lands is found in the Caribbean coast region (38.2 percent), followed by the zone comprising the Amazon, the Orinoco, and Chocó (34.5 percent), and rounded out by the Andean region (27.3 percent).

State inaction, even several years after the ruling, is especially glaring when contrasting figures on forced dispossession of lands with those on reparations via land grants awarded to the displaced: around 60,000 hectares – that is, 0.01 percent – of the territory usurped from this population.[30] This explains why the director of the Social Action Agency, in a public hearing before the Court in July 2009, described the land situation as "still dramatic."[31] An equally precarious situation is found in relation to the rights to truth, justice, and reparations, as documented by various studies on the right to land (Sánchez and Uprimny 2010; Salinas 2009). Indeed, the scarcity of information available is itself a vivid indicator of the profound deadlock around transitional justice policy (Restrepo 2009).

The lack of progress – and even the deterioration – of the effective enjoyment of these rights is, in fact, one of the issues that have remained most resistant to influence from the ruling and the follow-up process. The Court itself, in its survey of the ruling's first five years, concluded:

30 *Semana*, "They Are Killing Them," March 14, 2009.

31 Luis Alfonso Hoyos, Director of Social Action Agency, Public Hearing Before the Constitutional Court, July 10, 2009.

> As for the rights to truth, justice, reparations, and non-repetition, efforts ... remain insufficient. There remains a barbarous impunity toward the crime of displacement and current data only take into account complaints brought directly to the authorities' attention, even though this is a crime that must be investigated even if no complaint is filed (Article 159 of Law 599 of 2000). There are large procedural and institutional capacity obstacles in the way of advancement in these areas and no strategy to solve them has been developed.[32]

In 2011, the situation had not changed significantly. Hence, the Court concluded that it "found it difficult to conceive significant progress in the effective enjoyment of these rights, and thus, in the overcoming of the unconstitutional state of affairs."

In sum, how has the IDP's situation changed after the ruling and follow-up process? The data from this section suggest that there has been notable progress in certain rights (such as access to health and education). However, the general situation is one of profound precariousness and continued violation of fundamental rights of displaced persons. In fact, this situation led the Court to declare the continuation of the unconstitutional state of affairs in Decision 8 of 2009, wherein it concluded:

> Bearing in mind that the reports presented demonstrate the extreme gravity of the poverty situation of the displaced population, the deficient coverage of several aid programs, the inadequacy of policies on housing, land, and income generation, and the continued phenomenon of displacement as reflected in the large number of newly displaced persons each year since 2004 (a yearly average of 240,000), it would be impossible to declare a partial correction of the unconstitutional state of affairs, in spite of improvements in some rights.

In 2011, when the Court last evaluated the unconstitutional state of affairs right-by-right, it declared that the unconstitutional state of affairs remained, except as noted above, for the right to health for the general IDP population (Decision 219 of 2011).

If material effects on the displaced population have been limited, what of symbolic effects? The next section closes the chapter by addressing this question.

7.3. SYMBOLIC EFFECTS ON THE DISPLACED POPULATION

Previous chapters have analyzed the principal symbolic effects of T25, including those concerning displaced population organizations and their leaders.

[32] Constitutional Court, Decision 8 of 2009, number 94.

Chapter 6, for example, recounted how leaders came to frame their complaints in the language and procedures of human rights law. Chapter 5 examined political and discursive spaces opened by T25 for certain displaced population organizations, although carefully noting that these spaces are more restricted for social organizations lacking specialized legal experience and knowledge.

To complete this analysis, the present section analyzes symbolic effects on anonymous displaced individuals who do not belong to organizations or exercise leadership roles. The analysis is difficult for two reasons. First, the displaced population, by definition, is highly dispersed and diverse. Thus, the type of fieldwork undertaken for this study – based on interviews with government agencies and social organizations – offers only indirect evidence on the subject. Second, existing sources of data (such as II and III ENV) focus on the material situation of the displaced, for obvious reasons, and do not provide in-depth information on questions such as knowledge of the ruling and the degree to which its language and resources have been appropriated to demand rights.

The displaced population's use of writ of mandamus actions (*tutelas*) offers a source of data for analysis of the symbolic effect of judgment T25. According to Social Action Agency figures for 2009, displaced citizens presented close to 5,000 *tutelas* monthly.[33] The massive presentation of close to 60,000 annual *tutelas* suggests a high level of knowledge of human rights and judicial mechanisms on the part of IDPs. In 2013, the Ombudsman's Office reported that citizens presented 86,578 *tutelas* against the Victim's Unit alone (Ombudsman's Office 2014: 214). This figure makes the Victim's Unit the government agency with the most *tutela* actions filed that year (19 percent of all *tutelas*). It is safe to assume that the majority of these *tutelas* were presented by victims, most of whom are IDPs. This suggests a sharp increase in the amount of *tutelas* presented by IDPs, as this number is an underestimate of the total number of *tutelas* presented by IDPs because *tutelas* could have been presented against other government agencies. This knowledge could therefore represent an important symbolic effect of ruling T25, as suggested in an interview with an official from the Ministry of Environment, Housing, and Development, who stated that "the ruling has served as input for the filing of many *tutelas*. Today, we at the National Housing Fund handle close to 1,000 *tutelas* per year."[34]

[33] *El Tiempo*, "Three is Enough," October 4, 2009.

[34] Interview with Luis Domingo Gómez, Ministry of Environment, Housing, and Territorial Development, January 2009.

This conclusion, however, should be qualified. First, the explosion in *tutelas* is an ambiguous indicator of impact. On the one hand, it may indeed represent the genuine legal empowerment of the displaced population. On the other, it may also be a symptom of the lack of impact the ruling has had, and the continuation (or even worsening) of the flaws that led the Court to declare an unconstitutional state of affairs. As one interviewed leader mentioned, the *tutela* is a dysfunctional instrument for the effective guarantee of rights of IDPs, and the ruling and follow-up decisions were simply "band-aids on the larger problem because in order to enforce your rights you have to present a *tutela*."[35]

Interviews with several actors in the displacement field also demonstrated that while some displaced population leaders are quite familiar with the ruling, the majority remains in the dark. The clerk working on T25 emphasized that the ruling "is constantly invoked, [but only] by organized leaders."[36] The director of the Consultancy for Human Rights and Displacement (Codhes), when asked whether displaced persons were familiar with the ruling, answered: "Yes, many people are familiar with the ruling. But the displaced population is a very large, complex, and diverse group. For example, The National Office of the Displaced is very familiar with it. The regional leadership is, too, in general ... But at the grassroots level, not really."[37] A displaced leader and Fundagro Organization's legal representative shared this opinion, stating that "the general population isn't [aware of the ruling]. Only the ones who have been active from the beginning, who have been at workshops, know about it."[38]

Finally, the use of legal mechanisms by lawyers and intermediaries exploiting the economic opportunity brought by providing aid to the displaced could explain, in part, the increase in *tutelas*. In fact, an entire industry of unscrupulous intermediaries that game the system has sprung up, and grown to such a point that it now represents a significant source of loss to agencies such as the Social Action Agency. In 2009, for example, *El Tiempo* newspaper reported on a "mafia" of lawyers dedicated to applying for aid on behalf of displaced persons, in exchange for an elevated percentage of the aid awarded, or lawyers who offered "legal 'packages' or 'combos' whose value varied between 40,000

35 Interview with Ana Cecilia Prada, displaced leader, legal representative of Fundagro, January 16, 2009.

36 Interview with Clara Helena Reales, Colombian Constitutional Court clerk, December 18, 2008.

37 Interview with Marco Romero, Director of Codhes, December 19 and 23, 2008.

38 Interview with Ana Cecilia Prada, displaced leader, legal representative of Fundagro, January 16, 2009.

and 300,000 pesos [which] include[d] presenting petitions, *tutelas*, and contempt of court."[39]

Although far from pervasive, interviews suggested that the gaming of legal processes by intermediaries is not uncommon. For example, a high official of the Ministry of the Interior reported, "knowledge of the ruling and the follow-up decisions is still restricted to a privileged few and those in the know either don't share it or keep people misinformed so that they can take advantage of others. For example, they make up some type of fee and live off that."[40] The previously cited displaced leader offered an impression that coincides with this outlook: "Most of the people are victims, they're victims of a bunch of crooks that live off the recently arrived victims."[41]

In short, there is no definitive evidence on the existence or absence of symbolic effects of T25 on the majority of the displaced population – that is, those who are neither members of an organization nor occupy leadership roles. Due to the lack of comparative, long-term data and the ambiguity of *tutela* use, we lack clear indicators of this type of impact.

7.4. CONCLUSIONS

This chapter aimed to evaluate the impact that the ruling has ultimately had on the target beneficiary population. Multicausality and data limitations impede us from drawing strong, definitive conclusions about the socioeconomic effect. Following the book's analytic framework and bearing in mind the data restrictions, we followed two paths.

First, we addressed the material component of the socioeconomic effect. To that end, we presented the situation of the displaced population before the ruling and then analyzed the data from the I, II, and III National Verification Surveys on the degree of IDPs' effective enjoyment of rights. Although the data from both periods are not strictly comparable and it is difficult to determine whether improvements came directly from the Court's ruling and follow-up process, we found that the situation before the ruling was dire (leading the Court to declare an unconstitutional state of affairs), and even a decade after the Court handed down the ruling we found a mixed record for the judgment's effect on the enjoyment of rights. There has been notable progress in access to

39 *El Tiempo*, "Lawyer Mafia Prepares Applications for the Displaced and Then Keeps 20 and Even 100% of Benefits," April 26, 2009.

40 Interview with Liliana Guzmán, Coordinator of the Special Protection Programme for the Displaced Population, Ministry of the Interior and Justice, January 13, 2009.

41 Interview with Virgelina Chará, displaced leader, director of Asowomens and Work Organization, January 15, 2009.

health and education. In fact, seven years after the T25, the Court acknowledged that the government had overcome the unconstitutional state of affairs regarding the right to health of the general displaced population. However, we find little of evidence of a tangible socioeconomic effect due to the ruling regarding the rights to food, housing, immediate and humanitarian aid, and adequate income. Thus, the general situation continues to be characterized by profound precariousness and violations of IDPs' rights.

The second path consisted in evaluating the symbolic effects on displaced individuals not belonging to organizations. Here we found no definitive evidence on the existence or absence of symbolic effects. While the IDP population's use of constitutional writs of protection (*tutelas*) represents the legal empowerment of the displaced population, interviews revealed IDPs' uneven familiarity with the ruling.

With this analysis on the socioeconomic effect of the ruling we conclude Part II of the book, which documents in detail the direct, indirect, material, and symbolic effects of the most ambitious rulings in contemporary Latin American constitutionalism. In the last part of the book we again widen our field of vision and place T25 in comparative perspective to identify what types of judicial activism have the greatest potential to ameliorate situations of radical deprivation, what explains the varying impacts of SER judgments, and what the answers to these questions tell us about the justification and capacity for courts to carry out structural interventions.

PART III

DIALOGIC JUDICIAL ACTIVISM IN COMPARATIVE PERSPECTIVE

8

Explaining Impact in Comparative Constitutionalism: An Empirical Case for Dialogic Judicial Activism

The chapters that make up Part II have a predominantly descriptive focus and purpose. Given the lack of empirical analyses about the implementation of rulings in comparative constitutional studies, in Part II we used our analytical framework to document in detail the direct, indirect, material, and symbolic effects of an iconic case of SERs judicial activism.

However, as we explained in Chapter 1, T25 is a magnified version of similar developments in other courts in the Global South. Thus, the case study's findings provide a more general menu of responses to the central questions of contemporary comparative constitutionalism. What types of judicial interventions have the greatest potential to help ameliorate situations of radical deprivation? What kinds of judicial activism can better respond to classic objections regarding courts' lack of democratic legitimacy and capacity to decide cases of massive violations of SERs?

In this chapter we widen our analysis to tackle these questions. We proceed in two steps. In the first section, we turn to an explanatory question: what accounts for the different levels of impact of SER rulings? Why do some decisions have deep and multifarious effects while others remain on paper? Since the fate of judicial decisions hinges on responses from a wide array of actors – for example, the post-judgment strategies of activists and litigators, governmental reactions to court orders, and the role of the courts in the implementation phase – multicausality makes these questions intractable unless we restrict the analysis to a specific set of variables. We thus focus on the factors that are within the Court's purview. All other things being equal, there is a question of concern: what types of judicial decisions are more likely to have a broader impact on the fulfillment of SERs? Or, in prescriptive terms, what can courts do to enhance the impact of their rulings on SERs?

To empirically ground our response to these questions, we contrast the evidence from T25 with findings from case studies on two other key structural rulings by the Colombian Constitutional Court (CCC): T-153 of 1998 (on prison overcrowding), and T-760 of 2008 (on the health care system).[1] In addition, we briefly discuss secondary evidence on the impact of the *PUCL* (right to food) case in India and the *Grootboom* ruling in South Africa. Methodologically, we use the latter two rulings as shadow cases, in order to bolster the potential applicability of our findings to different national contexts.

In the chapter's second section, we use the evidence from this selection of cases to offer empirical responses to objections about courts' legitimacy and capacity. To do so, we critically examine the institutional assumptions underlying these objections and we contrast them with the political and legal realities that result in structural SER litigations. In actually existing democracies such as Colombia, India, or South Africa, which situations justify court interventions in structural SER disputes? What type of judicial activism can circumvent the objections regarding legitimacy and capacity in those contexts?

We posit that a dialogic approach to the justiciability of SERs enhances courts' impact, legitimacy, and capacity. As explained in Chapter 1, the degree to which an SER judgment is dialogic depends on a court's choices with regards to three components of the ruling: substantive content, remedies, and monitoring mechanisms. The decision's substantive content relates to the extent to which the Court declares that there has been a violation of a justiciable SER. In terms of Tushnet's (2009) typology, the choice that a court faces at this juncture is whether to affirm the justiciability of an SER in the case at hand, and, if it finds for the plaintiff, how strongly to interpret the scope of the plaintiff's rights. Thus, activist rulings, of both the monologic and dialogic varieties, shy away from weak conceptions of SERs by affirming justiciability of the latter in either strong terms (as in the "minimum core" approach of the CCC) or moderate terms (as in the "reasonableness" doctrine of the South African Constitutional Court).

With regard to remedies, whereas monologic judgments involve detailed, outcome-oriented orders, dialogic judgments tend to outline goals and procedures and, in line with the principle of separation of powers, place the burden on government agencies to design and implement policies. In terms of Tushnet's parameters to differentiate "strong" and "weak" remedies – that is,

[1] An earlier version of these comparative case studies can be found in Rodríguez-Garavito (2011a), from which we partially take this chapter.

the scope of orders and the extent to which orders are compulsory and peremptory – dialogic remedies tend to be weaker.[2]

Dialogic decisions also open up a monitoring process that encourages discussion of policy alternatives to solve the structural problem detected in the ruling. Unlike monologic judicial proceedings, the minutiae of the policies arise during the course of the monitoring process, not in the judgment itself. Dialogic courts often issue new decisions in light of progress and setbacks in the process and encourage discussion among actors in the case through deliberative public hearings. This constitutional dialogue involves a broader spectrum of stakeholders in the monitoring process. In addition to the court and state agencies directly affected by the judgment, implementation involves victims whose rights have been violated, relevant civil society organizations, international human rights agencies, and other actors whose participation is useful for the protection of the rights at issue, including grassroots organizations and academic experts.

There are stark differences among activist courts (and among decisions of the same court) on each of the three dimensions. As we will see, although in T25 the CCC has explicitly adopted a dialogic approach, in previous structural rulings such as the one on prison overcrowding (T-153 of 1998, hereafter T153) it leaned toward a monologic combination of strong rights, strong orders, and no monitoring. Yet in other structural decisions, such as T-760 of 2008 (hereafter T760) on the right to health, it has stood somewhere in between monologic and dialogic approaches.

The South African Constitutional Court has tended to adopt a combination of moderate rights, weak remedies, and no monitoring. In cases like *Soobramoney*[3] (on the right to health) and *Mazibuko*[4] (on the right to water), its moderate-rights approach has led it to reject SER claims on the basis that the state had not breached the reasonableness standard in refusing to provide, respectively, kidney dialysis to a terminally ill patient, and sufficient amounts of free water to impoverished citizens (Davis 2010; Dugard 2013; Wilson and Dugard 2013). In other cases, such as *Grootboom*, it has found for the plaintiff but chosen not to set deadlines or follow-up proceedings for enforcement. In the

[2] Given our focus on structural rulings that mandate positive actions by the executive or the legislature, we do not dwell on negative remedies here – that is, those that order elected authorities to abstain from a given course of action found to violate an SER, such as disproportionately taxing the poor.

[3] *Soobramoney v. Minister of Health, KwaZulu-Natal* (1) SA 765 (CC) (1998).

[4] *Mazibuko v. City of Johannesburg* (4) SA 1 (CC) (2010).

exceptional case of *Treatment Action Campaign* (TAC)[5], it handed down a strong remedy (i.e., an order for the state to provide nevirapine to pregnant mothers across the country to avoid mother-to-child transmission of HIV at birth), but reaffirmed its preference for moderate rights (through the reasonableness test) and no monitoring. A more dialogic approach is evident in the *Olivia Road* case[6], where the Court directed the state and the applicants to engage meaningfully with each other in order to find an adequate housing alternative in the face of the need to relocate the applicants from their informal dwellings (Pillay 2012). By turning "meaningful engagement" into a requirement of reasonable state action, and by reviewing the agreement between the parties to assess compliance, the Court took on a dialogue-promoting, mediating role.

The Indian Supreme Court's jurisprudence has oscillated among different understandings of rights, remedies, and monitoring (Pillay 2014). It has oftentimes resorted to a monologic mixture of strong rights, strong remedies, and strong monitoring mechanisms (Muralidhar 2008). Its strong-rights approach is noteworthy given that the 1949 Constitution did not enshrine SERs as enforceable rights, but rather as directive principles of state policy. The Court has thus built its approach by interpreting the constitutional provisions on the protection of the right to life as including the right to livelihood, in cases like *Francis Mullin*[7] and *Olga Tellis*.[8] However, its recent jurisprudence can be better characterized as dialogic (Chandrachud 2009), as the Court has taken up the role of an "embedded negotiator in facilitating the dialogue between the state and citizens" through strong rights, moderate remedies, and strong monitoring (Shankar 2013: 103). This has notably been its approach in the *PUCL* case on the right to food. Nonetheless, the Court has at times reverted to a weak rights approach in key cases such as *Narmada Bachao Andolan*, where it failed to find violations of the rights of 41,000 families displaced from their homes as a result of the building of a dam (Rajagopal 2005, 2007).

Do these different combinations of rights, remedies, and monitoring have a bearing on judicial impact? Evidence from the comparative case study of the CCC's rulings suggests that they do. We now turn to this evidence.

[5] *Minister of Health v. Treatment Action Campaign* (5) SA 721 (CC) (2002).

[6] *Occupiers of 51 Olivia Road, Berea Township and 197 Main Street Johannesburg v. City of Johannesburg* (3) SA 208 (CC) (2008).

[7] *Francis Mullin v. The Administrator*, 1 SCC 608 (1981).

[8] *Olga Tellis v. Bombay Municipal Corporation*, 3 SCC 545 (1985).

8.1. THE IMPACT OF DIALOGIC ACTIVISM

8.1.1. *Comparing Monologic and Dialogic Rulings*

Our findings on the impact of T25 contrasts with the more modest effects of two other structural CCC rulings: T153 and T760. In 1998 the CCC ruled T153, declaring that the dire situation of detainees in overcrowded prisons amounted to an unconstitutional state of affairs. Although the Court issued a number of short-term orders aimed at addressing the gravest administrative and budgetary flaws underlying prison overcrowding, it stopped short of establishing any meaningful monitoring mechanism. In T760, albeit not formally using the doctrine of unconstitutional states of affairs, the CCC issued a set of structural injunctive remedies and launched an ambitious monitoring process not unlike that of T25, including the creation of a specialized monitoring chamber within the Court. The Court took these actions in order to nudge the government to address long-standing administrative and legislative bottlenecks that crippled the health care system and overwhelmed courts with a yearly average of close to 100,000 writs of protection (*tutelas*) for basic medicines and treatment. Nevertheless, the monitoring quickly lost steam; by the time of writing, six years after the decision, it continues but has turned into a series of largely formalistic reports from government agencies to the Court.

Our interviews with CCC justices, civil society actors, and state officials involved in the three rulings show that while T153 had the lowest impact in the sample, T25 had the highest, with T760's impact ranking in between.[9] Indeed, fifteen years later, the persistence of prison overcrowding and the state bureaucracy and policies underlying it had changed so little that in 2013 human rights advocates unsuccessfully attempted to get the CCC to reopen the case. In contrast, the T760 Court, albeit far from achieving the structural changes in the health care system it had envisaged, managed to spur important legal reforms (e.g., the regulation of skyrocketing prices for medicines) and put the crisis of the health care system at the center of public debate.

How do these decisions compare in terms of our variables of interest? The three rulings share a strong rights approach. The first decision (T153) – in which the CCC created the doctrine of unconstitutional state of affairs – strongly condemned prison overcrowding for violating detainees' SERs rights; the Court also decisively affirmed the justiciability of these rights. Similarly

[9] We use here a synthetic assessment of the rulings' impact, which aggregates the four types of effects – direct, indirect, material, and symbolic.

painstaking accounts and condemnation of repeated violations of the right to health can be found in T760. In light of this, the Court explicitly adopted a stronger understanding of the right to health, by making it directly justiciable instead of conditioning its judicial enforcement on its connection to the right to life with dignity, as it had done in the past.

With regard to remedies, however, a sharp break is evident between earlier rulings and more recent jurisprudence. In T153, the CCC adopted a strong-remedies approach by handing down detailed orders for the government to (1) immediately suspend a contract for the renovation of one of the largest prisons in Bogotá; (2) formulate, in three months, a comprehensive plan for the renovation of existing prisons and the construction of new ones, which was to be executed within a four-year period; and (3) put an end, in four years, to the confinement of detainees under trial in the same prisons as convicted detainees.

As documented in the previous chapters, the T25 Court adopted a more procedural, dialogic approach by leaving it to the government to decide the content of IDP programs and the requisite funding for carrying them out. At the same time, however, it set stringent deadlines and handed down an outcome-oriented order requiring the government to begin protecting the most basic rights of IDPs in the short term (within six months). Thus, in terms of the above classification, this decision entailed moderate remedies.

A similarly moderate, intermediate approach to remedies is evident in the more recent decision on health care. Most of the decision's orders are means-oriented, mandating that the government formulate a contingency plan to deal with the impending bankruptcy of the health care system, create administrative protocols for resolving patients' complaints, and establish mechanisms to efficiently oversee private healthcare providers. The orders sought five main objectives: (i) promote the precision, updating, unification, and access to benefits plans; (ii) improve the sustainability and flow of financial resources; (iii) enhance the transparency of the health system through the creation and dissemination of patients' bills of rights and duties; (iv) move toward universal health coverage; and (v) develop indicators for periodic monitoring of compliance with the Court's orders. These orders' relative weakness is offset by stringent deadlines and a strong injunction ordering the government to unify the basic coverage for patients in the private and the public health care systems, as mandated by a 1993 law that had not been implemented (Rodríguez-Garavito 2013).

Finally, with regard to monitoring, T25 stands apart from the other rulings. Through twenty follow-up public hearings involving a wide array of

TABLE 8.1. *Comparison of Colombian Constitutional Court's Structural Rulings*

	Rights	Remedies	Monitoring	Impact
T-25 (2004–)	Strong	Moderate	Strong	High
T-760 (2008–)	Strong	Moderate	Weak	Moderate
T-153 (1998)	Strong	Strong	Weak	Low

governmental and non-governmental actors, as well as 289 follow-up decisions, the CCC has instituted a remarkably strong monitoring process.

In contrast, the earlier approach of T153 did not include any court-sponsored monitoring mechanisms. Instead, the CCC limited itself to asking the Ombudsman's Office and the Inspector General's Office to oversee the decision's enforcement. Likewise, the T760 Court, despite having outlined in the decision a monitoring mechanism akin to that of T25, has largely remained passive: it has held only two public hearings, failed to promote meaningful citizen participation, and limited its follow-up injunctions to petitions for information from the government (Lamprea 2014; Yamin and Parra-Vera 2010).[10] Weak monitoring, therefore, has characterized these two cases.

Table 8.1 sums up the comparison among the three cases, as well as the results of above-mentioned impact assessment.

Although a larger sample of cases is needed to extract firm conclusions, this comparison offers useful hints on the relationship between dialogic activism and judicial impact. The results suggest that, all other things being equal, dialogic rulings such as T25 hold out the prospect for greater overall impact on the fulfillment of SERs, whereas monologic rulings such as T153 are likely to have less impact. In between these two extremes are different combinations of rights, remedies, and monitoring that are likely to have moderate effects.

Impact studies of comparable rulings in India and South Africa provide additional support for this hypothesis. Using an earlier version of our analytical framework (Rodríguez-Garavito 2011a), Chitalkar and Gauri (forthcoming) examined the effects of the *PUCL* litigation, while Langford (2013) studied those of the *Grootboom* case. Their findings suggest that the combination of rights, remedies, and monitoring that characterize dialogic activism can

[10] One exception to the Court's passivity is a follow-up decision that ordered the government to immediately comply with the Court's previous order to unify coverage for underage patients in the public and the private health care systems (Decision 342 of 2009).

increase the probability that judicial interventions have the direct, indirect, material, and symbolic effects that activist courts envisage.

PUCL is a clear instance of dialogic adjudication. As Chitalkar and Gauri (forthcoming) comment:

> [T]he Supreme Court's approach in the right to food case appears to have been strategic in that the Court began by strongly and clearly declaring the right to food as a fundamental right, and further by defining the contours of that right in the form of legal entitlements. It then framed remedies, which although only re-affirming the government's existing responsibilities, clearly detailed milestones to be fulfilled. Most importantly, the Court created a robust mechanism for compliance monitoring, by appointing two commissioners to monitor enforcement of its decisions and report back to the Court in case of non-compliance.

Thus, in its first decision on the case in November 2001, the Court began by strongly recognizing the fundamental right to food. In addition to acknowledging its justiciability as a component of the right to life, it explicitly detailed state obligations that derived from it. As Birchfield and Corsi elaborate, "what is significant about the Indian example, is that the Supreme Court has taken these general obligations and given them teeth by specifically explicating the right in concrete policy terms and by establishing oversight mechanisms" (2010: 718). Specifically, the Court gave the status of legal entitlements to state programs fighting hunger and malnutrition such as: targeted public distribution system of grain to impoverished families; programs to provide take-home rations or cooked meals for adolescent girls, pregnant and lactating women, and children less than six years of age; and a mid-day meal scheme to supply every student in a public elementary school with a cooked meal (Birchfield and Corsi 2010). Although they had existed for some time, these and other programs were riddled with inefficiency and corruption, which helps to explain why in India, even today, nearly half of all children – approximately 60 million – are underweight (World Bank 2013).

In terms of remedies, the Court decided to maintain "continuous mandamus" over the case, giving orders throughout the years in order to take account of the level of enforcement and order new actions for state and national governments. More than a decade later, the Court maintains supervisory jurisdiction over the case and has given forty-four follow-up interim orders.

Nevertheless, the Court's most important innovation has been to delegate detailed monitoring to two high-profile commissioners, beginning in 2002. They report to the Court about implementation advances and setbacks. The commissioners have the power to investigate breaches of the Court's orders, demand enforcement and work with government authorities to overcome implementation obstacles, monitor data on hunger and malnutrition, and receive citizen complaints.[11]

The way in which the Court and the commissioners have monitored the case illustrates the dialogic approach of "judging as nudging" (Klein 2008). Instead of focusing on monologic and peremptory orders, the Court has favored continuous engagement, dissemination of information, and public deliberation as points of pressure to achieve government compliance. For example, in their first report to the Court, the commissioners explained, "we wish to emphasize that the approach of the commissioners is not fault finding. The State and Union Territories must take us as a friend and cooperate in a common endeavour to tackle food insecurity."[12]

This approach has enabled the coordination among the Court, the commissioners, and the right-to-food social movement to pressure government authorities. This combination, facilitated by the Court's dialogic judicial activism, is responsible for a good part of the case's impact (Chitalkar and Gauri forthcoming). Although the level of enforcement of the Court's orders has varied, some have had considerable effects. For example, the mid-day meal program benefited 60.8 million children from 2001–2006 and increased the intake of calories, proteins, and carbohydrates by an average of 49–100 percent (Brinks and Gauri 2014). The ruling has also had equally important symbolic and indirect effects, insofar as it has contributed to highlighting in public debates the need to urgently respond to malnutrition and hunger.

The *PUCL* case in India contrasts in various relevant aspects with *Grootboom* in South Africa. While the former followed a dialogic model that closely resembled T25 in Colombia, the latter opted for a less activist and dialogic approach, closer to the CCC's T760 judgment about the health care system. In effect, we characterize the South African Court's behavior as a combination of moderate rights, weak remedies, and weak monitoring. In terms of the rights' content, the Court affirmed the justiciability of the right to housing of the 390 adults and 510 children represented by the plaintiff, Irene Grootboom. By order of the Cape Town municipality, the community had been evicted from the informal settlement where they lived (Liebenberg 2010). According to the Court's ruling, the precariousness of the nationwide housing program (which failed to attend to the needs of millions of informal settlement dwellers) fell short of the state's obligation in regards to the right to housing,

[11] Interview with Harsh Mander, special commissioner to the Supreme Court of India in the *PUCL* case, April 30, 2015. See generally www.sccommissioners.org/

[12] See www.sccommissioners.org/Reports/Reports/SCC1_0802.pdf (accessed October 31, 2014).

and the manner in which the municipality had evicted the community was unconstitutional. In finding for the plaintiff, however, the Court used the reasonableness standard – and, thus, a weaker interpretation of the content of SERs than other courts such as the CCC and the Indian Supreme Court have acknowledged (Bilchitz 2013; see Chapter 1). We therefore classify *Grootboom* as moderate-rights ruling.

In regards to remedies, the Court refused to give individual orders, such as giving Ms. Grootboom a house. Instead, it expedited a structural injunction that sought to attend to the systemic flaws in the housing system. It thus ordered the state to design and implement a housing public policy that took account of the needs of the poorest South Africans. Even though the structural and means-oriented remedies suggest dialogic activism, the South African Court, in contrast to its Indian and Colombian counterparts, left implementation completely to state discretion by not establishing deadlines or procedures to comply with the order. In this sense, we categorize the judgment's remedies, like those of the majority of its jurisprudence, as weak.

The weakness of the remedies is accentuated by the lack of monitoring. Interestingly, in *Grootboom*, the South African Court explicitly refused to carry out the type of monitoring that the CCC has done in T25 or T760, or that the commissioners have done in the right-to-food case in India. In effect, in its *Grootboom* decision, the Court mentioned the fact that the South African Human Rights Commission (SAHRC), in an amicus brief submitted to the Court, had announced that it would "monitor, and if necessary, report in terms of these powers on the efforts made by the State to comply with its Section 26 obligations in accordance with this judgment."[13] Nevertheless, when SAHRC presented the Court with a detailed monitoring report of the case in 2011, it refused to consider it, claiming that it did not have supervisory jurisdiction over the case.

Langford's (2013) nuanced study about the ruling's effects supports our hypothesis about dialogic activism: the remedies' weaknesses and the lack of monitoring help to explain why *Grootboom* has not had the same level of impact as T25 and *PUCL*. However, Langford also empirically shows that the case has had some important effects, contrary to what more skeptical authors have argued about *Grootboom* (Berger 2008; Hirschl and Rosevear 2011). Using an expanded version of our analytical paradigm, Langford finds that the ruling has had material, political, and symbolic effects. Among other impacts, the

[13] *Grootboom*, para. 97

TABLE 8.2. *Comparison of Landmark Structural Rulings in Colombia, India and South Africa*

	Rights	Remedies	Monitoring	Impact
PUCL (2001–)	Strong	Moderate	Strong	High
T-25 (2004–)	Strong	Moderate	Strong	High
T-760 (2008–)	Strong	Moderate	Weak	Moderate
Grootboom (2001)	Moderate	Weak	Weak	Moderate
T153 (1998)	Strong	Strong	Weak	Low

case helped to protect the community from eviction and accelerate the provision of permanent housing (although Ms. Grootboom unfortunately never enjoyed these benefits before her death in 2008). Likewise, it led the state to modify its housing policy, slowed down eviction programs against informal settlement dwellers, and established an important precedent for other right to housing cases (Langford 2013: 195).

Table 8.2 sums up the comparative evidence on the features and impact of the five cases under consideration, ranked from highest to lowest impact.

As noted, our hypothesis regarding the greater impact of dialogic activism limits itself to court-controlled factors that have an influence on the impact of the aforementioned rulings and other activist decisions. In practice, external factors – from the reaction of affected parties in public and private sectors, to the degree of support from the media and civil society organizations – equally influence the effects of judicial interventions. For instance, T25 and T760 differ in one important respect: whereas in the former case the Court did not face resistance from vested interests outside the state, in the latter it encountered considerable pushback from beneficiaries of the dysfunctional system, including private health care providers and pharmaceutical companies that had found ways to make considerable profits by exploiting regulatory loopholes in the system. In contrast to the *TAC* right-to-health case in South Africa (Heywood 2009), the CCC could not rely on a strong social movement capable of countering such resistance. Additional research would be needed to parse out the interaction between court-controlled and external factors that affect the impact of judicial interventions. To contribute to that endeavor, we conclude this section by offering some hypotheses.

8.1.2. *Explaining the Impact of Dialogic Rulings*

We hypothesize that dialogic rulings have greater impact because they address the two key practical obstacles to the implementation of structural decisions: political resistance and institutional capacity. With regard to the former, structural injunctions on SERs naturally elicit resistance from powerful sectors with vested interests in the status quo. In the cases under consideration, these sectors included private health care providers and pharmaceutical companies reaping huge profits from thousands of lower court rulings ordering the government to pay for brand-name medicines in T760 (Lamprea 2015; Rodríguez-Garavito 2013); indifferent public officials in sclerotic bureaucracies responsible for programs on IDPs in the follow-up process to T25; negligent or corrupt personnel in the overcrowded prison system in T153; corrupt or inefficient public officials and food providers in *PUCL*; and dysfunctional bureaucracies and private construction companies in *Grootboom*.

By empowering a broader range of social actors to participate in monitoring, courts unleash direct and indirect effects that may help them overcome political resistance. The main effect is the direct involvement of political actors, such as human rights NGOs, reform-oriented public agencies, and grassroots organizations that are likely to adopt the ruling's implementation as part of their own agenda and thus become a source of countervailing power against the status quo. Moreover, orders of this nature may prompt the formation of political coalitions in support of the court or elicit media coverage that magnifies the material and symbolic effects of the case. As noted, this was the case after T25, which prompted the organization of a civil society Monitoring Commission that turned into a key ally of the Court as well as a provider of valuable information and recommendations. The right-to-food case in India is a paradigmatic instance of this indirect effect. The Supreme Court's 2001 ruling spurred the formation of the Right to Food Campaign, an informal network of organizations and individuals that mobilize against malnutrition and hunger.[14] In a positive feedback loop, the Campaign has become instrumental to the implementation of the Court's orders and to the broader cause, by not only petitioning the Court to demand that the government reform food distribution systems, but also by pursuing actions directly before the executive, the legislature, and the public at large. Through an extensive network of grassroots organizations, it has provided the type of

[14] See www.righttofoodcampaign.in/ (accessed October 15, 2014).

on-site information gathering and monitoring that Commissioners need to push forward the implementation of the Court's decisions. In this respect, Indian civil society has gone even farther in its contribution to the Court proceedings than its Colombian counterpart in T25.

Second, the mechanisms of dialogic activism may help courts address institutional shortcomings in dealing with complex socioeconomic issues. Although courts do not, by themselves, have the technical knowledge, personnel, and resources to find and implement solutions to problems as complex as massive forced displacement, informal housing, or malnutrition, they can provoke and moderate a dialogue among public authorities and civil society actors on these issues. By calling on not only government officials but also a wide variety of actors with relevant knowledge – for example, leaders and members of the beneficiary population, academic experts, and international human rights agencies – dialogic courts may promote a collaborative search for solutions, or at least a public discussion on alternative courses of action. As Gauri and Brinks (2012) have argued, courts can thus foster problem-solving, communicative action by serving as focal points for public conversations aimed at specifying the content and means of SERs implementation.

Direct and indirect effects potentially stemming from this dialogue include unlocking policy processes, improving coordination among disconnected state agencies, and creating public policies framed in the language of rights. As shown in the previous chapters, T25 provides an interesting illustration of these effects. A particularly useful feature of the monitoring process has been the collaborative formulation of progress indicators on the effective enjoyment of IDPs' rights. Through an iterative, multi-year process that has included numerous follow-up court orders and proposals by governmental and non-governmental agencies, the CCC adopted a list of quantitative, rights-based indicators to assess progress (see Chapter 4). These indicators have provided a shared monitoring framework for all the stakeholders, as well as a tool for the Court to fine-tune its follow-up injunctions in response to evidence on the evolution of policies and the situation of IDPs.

In sum, by combining the rights, remedies, and monitoring mechanisms of dialogic activism, courts may offset some of the political and institutional shortcomings that render their interventions ineffectual in complex distributional issues and enhance courts' overall impact on the fulfillment of SERs. They can also address some of the classical objections to judicial activism, as we discuss in the next section.

8.2. JUDICIAL ACTIVISM AND ITS CRITICS: A DIALOGICAL RESPONSE TO THE LEGITIMACY AND CAPACITY OBJECTIONS

The empirical study of the implementation of structural rulings sheds new light on responses to the classic objections against judicial activism. Based on the evidence from T25 presented in the previous chapters, as well as the comparative discussion in this chapter, we elaborate on the responses that we sketched in Chapter 1.

We focus on the two recurrent criticisms: the first regarding judicial activism's lack of democratic legitimacy, and the second regarding courts' inability to promote structural changes, such as those necessary for the fulfillment of SERs.[15]

8.2.1. *Courts and Democratic Accountability in Actually Existing Democracies*

The first argument, although usually treated as one, in fact consists of two different criticisms. On the one hand, the traditional objection concentrates on judges' undemocratic *origins*. According to this claim, because citizens do not democratically elect judges, their interference with public policy issues erodes the two pillars of democracy: electoral legitimacy and separation of powers. Adding to this criticism is an accountability argument: since judicial action is not subject to citizen control through elections that reward or punish prior performance, activist judges exercise considerable power without being held accountable for their performance.

On the other hand, some critiques focus on the possible anti-democratic *effects* of judicial activism. Proponents conventionally argue that judges' intervention may end up replacing public debate and social mobilization as the channels for conflict resolution and democratic decision-making (Rosenberg 1991). A more recent, empirically informed variation of this argument claims that elites have used "juristocracy" as a strategy to take over niches of power (such as constitutional courts) that are protected from electoral competition (Hirschl 2004).

The second main argument against judicial activism contends that even if they have democratic legitimacy, "courts lack the tools to readily develop appropriate policies and implement decisions ordering significant social

[15] Given the specific focus of this section, we do not systematically explore these arguments and the diversity of academic and political positions from which they arise. For a recent synthesis of the vast literature on this topic, see Tushnet (2009) and Fredman (2008). In relation to social rights, see Abramovich and Courtis (2002).

reform" (Rosenberg 1991: 21). By institutional design, courts usually deal with individual cases, have limited knowledge on matters of public policy, and rely on other branches of state power to enforce their judgments. Therefore, in this view, courts lack the overall vision, long-term planning, technical information, and coercive power to solve distributive justice problems.

These criticisms strategically targeted the type of monologic activism that undertook detailed transformations of complex institutions in past decades, such as dysfunctional prison systems (Feeley and Rubin 1998) or national banking systems inaccessible to the poor (Kalmanovitz 2001). Usually based on a neorealist view of law and social change, critics tended to support their case with empirical data on the limitations of court rulings' direct material effects (Rosenberg 1991).

Our case study and evidence on the implementation of other dialogic rulings such as *PUCL* suggest the need to revisit the terms and the merit of these arguments. In response to the criticism of the undemocratic origins of judges, we join proponents of experimentalist, dialogic judicial interventions in questioning the idealized and limited conception of democracy that underlies this objection (Sabel and Simon 2004). As we argued in Chapter 1, those advocating for judges' passivity assume that, unlike the judiciary, other branches of government are democratically legitimated and subject to accountability mechanisms. In reality, the legitimacy of actually existing democracies is far more complex and problematic than critics suggest.

Recall, for instance, the profound and recurrent policy flaws that led the CCC to declare an unconstitutional state of affairs in T25; they resulted from the executive and legislature's lack of political will to design any meaningful policy or regulatory response to the humanitarian emergency of over five million IDPs, to whom they were largely unaccountable. Recall also that the *PUCL* case was a reaction to the corruption and lack of accountability of government authorities responsible for the broken food distribution system in India. And that the dire situation of millions of slum dwellers in South Africa, encapsulated by the eviction of the *Grootboom* community, also had its roots in failures of the political system and the policy process. Although particularly acute and consequential in the Global South, limited accountability of elected officials is increasingly common in the Global North, as the capture of government sectors and parliaments by the powerful becomes a regular feature in growingly unequal societies.

Moreover, democratic accountability does not consist only in the electorate's control of public officials. Nor does the principle of separation of powers preclude that elected officials be accountable to unelected state entities. In the type of complex bureaucracies that make up contemporary democratic states, government transparency and accountability cannot be guaranteed through election mechanisms alone (Sabel and Simon 2004). As O'Donnell (1999, 2003) has shown, "vertical accountability" – whereby public authorities are subject to the scrutiny of voters, the media, and civil society actors – is but one of two forms of accountability in democratic systems. The second type, "horizontal accountability," is exercised *among* state institutions. Specifically, horizontal accountability controls "are undertaken by a state agency with the explicit purpose of preventing, cancelling, redressing and/or punishing actions (or eventually non-actions) by another state agency that are deemed unlawful, whether on grounds of encroachment or of corruption" (O'Donnell 2003: 38).

As O'Donnell's definition suggests, courts are the primary actors of horizontal accountability. They are responsible for checking the power of the executive and the legislature through a range of institutional mechanisms, from judicial review of congressional laws to criminal trials against corrupt officials to constitutional rulings on the state's failure to fulfill human rights. This horizontal dimension requires the courts to take precisely the type of action that critics condemn, including decisions to effectively nudge government officials to cease actions or omissions that contribute to massive violations of SERs.

8.2.2. *Destabilizing Rights: Institutional Paralysis and Courts' Unlocking Effect*

Judicial nudging and horizontal accountability are particularly important in situations of institutional paralysis or stalemate. As Sabel and Simon note with regards to the type of public interest litigation that underlies structural SER cases:

> [I]t is remarkable how rarely the practices that the plaintiffs attack seem to have been the result of an exercise of authority by anyone. The situation is more often the consequence of a failure or refusal to make policy. The most characteristic component of current structural decrees is a demand that the defendant simply promulgate some policy, often with minimal or uncontroversial constraints as to what it shall be (2004: 1092).

In such situations of chronic government inaction, the judiciary is oftentimes the only state organ with the independence and power to nudge bureaucracies into action (Chayes 1976). As explained in Chapter 3, the situation of

IDP policies before T25 closely resembled this scenario. Although the government had put in place an incipient legal framework and published disparate policy documents on the matter, it had largely remained paralyzed in the face of IDPs' humanitarian emergency. A similarly disastrous state policy failure explained India's status as one of the most malnourished countries in the world, despite a booming economy. Writing a year after the *PUCL* ruling, Jean Dreze and Amartya Sen described the situation as a "silent emergency" (Dreze and Sen 2002).

Institutional blockage may have various origins (Sabel and Simon 2004: 1064–1065). It may arise from a prisoner's-dilemma situation, as evident in the performance of the Colombian state prior to T25. Agencies engaged in a bureaucratic maze that was not optimal for any of them, yet it could only be resolved through an explicit overall coordination effort that none of them could undertake. The deadlock may also arise when one government agency or powerful social group has captured the political process or public policy on a subject, to the detriment of less powerful groups' interests and rights. This was the situation in the CCC's T760 ruling, as the health care system had been captured by a corrupt alliance of private providers and government regulators that were bleeding the system's finances by charging severely overpriced medicines and treatments to the state's budget.

The five cases under analysis in this chapter illustrate a third institutional blocking factor that, albeit commonly found in the Global South, remains invisible in studies on the subject that focus on European or U.S. legal and institutional practice (Hirschl 2004; Rosenberg 1991; Sabel and Simon 2004). While those studies focus on institutional coordination or accountability failures, structural litigation on SERs often arises due to state agencies' lack of *capacity*. In other words, those studies tend to take for granted that the institutions have the basic infrastructure, resources, and technical capacity to address the problem. They therefore see judicial intervention as a way to refine its cooperation and coordination with other capable institutions. However, structural cases in the Global South have a shared inception arising from the responsible institutions' lack of core capacities. In terms of sociology of the state it comes down to the state's lack of "infrastructural power" to effectively implement public policy (Mann 2012).

As shown by the story of T25's implementation process, courts oftentimes have to start by promoting capacity- and infrastructure-strengthening processes within the relevant institutions. The ruling and the follow-up have encouraged the construction of basic institutional capacities, such as information gathering, the allocation of resources, and coordination between the central government and departmental and municipal governments.

This has also been the case for T760, which has notably resulted in the reinforcement of the state's regulatory capacity vis-à-vis private providers and pharmaceutical companies through new legislation and administrative procedures (Rodríguez-Garavito 2013). The two Commissioners in the right-to-food case have undertaken a similar task in working with provincial governments to bolster their capacity to deliver the access-to-food programs laid out in the *PUCL* interim decisions (Birchfield and Corsi 2010). Against those skeptical of courts' capacity, it is essential to remember that in actually existing democracies, institutional capacity problems in public administration may be endemic as well.

In these contexts, judicial interventions first affect the state by shaking up institutional apparatuses that are locked in dysfunctional arrangements. This is the unlocking effect of SER structural litigation and adjudication (see Chapter 3). Legal interventions of this type aim to drive a wedge into those arrangements through the mobilization of constitutional norms and discourses. These "destabilizing rights" justify judicial interventions when courts hold chronically underperforming institutions accountable to constitutional rules and principles (Unger 1987).

The unlocking effect operates through a variety of mechanisms. For instance, the immediate state reactions to T25 show that the Court broke the institutional inertia on issues such as the budget allocated to provide services to IDPs, the revival of the inoperative inter-agency coordination system, and the delivery of some emergency services (see Chapters 3 and 4). Also, the T25 ruling alone, by agreeing with the plaintiffs and holding state institutions publicly accountable for serious rights violations, altered the balance of power between plaintiffs and defendants. This new political terrain likely creates new possibilities for collaboration, discussion, and negotiation among stakeholders, which can result in solutions that would have been infeasible under the pre-ruling balance of power. For example, the Constitutional Court, in condemning the Colombian state and identifying the unconstitutional state of affairs, gave legitimacy to NGOs and the IDP population as participants in the T25 monitoring process (see Chapter 5). By altering the political terrain of the discussion on forced displacement, the Court triggered processes unthinkable before the ruling, such as the joint effort between the state and NGOs to identify and design assessment indicators of public policies based on IDPs' effective enjoyment of rights (see Chapter 4). Langford (2013) found that the *Grootboom* case had a similar unlocking political effect, by increasing the leverage of communities of informal settlers in dealing with their municipalities.

In sum, by leveraging destabilization rights through dialogic rulings, activist courts can not only avoid eroding democratic accountability, but can also deepen and enhance it.

8.2.3. *Capacity for What? Courts as Authoritative Mediators of Problem-Solving Dialogues*

Regarding the second classical objection, on judicial capacity, our case study requires that we rethink its terms: capacity for what? As explained in Chapter 1, critics such as Rosenberg tend to direct their arguments against the type of heroic capacity that activist monologic courts would need in order to force recalcitrant governments and private actors into compliance with their detailed, strong remedies. In fact, as shown by T153 and other ambitious judicial efforts to reform prisons through strong remedies (Feeley and Rubin 1998), courts have scarce institutional resources – from budgets to coercive power to technical knowledge – to implement alone their detailed orders to mitigate the structural flaws of public policy.

The incapacity argument, however, does not as adequately apply to the type of experiential and dialogic activism we defend. In this version, the court capacity needed is not principally of designer or executor of public policy, nor of sanctioning government authorities that do not fulfill their obligations. While courts need the sanctioning power in extreme cases, the dialogic courts primarily need the capacity to serve as an authoritative focal point to moderate and drive collective problem-solving processes. As Gauri and Brinks have argued, courts exercise this capacity through three types of tasks:

> First, [courts] attempt to move parties from an adversarial to an investigative mode in an effort to find a new definition of a problem and its solutions. Second, they impose requirements that parties argue in good faith, reserving their most vehement admonitions and penalties for communication that is not "serious" or information that is inaccurate. Third, and related, these courts structure a public forum of communication by empowering new actors, facilitating or requiring the flow of information in the public sphere, and imposing reporting requirements (Gauri and Brinks 2012: 425–426).

Our case study shows that courts can fulfill these tasks without unduly compromising their institutional capacity or violating the separation of powers principle. Although the T25 process shows that adopting this role implies a considerable amount of work for an already overburdened court, it also suggests that there are institutional alternatives to manage it. The CCC has used the first option: create a specialized chamber dedicated to monitoring the case. In 2014, this chamber was composed by three of the nine CCC judges, supported by six clerks solely dedicated to this task.[16] This institutional arrangement has allowed the CCC to continue the monitoring process and handle the immense quantity of documents sent by state authorities and civil society. They sometimes present these documents in response to Court requests, while at other times they do so spontaneously to show results or file new complaints.

However, a special monitoring chamber's very existence and costs may be difficult to sustain in other political and institutional contexts. Even in Colombia, various interviewees within the Court expressed doubts about the long-term sustainability of this arrangement. In fact, our comparative case study has revealed a second alternative: the naming of case commissioners or rapporteurs, as the Indian Court has done in the right-to-food case. In a similar manner to how the special rapporteur offices function in the UN system, this type of expert can serve as an appropriate mechanism to combine moderate remedies with strong monitoring. In addition to not increasing the institutional framework's workload or the courts' budget (because the rapporteurs typically raise funds to compensate their own and their staff's time), this solution has the added benefit of charging detailed monitoring to independent experts that have intimate knowledge of the issue at hand. Indeed, from this point of view, this option possibly seems more appropriate than the special chamber solution as these are typically staffed by professionals (as happens in Colombia) with similar backgrounds to the judges – that is, expertise in constitutional law, and without knowledge in the public policy areas they have to monitor. The commissioner solution has the additional advantage of its proximity to civil society, with which it can more easily develop the type of collaborative and supportive relationships essential to sustain dialogic monitoring processes. In this way, the Court, the commissioners, and civil society can develop a triangulated approach that reinforces the monitoring process.

A third option courts can take in order to develop their institutional capacity involves the recognition of civil society coalitions as authorized interlocutors

[16] Interview with Luis Ernesto Vargas, Constitutional Court Justice and President of T25 Special Chamber, Ibagué, September 29, 2014.

that can provide information and act as a source of pressure in order to continue the monitoring process and measure advances. This option can complement the work of a special commissioner or chamber, as has occurred in the T25 monitoring, in which the CCC's special chamber has encouraged the Monitoring Commission's participation and used its reports, although it has not granted it official status or similar powers as the Indian Supreme Court has done with the commissioners.

A fourth alternative, also complementary to the previous three, consists of courts rationalizing the monitoring workload, prioritizing particularly severe or urgent problems and developing fulfillment indicators for its orders that enable evaluation for this very prioritization. In this respect, T25's monitoring process has been deficient, as the CCC has worked with an overly long list of rights and fulfillment indicators and has been reluctant to create a systematic prioritization strategy in regards to rights or population groups. Such an approach would allow it to thoroughly and efficiently monitor the case as the dossier expands and the process lengthens. In order to be loyal to its strong legal conception of all rights in question, the CCC has had notable difficulties in establishing priorities and progressive strategies in relation to the fulfillment of said rights (Rodríguez-Garavito 2009b). Due to the aforementioned, the Court has been reluctant or inefficient in declaring some of its orders as fulfilled and concentrated on those that are still pending. Although it continues to monitor, this has resulted in possibly risking its future institutional capacity to do so as petitions, orders, and documents accumulate.

Beyond the details of T25, we wish to highlight that these and other solutions render courts' roles manageable in structural cases so long as they understand their role as authoritative moderators of collective processes based on dialogues that seek to solve situations of radical deprivation. Through what we have termed the "participatory effect," dialogic courts are capable of fulfilling these mediation tasks and simultaneously complement said capabilities with the collective expertise of relevant actors, from state agencies to victims' organizations, to solve the issue at hand.

In order to be effective, this authoritative moderator role must be developed in the shadow of possible sanctions in particularly serious cases of non compliance. However, as shown by the T25 process, in which the CCC has preferred to use a combination of constructive engagement and public shaming for noncompliance in hearings and follow-up decisions, the soft power of persuasion and transparency can be more effective than the hard power of sanctions. Contrary to what judicial activism critics argue, courts have not only the ability, but also the obligation to use their power in order to contribute to the fulfillment of SERs and put into practice a separation of powers that reflects the institutional realities of actually existing democracies.

8.3. CONCLUSIONS

In this chapter, we inquired into the features of courts' decisions that can have bearing on the overall impact of structural decisions on SERs. We singled out the strength of the judgments' (1) declaration of rights, (2) remedies, and (3) monitoring. We hypothesized that dialogic rulings characterized by strong rights, moderate remedies, and strong monitoring are likely to have the greatest overall impact on the fulfillment of SERs. We illustrated this hypothesis by contrasting the findings from our core case study on T25 with findings from studies on two other CCC structural rulings (T153 on prison overcrowding and T760 on health care), as well as from secondary evidence from the right-to-food case in India and the *Grootboom* ruling in South Africa.

Our empirical case for dialogic activism also sheds new light on criticisms against judicial activism. To the criticism that judges are democratically unaccountable, we respond that a broader conception of accountability and separation of powers is needed in order to take into account the realities of democratic practice. In this conception, dialogic courts promote rather than erode democracy, by exercising horizontal accountability over other branches of government and by helping to break institutional deadlocks that contribute to massive violations of SERs. Further, they foster, rather than inhibit, democratic participation and collective deliberation to solve distributive justice dilemmas. In response to the criticism that courts lack the requisite institutional capacity to implement their activist rulings, we posit that, once the courts' role is reconceptualized as one of an authoritative mediator of problem-solving dialogues, it becomes clear that they have or can develop this capacity through institutional mechanisms such as specialized monitoring chambers or the appointment of independent experts to monitor rulings' implementation. Dialogic activism reduces, but does not eliminate, the risk of courts' being overwhelmed by mounting demands and the complexities of structural cases.

9

Conclusions: Comparative Constitutionalism as Institutional Imagination

Over the last two decades, courts, advocates, and scholars in the Global South have developed theories, strategies, and doctrines aimed at fulfilling the promise of socioeconomic rights in contexts marked by radical deprivation and unacceptable inequalities. Together with parallel developments in the Global North, those legal innovations have been fundamental contributions to comparative constitutionalism and international human rights.

Missing from the literature and the jurisprudence is a systematic reflection on the actual impact of SER rulings. In this book, we have sought to contribute to filling this scholarly and practical void by tackling the question of impact from two angles. First, we offered an analytical and methodological framework aimed at capturing the full range of court rulings' effects. We argued that, in addition to the direct material outcomes that courts and analysts tend to focus on, judicial impact includes a broader array of indirect and symbolic effects that can be as consequential for the fulfillment of SERs as those directly stemming from court orders. We illustrated this broader typology of effects with detailed evidence on the multifarious impacts of the most ambitious structural ruling of contemporary Latin American constitutionalism: the Colombian Constitutional Court's T25 ruling on the plight of internally displaced persons and its decade-long follow-up process. To bolster the potential usefulness of our case study for comparative constitutional studies and practice, we contrasted other structural rulings by the Colombian Court, as well as the *PUCL* right-to-food case in India and the *Grootboom* case on housing rights in South Africa, with our empirical findings on T25. In order to do this we applied our analytical framework to these other cases.

Second, we used empirical evidence from those case studies to tackle an explanatory question: why do different courts' efforts at addressing violations of SERs have disparate impacts? Why do some rulings, such as T25 or *PUCL*, have profound impacts, while others, such as *Grootboom*, have more modest effects? We focused on court-controlled factors that influence impact. We singled out three factors: the content of the rights recognized by a given ruling, the types of remedy handed down by the Court, and the existence and variety of monitoring that the Court pursues to ensure compliance with its ruling. We posited that dialogic judicial interventions are likely to have greater impact on the fulfilment of SERs than monologic rulings. We defined dialogic rulings as those that combine strong rights (i.e., the judicial enforcement of basic levels of material well-being), moderate remedies (i.e., open-ended orders that leave the details of public policy to government, but set specific deadlines and procedures that government must meet), and strong monitoring (i.e., follow-up decisions to assess progress, nudge recalcitrant public officials into compliance, and involve diverse stakeholders in a process of public deliberation and problem-solving on the underlying causes of SERs violations).

We argued that structural, dialogic decisions can deepen the positive effects of judicial interventions while simultaneously mitigating the risk of negative effects. With respect to positive effects, they can not only induce institutional and policy changes, but also enhance symbolic effects – for example, by making policy flaws visible to public opinion and thereby generating citizen pressure to address the causes of litigation. With regards to the negative effects, by definition, judicial interventions avoid uneven treatment of disperse individual litigation, and counteract, in this way, the risk of inequitable outcomes (see Brinks and Gauri 2014; Rodríguez-Garavito 2013).

More broadly, our empirical case for dialogic activism engages with canonical objections against activist courts – namely, the latter's alleged lack of democratic accountability and institutional capacity to foster social change. While recognizing that top-down, monologic judicial activism can present an anti-democratic risk and serious implementation challenges, we join proponents of experimentalist and dialogic activism in attempting to reformulate the rationale and mechanisms of judicial interventions, which can strengthen rather than erode democratic governance and human rights. Rather than abandoning the conception of law as a catalyst for social change, our task has been to put both monologic activists and their critics to the empirical test by analyzing the impact of rulings.

We advanced two arguments in response to the critics. First, in regards to courts' democratic accountability, our study takes as a point of departure the reality of institutional practice in actually existing democracies. In this context, the study showed that courts can deepen rather than erode democratic governance by acting as sources of horizontal accountability – that is, by breaking gridlocks within and among largely unaccountable government agencies, and nudging public officials to address systemic policy failures that lead to massive SERs violations. Second, our analysis reveals that courts' institutional capacity and potential for fostering democratic deliberation can be best developed through their continued post-judgment engagement by means of monitoring processes that provide opportunities for stakeholders' participation and public deliberation around the solution of distributive justice problems.

Judicial interventions of this type have two additional advantages over the case-by-case, monologic approach that has dominated SERs adjudication, especially in civil law countries. First, they respond to the objection regarding judges' lack of technical knowledge. By following up on compliance with their rulings through a monitoring process that involves not only public officials, but also a wide variety of actors with relevant knowledge (professional associations, NGOs, victims' organizations, academic experts, and so forth), dialogic courts can promote the collaborative search for solutions, or at least a public discussion about the alternatives for action. The direct and indirect effects that can emerge from this dialogue include unlocking public policy processes, improving coordination among previously disconnected public agencies, and creating public policy framed in the language of rights. These changes, in turn, can prevent the indiscriminate judicialization of disputes.

Second, this type of decision responds to the criticism that, when a judge grants a petition on SERs, she encroaches upon the government's and the legislature's competence. In judgments such as T25, the judge promotes the reform process, but does not decide its contents, since most of its orders are means-oriented rather than outcome-oriented. But, unlike other courts that use the procedural, structural approach (such as the South African Constitutional Court), the Colombian Court set strict time limits for compliance and the government's obligation to inform the Court on its progress, which the Court has enforced through a monitoring process that continues to this day.

In practice, what impact does this type of judicial intervention have? In the specific case of T25, our study concluded that, in the ten years subsequent to the judgment (2004–2014), the case has had a high degree of impact in unlocking the state apparatus and placing the issue at the heart of public policy and debate. It has also had a notable effect, albeit only partial, in the democratization of the issue, to the extent that it has created spaces for citizen participation and control. This has included legally sophisticated civil society organizations in the discussion, but has not been concomitantly effective in including internally displaced persons themselves.

Other effects have been more modest. In regards to the judgment's impact on the coordination of state entities we found that it had resulted in better cohesion among national government agencies, but has had limited success in increasing coordination among the public policies of national, departmental, and municipal governments. Moreover, governments continue to fundamentally lack clear definitions of responsibilities and inter-institutional communication.

There is also a mixed record for the judgment's effect on public policy. On one hand, the case has fundamentally influenced public policy design and the increase in funds allocated for their implementation. On the other hand, the government has inconsistently implemented these public policies and implementation continues to be a work in progress. In light of this and the continuation of the armed conflict that underlies forced displacement, it is not surprising that despite notable advances in essential rights such as health and education, it is still unclear as to whether the judgment will lead to a substantial improvement in the dramatic situation lived by more than five million IDPs in Colombia.

Looking forward, T25's trajectory raises legal and political questions that are relevant to the future of cases such as *PUCL*, and of judicial activism on SERs at large. For how long can activist courts such as the CCC sustain a monitoring process that has clear institutional and political costs? When can a court consider that the relevant government institutions have fulfilled the case's requirements and therefore put an end to its intervention? These questions remain unanswered for other scholars to study, in light of this and other structural cases in Colombia, India, South Africa, and elsewhere.

Based on previous studies we advance the following hypothesis: judicial interventions in structural cases are successful insofar as they become unnecessary (Rodríguez-Garavito 2009b). In other words, practitioners and scholars should assess judicial interventions' success based on the capacity of such interventions to make administrative bureaucracies and the legislature attend to the underlying structural problem without having the judiciary constantly pressuring these institutions. In T25, we define success as the moment when the CCC will be able to cease its protagonist role on remedying forced displacement, due to significant advances in public policy and IDPs' effective enjoyment of rights. In the other high-impact case in our sample (e.g. the right-to-food case in India), the Supreme Court and the two special commissioners will have accomplished their mission when state policies and programs regarding pervasive malnutrition and hunger have improved and become self-sustaining enough that the Court can lift its continuous mandamus.

In the meantime, as monitoring processes continue, dialogic activist courts such as Colombia's and India's face important challenges. As Shankar (2013: 127) has noted in relation to the *PUCL* case, the prolongation of the monitoring process "increases the load of an already overburdened judiciary and will lengthen backlogs in delivering justice. And if despite such supervision the executive fails to comply with Court directives, the institutional legitimacy of the judiciary will be besmirched." Our interviews with the Colombian Court's justices and clerks, as well as with civil society actors who have played key roles in the case over the years, reveal similar concerns about looming institutional burnout and the need for the Court to gradually withdraw from the case. A clear sense of how to do this, however, is not apparent in the interviews. Nor is an effort to strategically decide how to measure progress, determine when enough has been accomplished with regard to a given policy or right that the Court's nudging is no longer necessary, and focus instead on outstanding policy failures that need urgent attention.

Whether or not these and other activist courts manage to handle these risks while continuing to support the enforcement of SERs remains to be seen. In the meantime, their work has rekindled scholarly and practical interest in the role of courts in social change. Against the tradition of "rights essentialism" that has dominated constitutional theory and practice – with its focus on the creation and doctrinal clarification of legal standards on rights (Levinson 1999) – judicial involvement in distributive justice debates has brought renewed attention to how to craft remedies for SERs violations, and to effective institutional mechanisms to implement them. By moving from debate on *whether* to judicially enforce SERs to the debate on *how* to do it (Tushnet 2012), judges, advocates, and scholars are returning to the tradition of constitutional law as "institutional imagination" (Unger 1996) – that is, institutional arrangements that offer promising alternatives to realize the transformative potential of socioeconomic rights. By embarking on experiments in dialogic jurisprudence, crafting innovative judicial responses to the reality of radical deprivation, and reshaping conventional understandings of northern constitutionalism's concepts (like the canonical version of the doctrine of separation of powers), the work of courts in different corners of the Global South holds out the prospect for a more participatory and effective protection of human rights, in the South and the North alike.

In a world where ideas and practices disseminate rapidly through professional networks and the media, these innovations are gradually taking root in countries in different regions of the world. Our interviews with constitutional court justices from various countries show that they increasingly know about and have interest in using the precedents of activist courts such as the ones analyzed in this book. For instance, the Colombian Court's experience with T25 has elicited the interest of judges in apex courts responsible for enforcing bills of rights with strong SER components, such as that of Kenya's 2010 Constitution.[1] Similarly, academic and judicial associations in countries as different as Mexico, the Philippines, and South Africa have actively debated its applicability to and potential impact in their jurisdictions.[2]

The need for this type of transnational exchange is particularly pressing because the issue of SERs' impact ranks high on the minds of litigators and judges alike. After all, having a concrete impact on improved access and quality of basic goods and services – such as decent housing or health care – is what drives litigators and activists to resort to the courts in the first place. Similarly, if their rulings had no practical consequences, courts would be ill-advised to incur the considerable institutional costs associated with their activist rulings on SERs, especially in structural cases that entail protracted negotiations and tensions with government agencies responsible for implementing them. Once the dust has settled from a case, the question lingering on everyone's mind is this: was it worth the effort?

1 Interview with Willy Mutunga, Chief Justice of Kenya's Supreme Court, September 20, 2013.

2 Interview with Albie Sachs, former Justice of South Africa's Constitutional Court, September 19, 2013; interview with Manuel José Cepeda, former Justice of Colombia's Constitutional Court, May 27, 2014.

References

Abramovich, Víctor. 2005. "Courses of Action in Economic, Social and Cultural Rights: Instruments and Allies." *International Law Journal on Human Rights* 2.

Abramovich, Víctor and Christian Courtis. 2002. *Social Rights as Enforceable Rights* [Los derechos sociales como derechos exigibles]. México, D.F.: Ediciones del Castillo.

Afrodes and Global Rights. 2007. "Lights and Backlights about Exclusion." [Luces y contraluces sobre la exclusión]. Bogotá: Afrodes y Global Rights.

Alston, Philip. 2008. "Foreword." In Malcom Langford (ed.) *Social Rights Jurisprudence: Emerging Trends in International and Comparative Law*. New York: Cambridge University Press.

Arango, Rodolfo. 2003. "Basic Rights, Constitutional Justice and Democracy." *Ratio Juris* 16.

Baxi, Uprenda. 2013. "Preliminary Notes on Transformative Constitutionalism." In Oscar Vilhena, Uprenda Baxi, and Frans Viljoen (eds.) *Transformative Constitutionalism: Comparing the Apex Courts of Brazil, India and South Africa*. Pretoria: Pretoria University Law Press (PULP).

Bergallo, Paola. 2005. "Justice and experimentalism: The remedial function in public interest litigation in Argentina." ("Justicia y experimentalismo: la función remedial del poder judicial en el litigio de derecho público en Argentina"). SELA – (Seminario en Latinoamérica de Teoría Constitucional y Política) Papers. Paper 45.

2011. "Courts and Social Change: Lessons from the Struggle to Universalize Access to HIV/AIDS Treatment in Argentina." *Texas Law Review* 89.

Berger, Jonathan. 2008. "Litigating for Social Justice in Post-Apartheid South Africa: A Focus on Health and Education." In Varun Gauri and Daniel M. Brinks (eds.) *Courting Social Justice: Judicial Enforcement of Social and Economic Rights in the Developing World*. New York: Cambridge University Press.

Bilchitz, David. 2007. *Poverty and Fundamental Rights: The Justification and Enforcement of Socio-Economic Rights*. New York: Oxford University Press.

2013. "Constitutions and Distributive Justice: Complementary or Contradictory?" In Daniel Bonilla Maldonado (ed.) *Constitutionalism of the Global South: The Activist Tribunals of India, South Africa, and Colombia*. New York: Cambridge University Press.

Birchfield, Lauren and Jessica Corsi. 2010. "Between Starvation and Globalization: Realizing the Right to Food in India." *Michigan Journal of International Law* 31.

Bogotá Working Roundtable [Mesa de Trabajo de Bogotá sobre Desplazamiento Interno]. 2005. "Forced Displacement: Validity of the Unconstitutional State of Affairs" [Desplazamiento Forzado: Vigencia del Estado de Cosas Inconstitucional].

Bonilla, Daniel (ed.). 2013 *Constitutionalism of the Global South: The Activist Tribunals of India, South Africa and Colombia*. New York: Cambridge University Press.

Botero, Catalina. 2006. *Tutela Action in the Colombian Constitution* [La acción de tutela en el ordenamiento constitucional colombiano]. Bogotá: Escuela Judicial Rodrigo Lara Bonilla, Consejo Superior de la Judicatura.

Bourdieu, Pierre. 1987. "The Force of Law: Toward a Sociology of the Juridical Field." *Hastings Law Journal* 38.

2000. "The Force of Law: Elements for a Sociology of the Legal Field" [La fuerza del derecho: elementos para una sociología del campo jurídico]. In *Pierre Bourdieu y Gunther Teubner The Force of Law* [La fuerza del derecho]. Bogotá: Uniandes y Siglo del Hombre Editores.

Brinks, Daniel M. and Varun Gauri. 2014. "The Law's Majestic Equality? The Distributive Impact of Litigating Social and Economic Rights." *Perspectives on Politics* 12 (2).

Brinks, Daniel M. and William Forbath. 2013. "The Role of Courts and Constitutions in the New Politics of Welfare in Latin America." In Peter Peerenboom and Tom Ginsburg (eds.) *Law and Development of Middle-Income Countries*. New York: Cambridge University Press.

Cambio. 2008. "The Country According to José Obdulio" [El país según José Obdulio], August 13.

Center of Legal and Social Studies [Centro de Estudios Legales y Sociales] (CELS). 2008. *Strategic Litigation and Human Rights: The Fight for Rights* [Litigio estratégico y derechos humanos: La lucha por el derecho]. Buenos Aires: Siglo XXI Editores.

Chandrachud, Abhinav. 18 July 2009. "Dialogic Judicial Activism in India." *The Hindu*. Available: www.thehindu.com/todays-paper/tp-opinion/dialogic-judicial-activism-in-india/article232566.ece Accessed: October 27, 2014.

Chayes, Abram. 1976. "The Role of the Judge in Public Law Litigation." *Harvard Law Review* 89 (7).

Chitalkar, Poorvi and Varun Gauri. forthcoming. "India: Compliance with Orders on the Right to Food." In Malcolm Langford, César Rodríguez-Garavito, and Julieta Rossi (eds.) *Making It Stick: Compliance with Social Rights Judgments in Comparative Perspective*. Cambridge University Press.

Clavijo, Sergio. 2001. *Faults and Failures of the Constitutional Court: The Case of Colombia 1991–2000* [Fallos y fallas economicas de las altas cortes: El caso de Colombia 1991–2000]. Bogotá: Alfaomega.

Colombian Commission of Jurists and Colombia Jesuit Service for Refugees. [Comisión Colombiana de Juristas y Servicio Jesuita a Refugiados Colombia]. "Monitoring the Implementation of International Recommendations on Forced Displacement in Colombia 2004–2005. Report to the Representative of the Secretary-General of the United Nations on the Human Rights of Internally Displaced People"

[Seguimiento a la aplicación de las recomendaciones internacionales sobre desplazamiento forzando en Colombia 2004–2005. Informe para el Representante de Secretario General de las Naciones Unidas sobre los derechos humanos de las personas internamente deplazadas]. Bogotá: Códice Ltda.

Comptroller General's Office, Inspector General's Office, and the Ombudsman's Office [Contraloría General de la República, Procuraduria General de la Nación, Defensoría del Pueblo]. 2012. "First Follow-up Report to Law 1448 of 2011 on Victims and Land Restitution 2012" [Primer Informe de Seguimiento a la Ley 1448 de 2011 de Víctimas y Restitución de Tierras 2012], August 21, 2012.

Coomans, Fons (ed.). 2006. *Justiciability of Economic and Social Rights: Experiences from Domestic Systems*. Cambridge: Intersentia.

Davis, Dennis. 2010. "South African Constitutional Jurisprudence: The First Fifteen Years." *Annual Review of Law and Social Science* 6.

Dixon, Rosalind. 2007. "Creating Dialogue About Socioeconomic Rights: Strong-Form Versus Weak-Form Judicial Review Revisited," *International Journal of Constitutional Law* 5.

Dreze, Jean and Amartya Sen. 2002. *India: Development and Participation*. New York: Oxford University Press.

Dugard, Jackie. 2013. "Urban Basic Services: Rights, Reality and Resistance." In Malcolm Langford, Ben Cousins, Jackie Dugard, and Tshepo Madligozi (eds.) *Socio-Economic Rights in South Africa: Symbols or Substance?* New York: Cambridge University Press.

El Espectador, "The Displaced Population's Situation" [La situación de los desplazados], April 25, 2009.

El Tiempo, "32 Trillion to Attend to the Displaced Population" [32 mil millones para atender a la población desplazada], November 21, 2004.

El Tiempo, "600 Women Tell Their Emotionally Powerful Stories Before the Court" [Las 600 mujeres que conmovieron a la Corte], May 25, 2008.

El Tiempo, "Band-aids" [Pañitos de agua tibia], April 3, 2000.

El Tiempo, "The Year of IDPs" [El Año de los Desplazados], April 8, 2007.

El Tiempo, "Beyond Numbers, People" [Más allá de las cifras, personas], October 2, 2008.

El Tiempo, "Colombia Reached Record Rate of Displacement" [Colombia Alcanzó Tasa Récord de Desplazamiento], April 29, 2003.

El Tiempo, "Court Requests Concrete Data on Displaced" [Corte Pide Datos Concretos Sobre Desplazados], February 2, 2007.

El Tiempo, "Displaced Civilians of Caparrapí" [Deplzados Civiles de Caparrarpí]. April 22, 2000.

Episcopal Conference of Colombia [Conferencia Episcopal de Colombia]. 1995. "Human Rights and the Displaced in Colombia" [Derechos Humanos y desplazados por violencia en Colombia]. Bogotá.

Epp, Charles R. 1998. *The Rights Revolution: Lawyers, Activists and Supreme Courts in Comparative Perspective*. Chicago: Chicago University Press.

Farstein, Carolina, Gabriela Kletzel, and Paola García Rey. 2010. "Searching for Effective Judicial Remedies: New Challenges to the Justiciability of Socioeconomic Rights" [En Busca de un Remedio Judicial Efectivo: Nuevos Desafíos para la Justiciabilidad de los Derechos Sociales]. In Pilar Arcidiácono,

Nicolás Espejo Yaksic, and César Rodríguez-Garavito (eds.) *Social Rights: Justice, Politics, and Economics in Latin America* [Derechos Sociales: Justicia, Política y Economía en América Latina]. Bogotá: Siglo del Hombre Editores.

Feeley, Malcolm M. and Edward L. Rubin. 1998. *Judicial Policy Making and the Modern State: How the Courts Reformed America's Prisons*. New York: Cambridge University Press.

Ferraz, Octavio Luiz Motta. 2009. "The Right to Health in the Courts of Brazil: Worsening Health Inequities?" *Health and Human Rights Journal* 11 (2).

Fredman, Sandra. 2008. *Human Rights Transformed: Positive Rights and Positive Duties*. New York: Oxford University Press.

Fung, Archon and Erik Olin Wright. 2003. *Deepening Democracy. Institutional Innovations in Empowered Participatory Governance*. London: Verso.

García-Villegas, Mauricio. 2014. *The Symbolic Efficacy of Law* [La eficacia simbólica del derecho]. Bogotá: Debate.

Gargarella, Roberto. 2006. "Should Deliberative Democrats Defend the Judicial Enforcement of Social Rights?" In Samantha Besson and José Luis Martí (eds.) *Deliberative Democracy and Its Discontents*. Burlington: Ashgate.

2015. "Latin American Constitutionalism: Social Rights and the "Engine Room" of the Constitution." In César Rodríguez-Garavito (ed.) *Law and Society in Latin America: A New Map*. New York: Routledge.

Goertz, Gary and James Mahoney. 2012. *A Tale of Two Cultures: Qualitative and Quantitative Research in the Social Sciences*. Princeton: Princeton University Press.

Gauri, Varun and Daniel M. Brinks (eds.). 2008. *Courting Social Justice. Judicial Enforcement of Social and Economic Rights in the Developing World*. New York: Cambridge University Press.

Gauri, Varun and Daniel M. Brinks. 2012. "Human Rights as Demands of Communicative Action." *The Journal of Political Philosophy* 20 (4).

Guzmán, Diana Esther and Linda María Cabrera C. 2013. "Access to Justice for Women Victims of Sexual Violence. Fifth Monitoring Report to Decision 92 of 2008 from the Constitutional Court, Annex Reserved" [Acceso a la justicia para mujeres víctimas de violencia sexual. Quinto Informe de Seguimiento al Auto 092 de 2008 de la Corte Constitucional, anexo reservado]. Monitoring Table of the Constitutional Court, Annex Reserved [Mesa de seguimiento al Auto 092 de la Corte Constitucional, anexo reservado].

Haltom, William and Michael McCann. 2004. *Distorting the Law: Politics, Media, and the Litigation Crisis*. Chicago: University of Chicago Press.

Heywood, Mark. 2009. "South Africa's Treatment Action Campaign: Combining Law and Social Mobilization to Realize the Right to Health." *Journal of Human Rights Practice* 1 (1).

Hirschl, Ran. 2004. *Towards Juristocracy: The Origins and Consequences of the New Constitutionalism*. Cambridge: Harvard University Press.

2013. "From Comparative Constitutional Law to Comparative Constitutional Studies." *International Journal of Constitutional Law* 11 (1).

Hirschl, Ran and Evan Rosevear. 2011. "Constitutional Law Meets Comparative Politics: Socio-Economic Rights and Political Realities." In Tom Campbell,

K. D. Ewing, and Adam Tomkins (eds.) *The Legal Protection of Human Rights: Sceptical Essays*. New York: Oxford University Press.

Hogg, Peter W. and Allison A. Bushell. 1997. "The Charter Dialogue Between Courts and Legislatures (Or Perhaps The Charter of Rights Isn't Such a Bad Thing After All)." *Osgoode Hall Law Journal* 35 (1).

Human Rights Commission, United Nations. 1995. [Comisión de Derechos Humanos, Naciones Unidas] "Report of the Special Representative of the Secretary-General on Internally Displaced Persons Concerning the Visit to Colombia in 1994" [Informe del Representante Especial del Secretario General sobre la cuestión de los desplazados internos sobre la visita a Colombia en 1994]. Colombia Mission, Human Rights Commission, 51st period of sessions, Item 11 d) of the Provisional Agenda [Comisión Colombia, Comisión de Derechos Humanos, 51° period de sesiones, Tema 11 d) del programa provisional], E/CN.4/1995/50Add.1, October 3, 1994.

Human Rights Commission, United Nations [Comisión de Derechos Humanos, Naciones Unidas]. 2000. *Report of the Special Representative of the Secretary-General on Internally Displaced Persons. Follow-up Mission to Colombia.* [Informe del Representante Especial del Secretario General sobre la cuestión de los desplazados internos. Misión de seguimiento enviada a Colombia]. 56 Session, E/ CN.4/2000/83/Add.1, January 11, 2000.

Human Rights Watch. 2014. "The Crisis in Buenaventura: Disappearances, Dismemberment, and Displacement in Colombia's Main Pacific Port." Available at: www.hrw.org/sites/default/files/reports/colombia0314webwcover_1.pdf Accessed: November 8, 2014.

Ibáñez, Ana María. 2008. *Forced displacement in Colombia: An Irreversible Path towards Poverty* [El desplazamiento forzoso en Colombia: un camino sin retorno hacia la pobreza]. Bogotá: Universidad de Los Andes.

2009. "Return Programs for the Displaced Population" [Los programas de retorno para la población desplazada]. In César Rodríguez-Garavito (ed.) *Beyond the Displacement: Policies, Rights, and Overcoming Forced Displacement in Colombia* [Más allá del desplazamiento: políticas, derechos y superación del desplazamiento forzado en Colombia]. Bogotá: Ediciones Uniandes, ANCUR, and ASDI.

International Commission of Jurists (ICJ). 2008. "Courts and Legal Enforcement of Economic, Social and Cultural Rights: Comparative Experiences of Justiciability." Available: www.humanrights.ch/upload/pdf/080819_justiziabilitt_esc.pdf Accessed: November 10, 2014.

Jones, Charles O. 1970. *An Introduction to the Study of Public Policy*. Belmont: Duxbury Press.

Joubert, Pearlie. 2008. "Grootboom Dies Homeless and Penniless." *Mail and Guardian Online*. Available: http://mg.co.za/article/2008-08-08-grootboom-dies-homeless-and -penniless Accessed: June 16, 2014.

Kalmanovitz, Salomón. 2001 *Institutions and Economic Development in Colombia* [Las instituciones y el desarrollo económico de Colombia]. Bogotá: Norma.

Klein, Alana. 2008. "Judging as Nudging: New Governance Approaches for the Enforcement of Constitutional Social and Economic Rights." *Columbia Human Rights Law Review* 39 (2).

Kraft, Michael and Scott Furlong. 2007. *Public Policy: Politics, Analysis, and Alternatives*. Washington: CQ Press.

Lamprea, Everaldo. 2014. Colombia's right to health litigation in a context of healthcare reform", in Flood, Colleen and Aeyal Gross (eds). The Right to Health at the Public/Private Divide-A Global Comparative Study. Cambridge University Press.

2015. *Rights in Practice: Health Policy, Litigation, and Courts in Colombia (1991–2014)* [Derechos en la práctica: Políticas de salud, litigio y cortes en Colombia (1991–2014)]. Bogotá: Uniandes.

Landau, David. 2012. "The Reality of Socioeconomic Rights Enforcement." *Harvard International Law Journal* 53.

Langford, Malcolm. 2009. "The Justiciability of Social Rights: From Practice to Theory." In Malcom Langford (ed.) *Social Rights Jurisprudence: Emerging Trends in International and Comparative Law*. New York: Cambridge University Press.

2013. "Housing Rights Litigation: *Grootboom* and Beyond." In Malcolm Langford, Ben Cousins, Jackie Dugard, and Tshepo Madligozi (eds.) *Socio-Economic Rights in South Africa: Symbols or Substance?* New York: Cambridge University Press.

Langford, Malcolm, César Rodríguez-Garavito, and Julieta Rossi (eds.). forthcoming. *Making It Stick: Compliance with Social Rights Judgments in Comparative Perspective*. New York: Cambridge University Press.

Liebenberg, Sandra. 2010. *Socioeconomic Rights: Adjudication Under a Transformative Constitution*. Cape Town: Juta Academic.

Levinson, Daryl J. "Rights Essentialism and Remedial Equilibration." *Columbia Law Review* (1999): 857–940.

Mangabeira, Roberto. 1987. *False Necessity: Anti-Necessitarian Social Theory in the Service of Radical Democracy*. New York: Cambridge University Press.

Mann, Michael. 2012. *The Sources of Social Power: Volume 1, A History of Power from the Beginning to AD 1760*. New York: Cambridge University Press.

McAdam, Doug, Sidney Tarrow, and Charles Tilly. 2001. *Dynamics of Contention*. New York: Cambridge University Press.

McCann, Michael. 1994. *Rights at Work: Pay Equity Reform and the Politics of Legal Mobilization*. Chicago: Chicago University Press.

Minow, Martha. 2010. *In Brown's Wake: Legacies of America's Educational Landmark*. New York: Oxford University Press.

Mœstad, Ottar, Lise Rakner, and Octavio Ferraz. 2011. "Assessing the Impact of Health Rights Litigation." In Alicia Yamin and Siri Gloppen (eds.) *Litigating Health Rights: Can Courts Bring More Justice to Health?* Cambridge: Harvard University Press.

Monitoring Commission [Comisión de Seguimiento a la política pública sobre desplazamiento forzado]. 2008. First Report to the Constitutional Court. National Verification Process for the Rights of the Displaced Population [Primer Informe a la Corte Constitucional. Proceso Nacional de Verificación de los Derechos de la Población Desplazada]. 31 January 2008. Bogotá.

Monitoring Commission of Administrative Agencies [Comisión de Seguimiento de los Organismos de Control]. 2013. Second Follow-up Report to the Victims and Land

Restitution Law 2012–2013. [Segundo informe de seguimiento y monitoreo a la implementación de la Ley de Victimas y restitución de tierras 2012–2013]. August. Bogotá.

2008a. Fifth Report to the Constitutional Court. National Verification Process for the Rights of the Displaced Population [Quinto Informe a la Corte Constitucional. Proceso Nacional de Verificación de los Derechos de la Población Desplazada]. 4 June 2008. Bogotá.

2008b. Seventh Report on the Implementation of Rights to the Displaced Population. [Séptimo Informe de verificación sobre el cumplimiento de derechos a la población en situación de desplazamiento]. October 30, 2008.

2009. Eleventh Report: Quantification and Valuation of the Lands and Goods Abandoned or Dispossessed to the Displaced Population in Colombia. Basis for the Development of a Reparation Process [Décimo Primer Informe: Cuantificación y valoración de las tierras y los bienes abandonados o despojados a la población desplazada en Colombia. Bases para el desarrollo de procesos de reparación]. January 19, 2009.

2010. Third Verification Report on the Implementation of Rights to the Displaced Population [Tercer Informe de verificación sobre el cumplimiento de derechos a la población en situación de desplazamiento]. December 2010.

Monitoring Commission of Administrative Agencies [Comisión de Seguimiento de los Organismos de Control]. 2013. *First Follow-up Report and Monitoring of the Implementation of the Law Decrees of Indigenous, Black, Afro-Colombian, Palenquera, Raizalez, and Rom Victims* [Primer informe de seguimiento y monitoreo a la implementación de los Decretos ley de victimas indigenas, negras, afrocolombianas, palenqueras, raizalez y rom]. Executive summary.

Muralidhar, Shir. 2008. "India: The Expectations and Challenges of Judicial Enforcement of Social Rights." In Malcolm Langford (ed.) *Social Rights Jurisprudence: Emerging Trends in International and Comparative Law*. New York: Cambridge University Press.

National Planning Department and Ministry of Finance [Departamento Nacional de Planeación y Ministerio de Haciendo y Crédito Público]. 2014. "Report on Resources Assigned and Spent in the Framework of the Public Policy for the Population of Victims of Internal Displacement – Response to Order 5 of Decision 219 of 2011" [Informe sobre los recursos asignados y ejecutados en el marco de la política pública dirigida a la Población Víctima del Desplazamiento Forzado – Respuesta a la Orden 5a del Auto 219 de 2011]. Bogotá: DNP y MHCP. February 28.

Nino, Carlos Santiago. 1998. *Radical Evil on Trial*. New Haven: Yale University Press.

O'Donnell, Guillermo. 1999. "Horizontal Accountability in New Democracies." In Andreas Schedler, Larry Jay Diamond, and Marc F. Plattner (eds.) *The Self-Restraining State: Power and Accountability in New Democracies*. Boulder: Lynne Rienner Publishers.

2003. "Horizontal Accountability: Legal Institutionalization of Mistrust." In Scott Mainwaring and Christopher Welna (eds.) *Democratic Accountability in Latin America*. New York: Oxford University Press.

Office of the Mayor of Medellín [Oficina de la Alcaldía de Medellín]. 2013. "Effective Enjoyment of Rights Indicators: Perspective and Challenges" [Indicadores de

Goce Efectivo de Derechos: Perspectivas y Retos]. Municipal Unit of Assistnce and Reparation to Victims [Unidad Municipal de Atención y Reparación a Victimas].

Ombudsman's Office [Defensoría del Pueblo]. 2014. *The Tutela and the Rights to Health and Social Security 2013* [La tutela y los derechos a la salud y a la seguridad social 2013]. Defensoría del Pueblo: Imprenta Nacional de Colombia.

Peerenboom, Peter and Tom Ginsburg (eds.). 2013. *Law and Development of Middle-Income Countries*. New York: Cambridge University Press.

Pillay, Anashri. 2012. "Toward Effective Social and Economic Rights Adjudication: The Role of Meaningful Engagement." *International Journal of Constitutional Law* 10 (3).

2014. "Revisiting the Indian Experience of Economic and Social Rights Adjudication: The Need for a Principled Approach to Judicial Activism and Restraint" *International and Comparative Law Quarterly* 63.

Presidency of the Republic, Social Action Agency, and National Planning Department. 2007. "Sectorial Baseline of the Public Policy of Assistance to the Internally Displaced Population by Violence - Response to Decisions 109 and 233 of 2007" [Línea de base sectorial de la política pública de atención a la población desplazada por la violencia - Respuesta a los autos 109 y 233 de 2007]. Mimeo.

Profamilia. 2010. "The 2010 National Demographic and Health Survey" [Encuesta Nacional de Demografía y Salud del 2010 (ENDS)]. Available at: www.profamilia.org.co/encuestas/Profamilia/Profamilia/images/stories/PDF-capitulos/Capitulo-14.pdf Accessed: October 27, 2014.

Rajagopal, Balakrishnan. 2005. "Limits of Law in Counter-Hegemonic Globalization: The Indian Supreme Court and the Narmada Valley Struggle." In Boaventura Santos and César Rodríguez-Garavito (eds.) *Law and Globalization from Below: Toward a Cosmopolitan Legality*. New York: Cambridge University Press.

2007. "Pro-Human Rights but Anti-Poor?: A Critical Evaluation of the Indian Supreme Court from a Social Movement Perspective." *Human Rights Review* 18 (3).

Restrepo, Esteban. 2009. "The Displaced as Pariah: The Guarantee of the Rights to Truth, Justice, and Reparation of the Victims of the Crime of Forced Displacement in Colombia" [El desplazado como paria: la garantía de los derechos a la verdad, la justicia, la reparación de las victimas del delito de desplazamiento forzado en Colombia]. In Cesar Rodríguez-Garavito (ed.) *Beyond Displacement: Policies, Rights, and Overcoming Forced Displacement* [Más allá del desplazamiento: políticas, derechos y superación del desplazamiento forzado]. Bogotá: Uniandes, Ancur and ASDI.

Rodríguez-Garavito, César (ed.). 2009a *Beyond Displacement: Policies, Rights, and Overcoming Forced Displacement* [Más allá del desplazamiento: políticas, derechos y superación del desplazamiento forzado]. Bogotá: Uniandes, Ancur and ASDI.

2009b. "Beyond Displacement, or How to Overcome an Unconstitutional State of Affairs" [Más allá del desplazamiento, o cómo superar un estado de cosas inconstitucional]. In César Rodríguez-Garavito (ed.) *Beyond Displacement: Policies, Rights, and Overcoming Forced Displacement* [Más allá del desplazamiento: políticas, derechos y superación del desplazamiento forzado]. Bogotá: Uniandes, Ancur and ASDI.

2011a. "Beyond the Courtroom: The Impact of Judicial Activism on Socioeconomic Rights in Latin America." *Texas Law Review* 89.

2011b. "Toward a Sociology of the Global Rule of Law Field: Neoliberalism, Neoconstitutionalism, and the Contest over Judicial Reform in Latin America." In Yves Dezalay and Bryant G. Garth (eds.) *Lawyers and the Rule of Law in an Era of Globalization*. New York: Routledge.

2013. "The Judicialization of Health Care: Symptoms, Diagnosis and Prescriptions." In Peter Peerenboom and Tom Ginsburg (eds.) *Law and Development of Middle-Income Countries*. New York: Cambridge University Press.

2015. "Constitutions in Action: The Impact of Judicial Activism on Socioeconomic Rights in Latin America." In César Rodríguez-Garavito (ed.) *Law and Society in Latin America: A New Map*. New York: Routledge.

Rodríguez-Garavito, César, Natalia Orduz, Felipe Arias, Sebastián Boada, and Sebastián Rubiano. 2010. "Indigenous Displacement: Analysis of Compliance with Decision 4 of the Constitutional Court" [El desplazamiento indígena: análisis del cumplimiento Auto 004 de la Corte Constitucional]. Bogotá: Programa de Justicia Global y Derechos Humanos de la Universidad de los Andes.

Rodríguez-Garavito, César and Natalia Orduz. 2012. *Prior Consultation: Dilemmas and Solutions* [La Consulta Previa: Dilemas y Soluciones]. Bogotá: Centro de Estudios de Derecho, Justicia y Sociedad.

Rodríguez-Garavito, César, Tatiana Alfonso Sierra, and Isabel Cavelier Adarve. 2009. *Afro-Colombian Displacement: Land, Violence, and Rights of Black Communities in Colombia* [El desplazamiento afro: tierra, violencia y derechos de las comunidades negras en Colombia]. Bogotá: Universidad de los Andes, Facultad de Derecho, Cijus, Ediciones Uniandes.

Roldán, Mary. 2003. *Blood and Fire: Violence in Antioquia, Colombia, 1946–1953* [A sangre y fuego: la violencia en Antioquia, Colombia, 1946–1953]. Bogotá: Instituto Colombiano de Antropología.

Rosenberg, Gerald. 1991. *The Hollow Hope. Can Courts Bring About Social Change?* Chicago: The University of Chicago Press.

Sabel, Charles F. and William H. Simon. 2004. "Destabilization Rights: How Public Law Litigation Succeeds." *Harvard Law Review* 117.

Salinas, Yamile. 2009. "The Protection and Restitution of the Lands and Realty of the Victims of Forced Displacement" [La protección y restitución de las tierras y bienes inmuebles de las victimas del desplazamiento Forzado]. In Cesar Rodríguez-Garavito (ed.) *Beyond Displacement: Policies, Rights, and Overcoming Forced Displacement* [Más allá del desplazamiento: políticas, derechos y superación del desplazamiento forzado]. Bogotá: Uniandes, Ancur and ASDI.

Sánchez, Nelson Camilo and Rodrigo Uprimny. 2010. "Proposals for a Transformative Land Restitution" [Propuestas para una restitución de tierras transformadora]. In Catalina Díaz (ed.) *Pending Tasks: Proposals for the Formulation of Reparation Policies in Colombia* [Tareas Pendientes: Propuestas para la formulación de políticas públicas de reparación en Colombia] Bogota: ICTJ and Dejusticia.

Shankar, Shylashri. 2013. "The Embedded Negotiators: India's Higher Judiciary and Socioeconomic Rights." In Daniel Bonilla Maldonado (ed.) *Constitutionalism of the Global South: The Activist Tribunals of India, South Africa, and Colombia*. New York: Cambridge University Press.

Shankar, Shylashri and Pratap Bhanu Mehta. 2008. "Courts and Socioeconomic Rights in India." In Varun Gauri and Daniel M. Brinks (eds.) *Courting Social Justice: Judicial Enforcement of Social and Economic Rights in the Developing World*. New York: Cambridge University Press.

Sunstein, Cass R. 2004. *The Second Bill of Rights*. New York: Basic Books.

Semana, "The Final Judgement" [El Juicio Final], June 13, 2005.

Semana, "Good News, At Last" [Por fin, buenas noticias], February 12, 2006.

Semana, "Time's Up" [Se agota el plazo], December 12, 2004.

Snow, David, Burke Rochford, Steve Worden, and Rober Benford. 1986. "Frame Alignment Processes, Micromobilization, and Movement Participation." *American Sociological Review* 51.

Social Action Agency and National Planning Department [Acción Social y Departamento Nacional de Planeación]. 2007. Line of Sectoral basis of Public Policy Attention to the Population Displaced by Violence [Línea de base sectorial de la política pública de atención a la población desplazada por la violencia]. (Response to Decisions 109 and 233 of 2007 [Respuesta a los autos 109 y 233 de 2007]) (mimeo).

Summers, Nicole. 2011. "Colombian Victims' Law: Transitional Justice in a Time of Violent Conflict?" *Harvard Human Rights Journal*. Vol. 25.

Swidler, Ann. 1986. "Culture in Action: Symbols and Strategies." *American Sociological Review* 51.

Tushnet, Mark. 2009. *Weak Courts, Strong Rights: Judicial Review and Social Welfare Rights in Comparative Constitutional Law*. Princeton: Princeton University Press.

2012. "New Comparative Constitutional Scholarship on Enforcing Second Generation Rights." *Jotwell: The Journal of Things We Like (Lots)*. Available: http://conlaw.jotwell.com/new-comparative-constitutional-scholarship-on-enforcing-second-generation-rights/ Accessed: January 12, 2014.

Unger, Roberto. 1987. *False Necessity: Anti-Necessitarian Social Theory in the Service of Radical Democracy*. London: Verso.

1996. *What Should Legal Analysis Become?* London: Verso.

UNHCR [Acnur]. 2007. *Balance of Public Policy for Comprehensive Care to Forced Displacement in Colombia. January 2004-April 2007* [Balance de la política pública para la atención integral al desplazamiento forzado en Colombia]. Bogotá: Pro-Offset.

Uprimny, Rodrigo. 2000. "Constitutional Justice, Social Rights, and the Economy: A Theoretical Analysis and a Discussion of the UPAC Rulings" [Justicia constitucional, derechos sociales y economía: un análisis teórico y una discusión de las sentencias de UPAC]. *Legal Thought* 13 [Pensamiento Jurídico 13].

Uprimny, Rodrigo. 2015. "The Recent Transformation of Constitutional Law in Latin America: Trends and Challenges." In César Rodríguez-Garavito (ed.) *Law and Society in Latin America: A New Map*. New York: Routledge.

Uprimny, Rodrigo and Mauricio Villegas-García. 2004. "Constitutional Court and Social Emancipation in Colombia" [Corte constitucional y emancipación social]. In Boaventura de Sousa Santos and Mauricio Villegas-García (eds.)

Social Emancipation and Violence in Colombia [Emancipación social y violencia en Colombia]. Bogotá: Norma.

Victims Unit. 2014. "Follow up to Judgment T 025 of 2004. Response to the Order from 11 March 2014." April 2014.

Vilhena, Oscar, Uprenda Baxi, and Frans Viljoen. 2013. "Introduction." In Oscar Vilhena, Uprenda Baxi, and Frans Viljoen (eds.) *Transformative Constitutionalism: Comparing the Apex Courts of Brazil, India and South Africa*. Pretoria: Pretoria University Law Press (PULP).

Walzer, Michael (ed.). 1995. *Toward a Global Civil Society*. New York: Berghahn Books.

Wilson, Bruce M. 2005. "Changing Dynamics: The Political Impact of Costa Rica's Constitutional Court." In Rachel Sieder, Line Schjolden, and Alana Angell (eds.) *The Judicialization of Politics in Latin America*. New York: Palgrave Macmillan.

Wilson, Stuart and Jackie Dugard. 2013. "Constitutional Jurisprudence: The First and Second Waves." In Malcolm Langford, Ben Cousins, Jackie Dugard, and Tshepo Madligozi (eds.) *Socio-Economic Rights in South Africa: Symbols or Substance?* New York: Cambridge University Press.

World Bank. 2013. Helping India Combat Persistently High Rates of Malnutrition. Available: www.worldbank.org/en/news/feature/2013/05/13/helping-india-combat-persistently-high-rates-of-malnutrition.

World Health Organization (WHO). 2012. Global Database on Child Growth and Malnutrition. Available: www.who.int/nutgrowthdb/database/countries/ind/en/ Accessed: October 30, 2014.

Yamin, Alicia Ely and Oscar Parra-Vera. 2010. "Judicial Protection of the Right to Health in Colombia: From Social Demands to Individual Claims to Public Debates." *Hastings International and Comparative Law Review* 33 (2).

Yamin, Alicia Ely and Siri Gloppen (eds.). 2011. *Litigating Health Rights: Can Courts Bring More Justice to Health?* Cambridge: Harvard University Press.

Young, Katherine G. 2012. *Constituting Economic and Social Rights*. New York: Oxford University Press.

GOVERNMENT DOCUMENTS

National Council for Integral Attention to the Displaced Population [Consejo Nacional de Atención Integral a la Población Desplazada, CNAIPD]

CNAIPD, Act 4 of January 12, 2005
CNAIPD, Statement 1 of 2005
CNAIPD, Acts 1–21
CNAIPD, Act 10, July 18, 2006

Ministry of the Interior and Justice [Ministerio del Interior y Justicia]

Directive 3 of 2004
Directive 4 of 2004

Directive 2 of 2005

Unit for Victims' Attention and Reparation [Unidad para la Atención y Reparación Integral a las Víctimas]

Resolution 388 of 2013

National Development Plans (NDP) [Plan Nacional de Desarrollo (PND)]

NDP 2006–2010. "Communal State: Development for Everyone" [Estado Comunitario: desarrollo para todos].
NDP 2011–2014. "Prosperity for Everyone" [Prosperidad para Todos].

National Council for Economic and Social Policy [Consejo Nacional de Política Económica y Social]

Conpes document 2804 of 1995
Conpes document 2924 of 1997
Conpes document 3057 of 1999
Conpes document 3115 of 2001
Conpes document 3400 of 2001

COLOMBIAN CONSTITUTIONAL COURT [CORTE CONSTITUCIONAL DE COLOMBIA]

Judgments [Sentencias]

Judgment SU-559 of 1997
Judgment T-227 of 1997
Judgment T-068 of 1998
Judgment T-153 of 1998
Judgment T-590 of 1998
Judgment C-700 of 1999
Judgment T-535 of 1999
Judgment T-144 of 1999
Judgment SU-090 of 2000
Judgment SU-1150 of 2000
Judgment T-1635 of 2000
Judgment T-602 of 2003
Judgment T25 of 2004
Judgment T-760 of 2008

Decisions [Autos]

Decision 387 of 1997
Decision 1150 of 2000
Decision 185 of 2004
Decision 176 of 2005
Decision 177 of 2005
Decision 178 of 2005
Decision 218 of 2006
Decision 266 of 2006
Decision 333 of 2006
Decision 334 of 2006
Decision 335 of 2006
Decision 337 of 2006
Decision 27 of 2007
Decision 58 of 2007
Decision 101 of 2007
Decision 109 of 2007
Decision 200 of 2007
Decision 233 of 2007
Decision 2 of 2008
Decision 11 of 2008
Decision 52 of 2008
Decision 53 of 2008
Decision 68 of 2008
Decision 92 of 2008
Decision 116 of 2008
Decision 251 of 2008
Decision 1190 of 2008
Decision 4 of 2009
Decision 5 of 2009
Decision 6 of 2009
Decision 7 of 2009
Decision 8 of 2009
Decision 9 of 2009
Decision 11 of 2009
Decision 36 of 2009
Decision 52 of 2009
Decision 119 of 2009
Decision 314 of 2009

Decision 342A of 2009
Decision 266 of 2009
Decision 382 of 2010
Decision 383 of 2010
Decision 174 of 2011
Decision 219 of 2011
Decision A45 of 2012
Decision 29 of 2012
Decision 115A of 2012
Decision 116 of 2012
Decision 173 of 2012
Decision 299 of 2012
Decision of November 1, 2012
Decision 8 of 2013
Decision 98 of 2013
Decision 99 of 2013
Decision 119 of 2013
Decision 145 of 2013
Decision 234 of 2013
Decision 73 of 2014
Decision of March 11, 2014
Press Release, February 6, 2004

LAWS AND DECREES

Decrees [Decretos]

Decree 2591 of 1991
Decree 2569 of 2000
Decree 2007 of 2001
Decree 250 of 2005
Decree 2467 of 2005
Decree 4633 of 2011
Decree 4634 of 2011
Decree 4635 of 2011

Laws [Leyes]

Law 387 of 1997
Law 589 of 2000
Law 975 2005

Law 1151 of 2007
Law 1190 of 2008
Law 1448 of 2011 (Victims and Land Restitution Law)
Law Decree 4633 of 2011
Presidential Directive 06 of October 7, 2005

Index

Lightning Source UK Ltd.
Milton Keynes UK
UKOW06n0826131015

260429UK00005B/87/P

9 781107 078888